IMAGES
of Modern America

St. Louis Advertising

Frank Absher

ARCADIA PUBLISHING

ISBN 978-1-4671-1286-4

Published by Arcadia Publishing
Charleston, South Carolina

Printed in the United States of America

Library of Congress Control Number: 2014938126

For all general information, please contact Arcadia Publishing:
Telephone 843-853-2070
Fax 843-853-0044
E-mail sales@arcadiapublishing.com
For customer service and orders:
Toll-Free 1-888-313-2665

Visit us on the Internet at www.arcadiapublishing.com

For my wife, Barbara

Contents

ACKNOWLEDGMENTS

A book such as this one is enhanced when experts make themselves available to advise and consult. During the creation of this book, I was privileged to work with some of the area's most esteemed advertising veterans. Their insight into and comments about the ads are sprinkled throughout the text to give readers an idea of just how good the creative work in St. Louis has been over the years. The commentary from the professionals may help readers understand why a particular ad is so appealing or why it worked so well.

The knowledgeable St. Louis advertising veterans who offered assistance and input include Charlie Claggett Jr., Steve Kopcha, Gerry Mandel, Ken Ohlemeyer, Del Schwinke, Ted Simmons, Don Stork, and Kristy Tucciarone.

The St. Louis Public Library's St. Louis Media Archives are quickly becoming a repository for advertising history, and the help of library employee Sarah Cain was invaluable in assembling this collection of images. Jason Stratman, at the Missouri History Museum, put in countless hours helping me assemble the images, and St. Louis artist R.J. Shay contributed invaluable grunt work.

INTRODUCTION

Mention "advertising" to most people, and you may be in for a litany of complaints. Yet, many of these same people admit to watching special events such as the Super Bowl or the Academy Awards ceremony in part to see the advertisements that air during the telecasts.

It is easy to wax poetic about the economic impact of advertising in a capitalistic society. One can look at the amount of money spent to place ads in various media to get the attention of media consumers. There is also all the money spent in the creation and production of these ads. As a veteran of many years of work in the media, I can personally attest to the value of the money spent, but there is a lot more to the story of advertising in St. Louis.

In reality, the main function of most media is to deliver an audience that will be exposed to the advertising. At first, I had a difficult time accepting that truism after operating under the assumption that the media were there for entertainment and information, but pulling back to look at the big picture brings that main function into focus. This book, however, is meant to entertain—with advertisements.

The pages of this book are filled with ads that were created in St. Louis by people who were part of the fabric of the St. Louis area. There are ads that promoted locally made products and locally owned businesses. Glancing through these pages, readers will be entertained not only by the creativity of the ads but also by the glance into life in St. Louis through the years. These ads provide a window into life as it was. Some of them also show us life as consumers wished it could become.

Advertising had other major influences. When Listerine (manufactured in St. Louis) dredged up an obscure medical term—halitosis (bad breath)—to convince people to buy its product, the company saw immediate results with sales rising sixteenfold in seven years. Countless other brands promised remedies for problems people had not known they had. In the pages of this book are some early advertisements for these products.

The St. Louis area had a major impact on the development and growth of advertising around the world. Two local agencies, D'Arcy and Gardner, grew to be so large that they set up satellite offices in other major cities. This, in turn, gave them access to worldwide accounts. While most people are aware that ads for Anheuser-Busch products were created in St. Louis, not many know about the thousands of Coca-Cola ads made in St. Louis or of those for Pet Milk, Ralston Purina, Brown Shoe Company, and products with headquarters in other cities. Many of those ads—for brands such as Van Camp foods, Dazey home appliances, Popsicles, National Car Rentals, General Tires, Gerber Baby Foods, and Scripto writing instruments—were created in St. Louis.

Even though these two agencies were nationally known for their work, there were many, many more agencies in the region that created award-winning work, and while advertising is more about selling products or creating images than winning awards, it is nonetheless fascinating to see the beautiful art and copy in some of these advertisements.

The business of advertising is as unpredictable as is life itself. Where artists toiled to produce intricate images by hand a century ago, today's artists may never touch pencils or paintbrushes, instead performing all their creative work on computers. And the two major agencies that once brought so much business to St. Louis are gone, having been absorbed by huge conglomerates and then squeezed out of existence.

This does not mean, however, that the business of advertising has left St. Louis. Hundreds of people still make a living in the market: strategizing, creating, and producing ads for an ever-changing media environment. As in the past, the advertiser's job is to get the attention of potential consumers, no matter the medium, and deliver the message. This book purposely focuses on the past, for all intents and purposes, up to about 1980, and by necessity concentrates on ads that appeared in print.

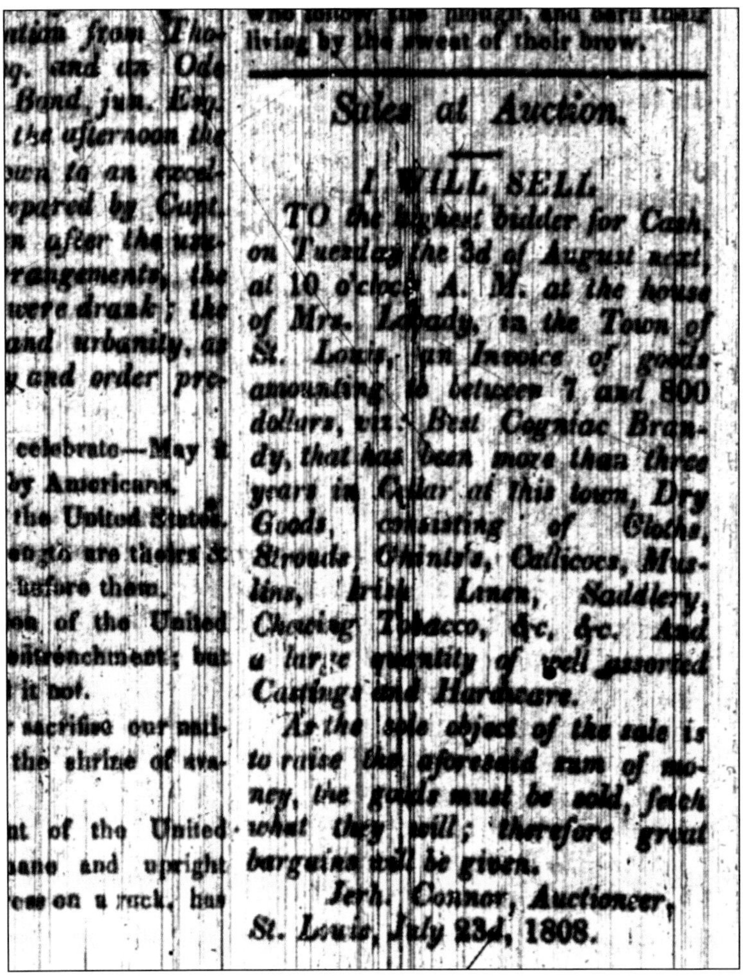
living by the sweat of their brow.

Sales at Auction.

I WILL SELL

TO the highest bidder for Cash, on Tuesday the 3d of August next, at 10 o'clock A. M. at the house of Mrs. Labady, in the Town of St. Louis, an Invoice of goods amounting to between 7 and 800 dollars, viz: Best Cogniac Brandy, that has been more than three years in Cellar at this town, Dry Goods, consisting of Cloths, Strouds, Chintz's, Callicoes, Muslins, Irish Linen, Saddlery, Chewing Tobacco, &c. &c. And a large quantity of well assorted Castings and Hardware.

As the sole object of the sale is to raise the aforesaid sum of money, the goods must be sold, fetch what they will; therefore great bargains will be given.

Jerh. Connor, Auctioneer,

St. Louis, July 23d, 1808.

This is probably one of the oldest existing advertisements found in St. Louis media. It appeared on the front page of the *Missouri Gazette* on July 26, 1808. Prior to newspapers, ads were propagated via posters and handbills. (St. Louis Media Archives.)

One

Outdoor Advertising

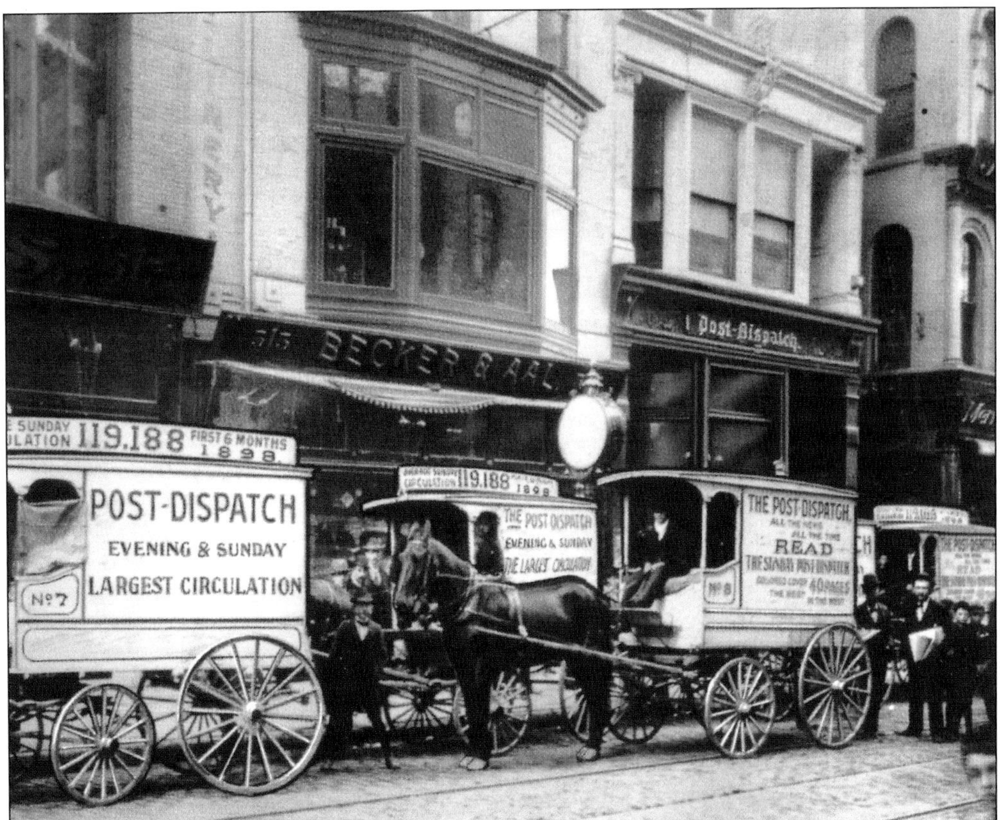

In 1898, the *St. Louis Post-Dispatch* used its delivery wagons to create rolling billboards. This photograph shows the wagons parked in front of the paper's building downtown at 530 Olive Street with advertising copy promoting the high circulation figures for the paper's Sunday edition. Bumpy streets, coupled with the slow gait of the horses, gave people on the sidewalks ample time to take in the ads' information. (St. Louis Media Archives.)

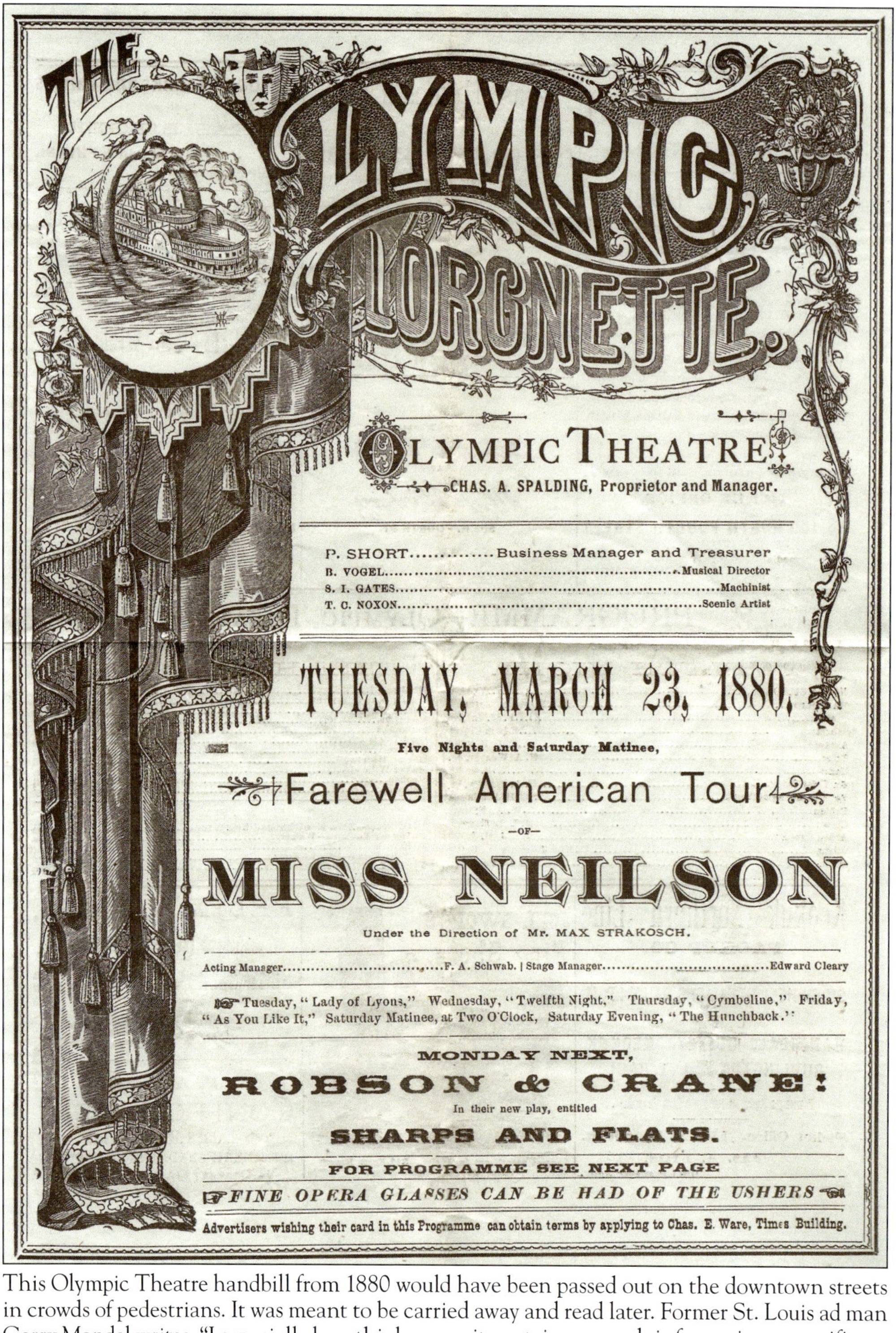
THE
OLYMPIC
LORGNETTE.
OLYMPIC THEATRE
CHAS. A. SPALDING, Proprietor and Manager.
P. SHORT............Business Manager and Treasurer
B. VOGEL..........Musical Director
S. I. GATES..........Machinist
T. C. NOXON..........Scenic Artist
TUESDAY, MARCH 23, 1880.
Five Nights and Saturday Matinee,
Farewell American Tour
—OF—
MISS NEILSON
Under the Direction of Mr. MAX STRAKOSCH.
Acting Manager..........F. A. Schwab. | Stage Manager..........Edward Cleary
Tuesday, "Lady of Lyons," Wednesday, "Twelfth Night," Thursday, "Cymbeline," Friday, "As You Like It," Saturday Matinee, at Two O'Clock, Saturday Evening, "The Hunchback."
MONDAY NEXT,
ROBSON & CRANE!
In their new play, entitled
SHARPS AND FLATS.
FOR PROGRAMME SEE NEXT PAGE
FINE OPERA GLASSES CAN BE HAD OF THE USHERS
Advertisers wishing their card in this Programme can obtain terms by applying to Chas. E. Ware, Times Building.

This Olympic Theatre handbill from 1880 would have been passed out on the downtown streets in crowds of pedestrians. It was meant to be carried away and read later. Former St. Louis ad man Gerry Mandel writes, "I especially love this because it contains so much information; magnificent copy, layout, illustration." (St. Louis Media Archives.)

Vandalia LINE.

FAST MAIL ROUTE.

Express Passenger Trains

Leave ST. LOUIS (Union Depot) every morning and evening (Saturdays and Sundays included) with PULLMAN HOTEL CARS and PALACE SLEEPING CARS without change, for

New York, Philadelphia, Harrisburg, Pittsburg, Columbus, Indianapolis, Cincinnati Louisville, and intermediate points.

One Change to Cleveland, Buffalo, Boston, Baltimore and Washington.

LOCATION IN THROUGH CARS SECURED AT

TICKET OFFICE,

No. 100 NORTH FOURTH STREET

E. A. FORD,

General Passenger Agent.

Chas. Humes & Co.,

DEALERS IN

FINE BUILDERS' HARDWARE,

Artistic Bronze Hardware a Specialty.

No. 11 North Sixth Street, ST. LOUIS.

W. H. GUMERSELL & CO.,

Emporium for those Perfect-Fitting

KID GLOVES

"Nonpareil," "Semper Idem," "Entre Nous," worn by the Elite of Society.

Bridal and Party Fans, Laces and Lace Goods, Embroideries, Dress Trimmings, French Corsets, Zephyr Worsteds, Fancy Goods, Etc.

413 N. FOURTH STREET.

Buy Your

HATS

AT

M. J. Steinberg

303 N. FOURTH ST.

For Good Trunks and Valises

GO TO

CHAS. BIEGER,

22 South Fifth St.

Repairing on Short Notice.

St. Louis Impenetrable Paint Co.,

Sole Manufacturers of

IMPENETRABLE PAINT

A glossy, durable, waterproof paint, prepared in all colors ready for use. Office and Factory, 421 N. Twelfth Street.

W. R. COTTRILL,

ST. LOUIS BILL POSTER,

221 North Third Street.

BUY YOUR

STATIONERY,

Pocket Cutlery, Pocket Books,

—AT—

CHAS. T. ULRICI,

DEALER IN

TOYS AND NOTIONS,

217 N. Fourth Street.

PROGRAMME—OLYMPIC THEATRE.

Saturday Matinee,

TWELFTH NIGHT.

MISS NEILSON as	VIOLA
MALVOLIO	EDWARD COMPTON
Orsino	F. W. Sanger
Sebastian	Edwin Cleary
Antonio	L. F. Rand
Friar	H. A. Weaver, Jr.
Curio	R. Smith
Sir Toby Belch	H. A. Weav r, Sr.
Sir Andrew Aguecheek	C. H. Bradshaw
Fabian	W. A. Eytinge
Clown	M. L. Leffingwell
A Sea Captain	J. H. Miller
Olivia	Miss Josephine C. Bailey
Marie	Miss Lizzie Goode

Saturday Evening,

THE HUNCHBACK.

JULIA	MISS NEILSON
SIR THOMAS CLIFFORD	EDWARD COMPTON
Master Walter	H. A. Weaver
Modus	F. W. Sanger
Fathom	C. H. Bradshaw
Lord Tinsel	W. A. Eytinge
Gaylove	J. H. Miller
Master Heartwell	Mr. Russell
Master Wilford	H. A Weaver, Jr.
Stephen	M. L. Leffingwell
Helen	Miss Josephine C. Bailey

MUSIC.

1	Overture—Zehn Maedchen und Kein Mann	Suppe
2	Wiener Bonbons—Walzer	Strauss
3	Reverie	Rosewig
4	Anna Polka—Solo by Kietz	Legendre
5	Selection—Le Petit Duc	Lecocq

Keokuk Northern Line

PACKET CO.

SIDEWHEEL STEAMERS DAILY 4 P. M.

FOR

HANNIBAL, QUINCY, KEOKUK, BURLINGTON and ST. PAUL.

Passenger Rates 50 Per Cent. Less Than Rail.

Ticket Office, 114 N. Fourth St.

JAS. A. LYON,

Gen'l Passenger Agent.

JOEL SWOPE'S

Fine Shoes.

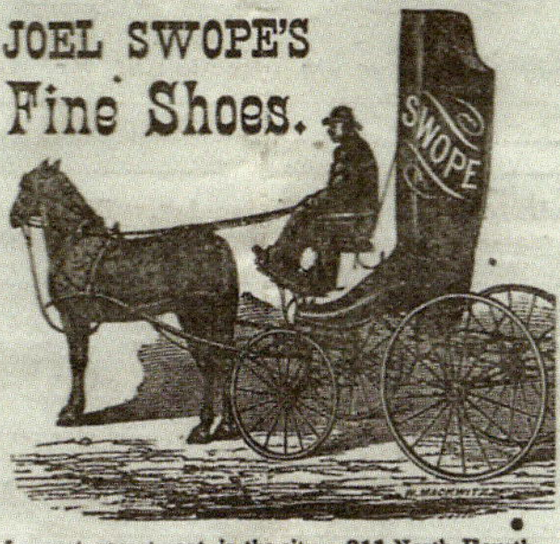

Largest assortment in the city. 311 North Fourth Street Opposite Everett House.

FELIX BARCHI,

Confectioner and Ladies' Restaurant.

Best Lunch and Dinner served. Open till 12 night. No. 408 Washington Avenue.

Regular Dinner, 40 Cents.

BISCUITS GLACES ALWAYS ON HAND.

P. ADAMS,

CONFECTIONERY

LADIES RESTAURANT,

ICE-CREAM AND OYSTER PARLOR.

414 MARKET ST., Opp. Court House.

The flip side of the Olympic Theatre handbill features paid advertisements for other businesses. In addition to giving these companies the attention of potential customers, the ads served to offset the cost incurred by the Olympic Theatre of having the handbills printed and distributed, just as advertising paid for the cost of publishing newspapers. (St. Louis Media Archives.)

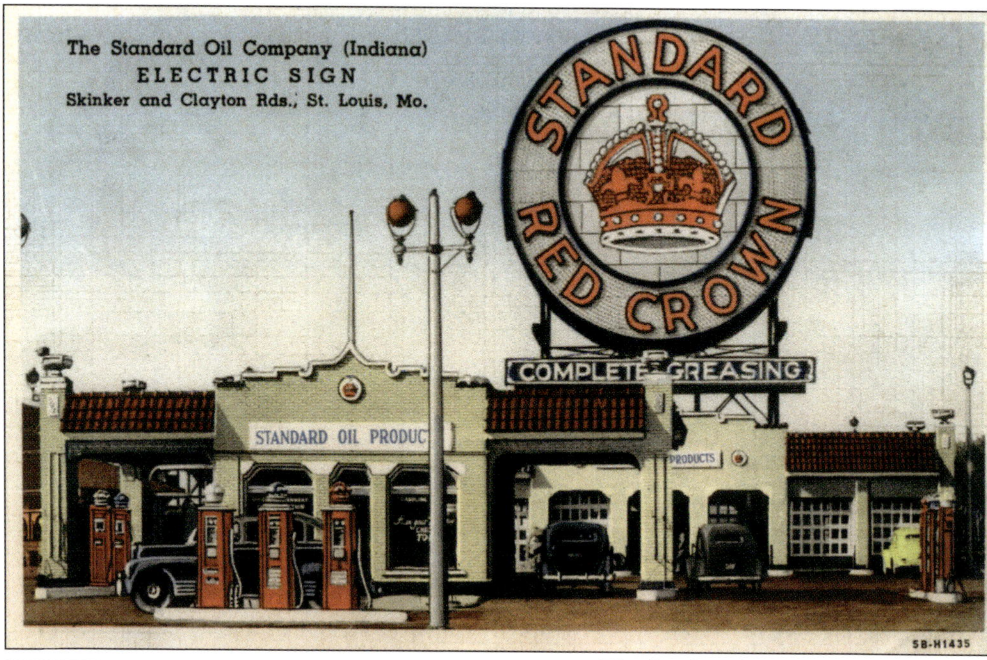

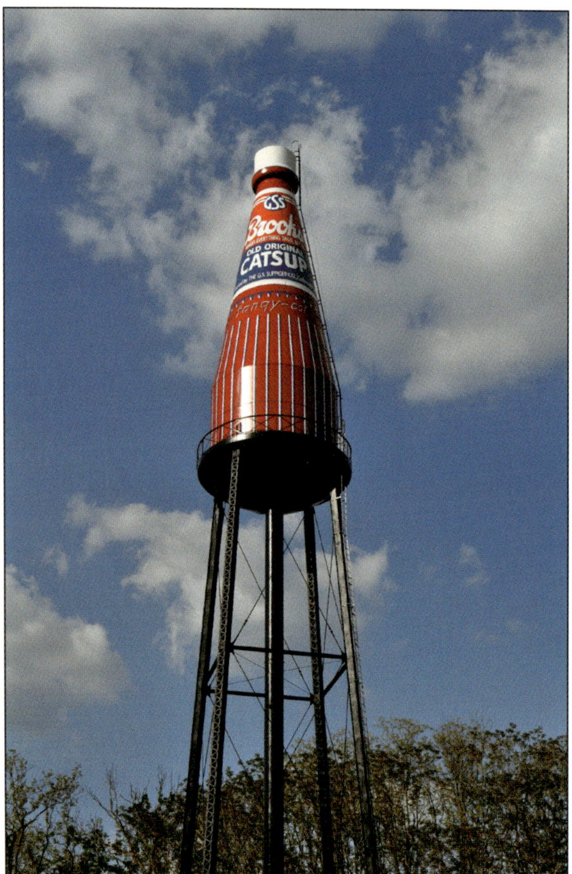

The landmark advertising sign at the Clayton Road–South Skinker Boulevard intersection has been there since the 1930s, although a change in the company name has sterilized the artistic value somewhat. The 5,800 lightbulbs inside the sign shown in this illustration have been replaced by external spotlights. Retired St. Louis ad man Gerry Mandel writes, "There was no way anyone could miss this sign. It was a work of art in lightbulbs." (St. Louis Media Archives.)

Brooks Catsup had a processing plant at this location in Collinsville, and this 70-foot-tall water tower was built by the W.E. Caldwell Tank Company in 1949. Retired ad man Don Stork calls it "a good example of '20th century roadside Americana.' " (Michael Gassmann/ World's Largest Catsup Bottle, Inc.)

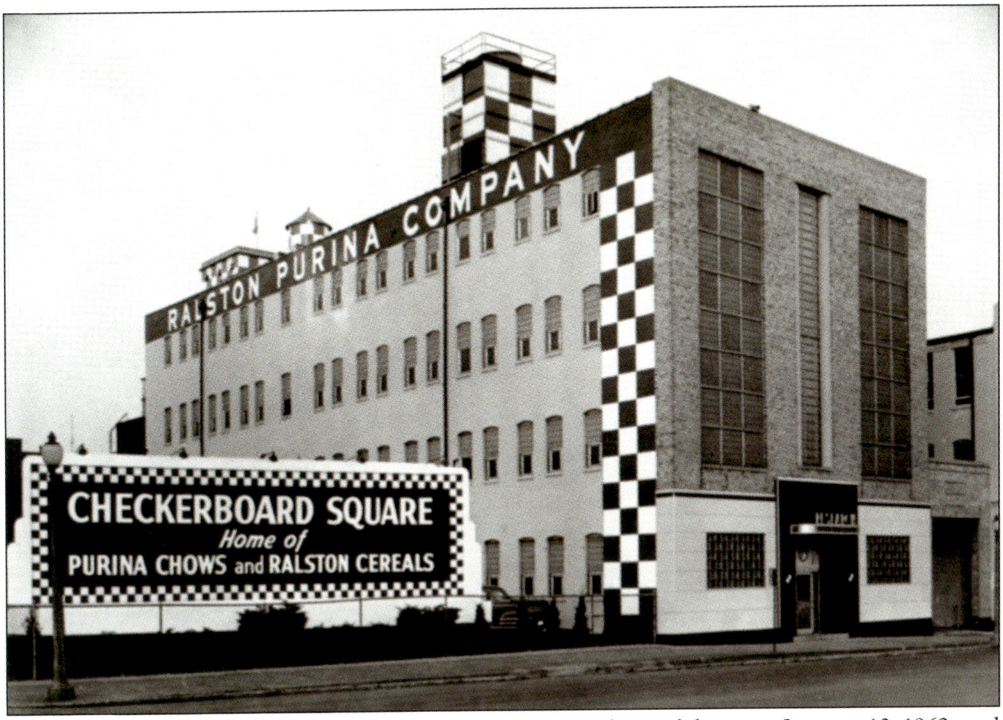

This building, which housed the offices of Ralston Purina, burned down on January 10, 1962, and was replaced by a modern structure. The name Checkerboard Square was retained. The company adopted the checkerboard logo after incorporating as Ralston Purina in 1902 and used it on all of its packaging. (Ralston Purina.)

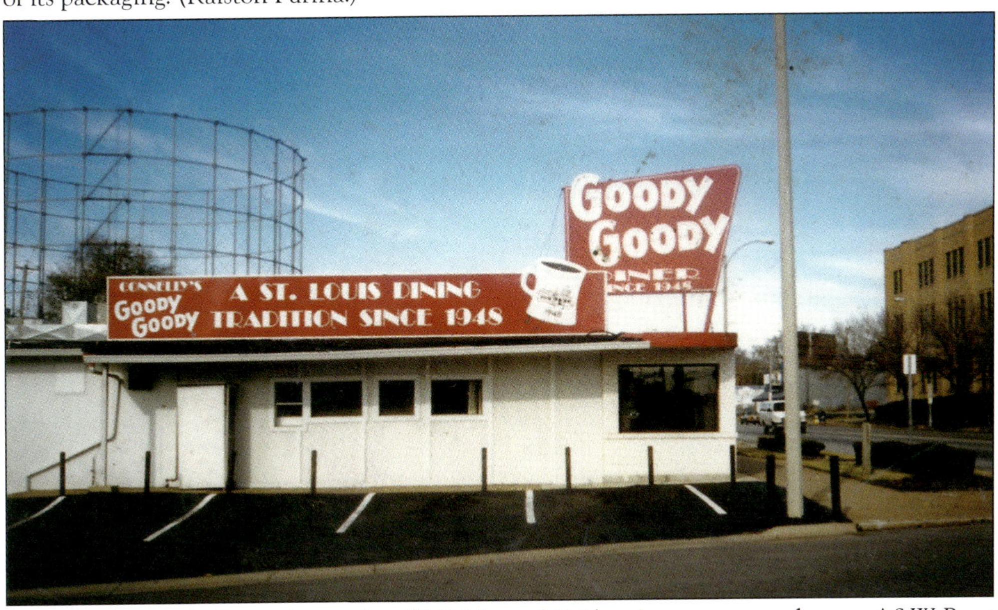

The Goody Goody Diner, located at 5900 Natural Bridge Avenue, opened as an A&W Root Beer stand in 1948. Today's signage, the work of sign painter Lonnie Tettaton, complements the building's late 1940s architecture and identifies the local landmark, which has set the scene for countless St. Louis memories. (Lonnie Tettaton.)

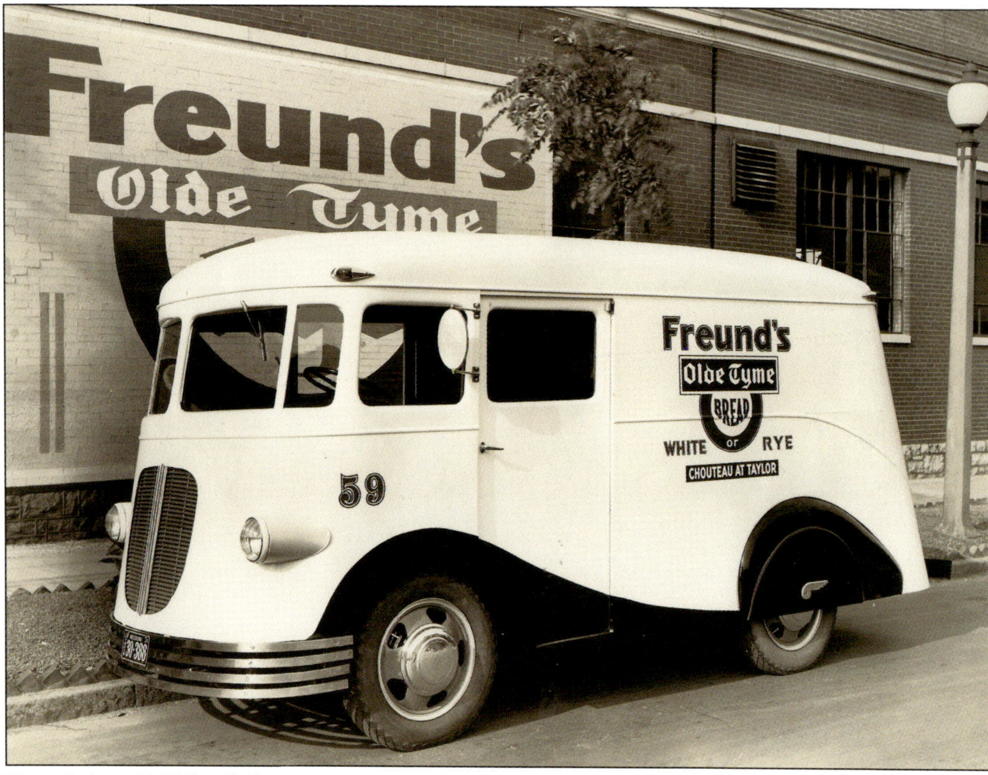

Founded in 1848 by Bohemian immigrants Moritz Freund and his wife, Jetta, Freund Baking Company was based in Soulard and relied on wagons and, later, trucks like this 1938 model to deliver baked products to stores and restaurants on 72 bread and 14 pie routes. (Duane Marburger.)

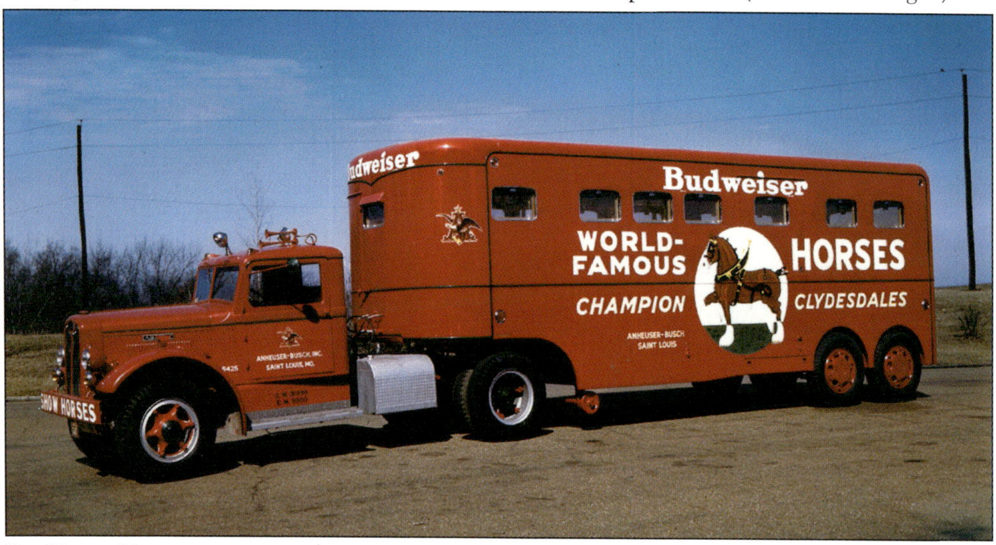

Dr. Kristy Tucciarone, associate professor of advertising and public relations at Lindenwood University, writes, "Anheuser-Busch's iconic team of Clydesdales became central to the brewer's rich history on April 7, 1933, a gift from August Busch Jr. to his father at the end of Prohibition. The traveling hitch provides instant recognition with a vibrant red palette." The signage on this 1946 truck heralded the arrival of the horse team. (Duane Marburger.)

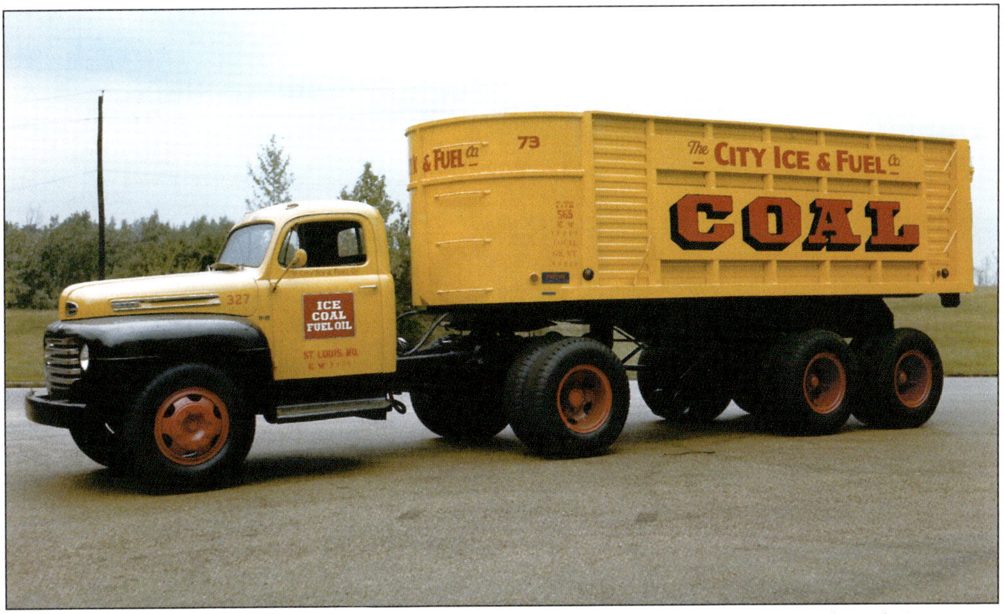

Even something as mundane as coal or ice can be branded. This City Ice and Fuel Company truck from the late 1940s was probably used to haul coal to customers' homes or places of business. (Duane Marburger.)

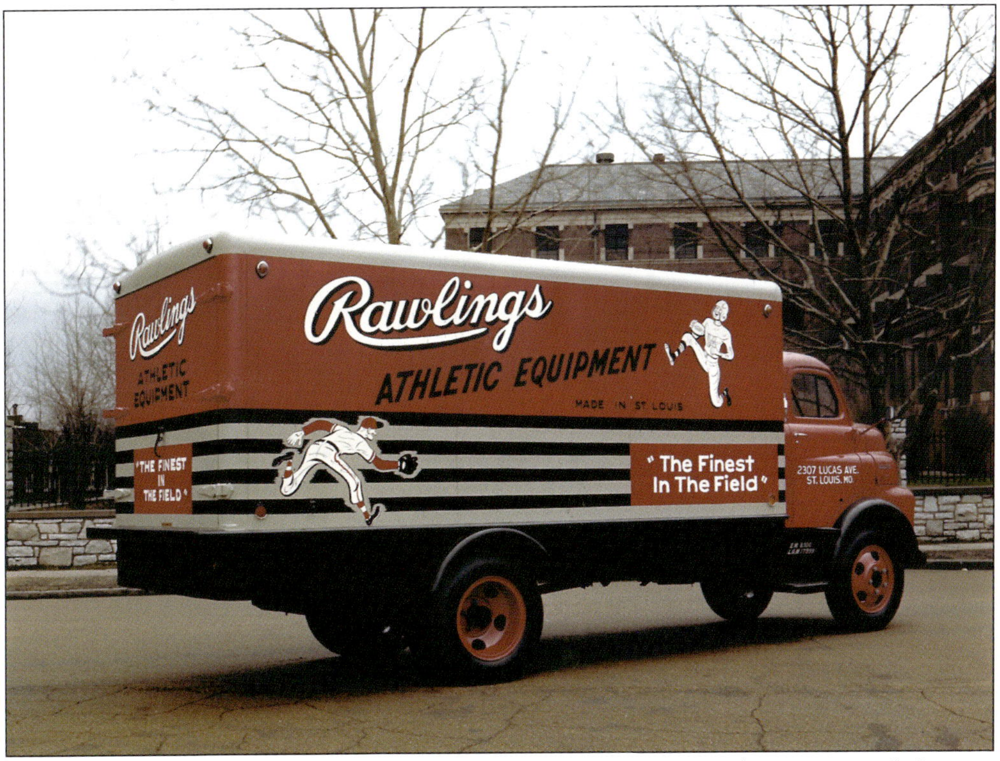

Founded in 1887, the Rawlings company name has been synonymous with sporting goods for more than a century. Its delivery trucks were used as rolling billboards with the company's colorful logo reinforcing the brand name. (Duane Marburger.)

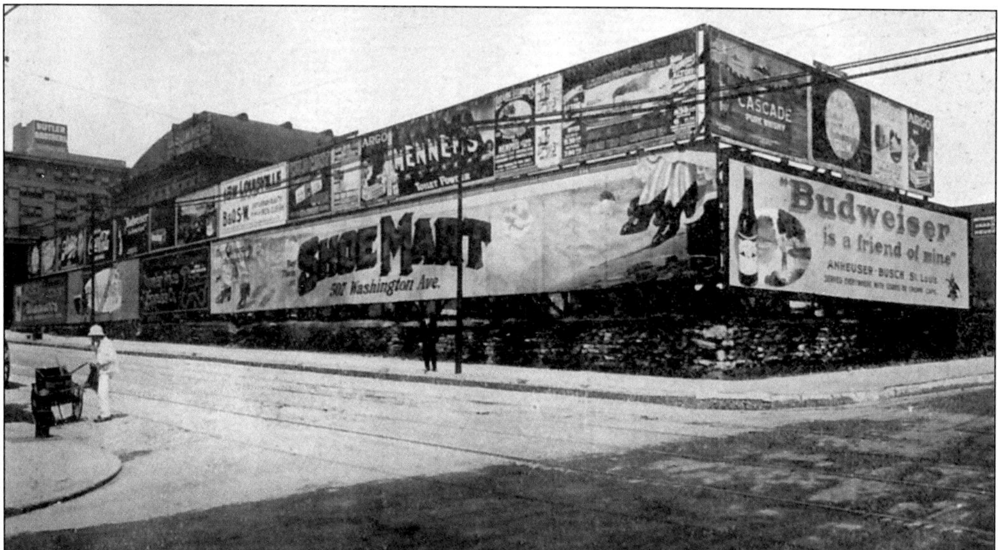

FIRST GREETINGS TO VISITORS
This double-decker occupies the entire block between Chestnut and Pine fronting on Eighteenth Street, near the Union Station. It leaves on the mind of the visitor a false impression of St. Louis.

At the turn of the century, a loud, vocal opposition began making their feelings known about the visual blight of billboards. This display on Eighteenth Street, between Chestnut and Pine Streets, greeted visitors as they left Union Station in the early 1900s. A civic report referred to the displays as "the unsightliness and rude aggressiveness of walls of lurid advertisements which line our important thoroughfares. The universally accepted indictment against billboards is the fact that they are unsightly and ugly." (St. Louis Public Library.)

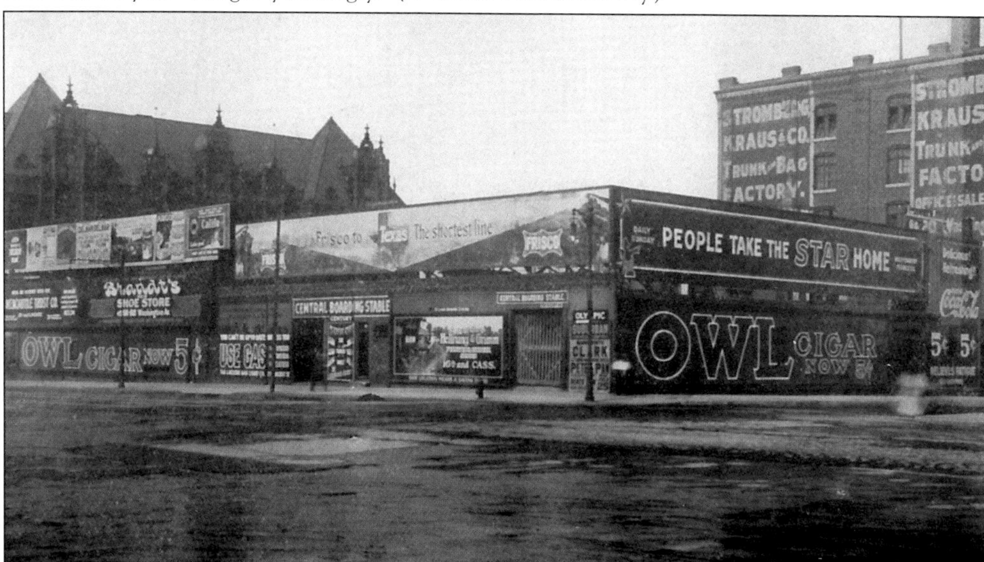

THE CITY HALL BEHIND A "TRIPLE-DECKER"
What is the use of "architectural symmetry and harmony" with such surroundings.

North of city hall, which is visible in the background of this image, another over-the-top billboard display was targeted by opponents, some of whom referred to the blight as "unsafe, unsanitary and even immoral." The Civic League Committee of St. Louis, an anti-billboard group, was able to persuade politicians to pass ordinances in 1906. (St. Louis Public Library.)

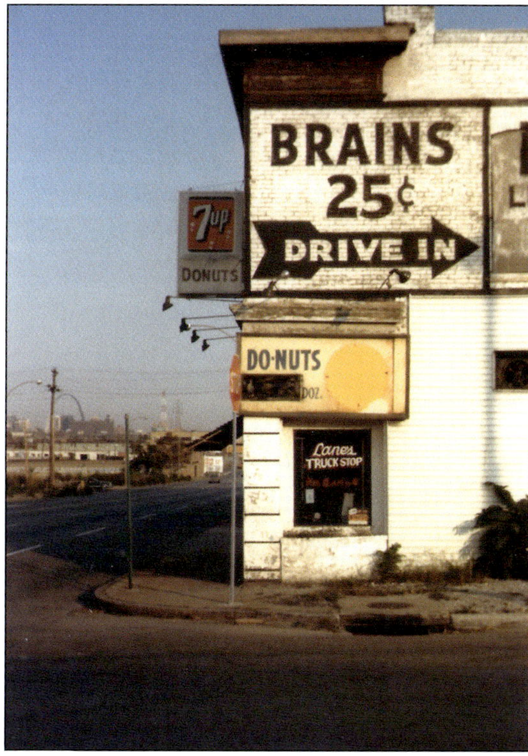

This vintage photograph by Wm. Stage has immortalized the now-defunct Lane's Truck Stop. Gerry Mandel calls the picture "a work of art," and another ad man, Don Stork, remembers, "This location, on Chouteau [Avenue] east of Grand [Boulevard], packed in customers from all walks of life; truckers, locals, business people and St. Louis University Medical School staff and students. It was one of many St. Louis establishments using its own space for advertising." (Wm. Stage.)

Busch Bavarian Beer was introduced in 1955 as a regional beer. Dr. Kristy Tucciarone calls this billboard an excellent example of outdoor advertising that gains attention—the skier literally flies overhead. It captures the essence of Bavaria. (Copyright © Anheuser-Busch, LLC. Used with permission of Anheuser-Busch, LLC. All rights reserved.)

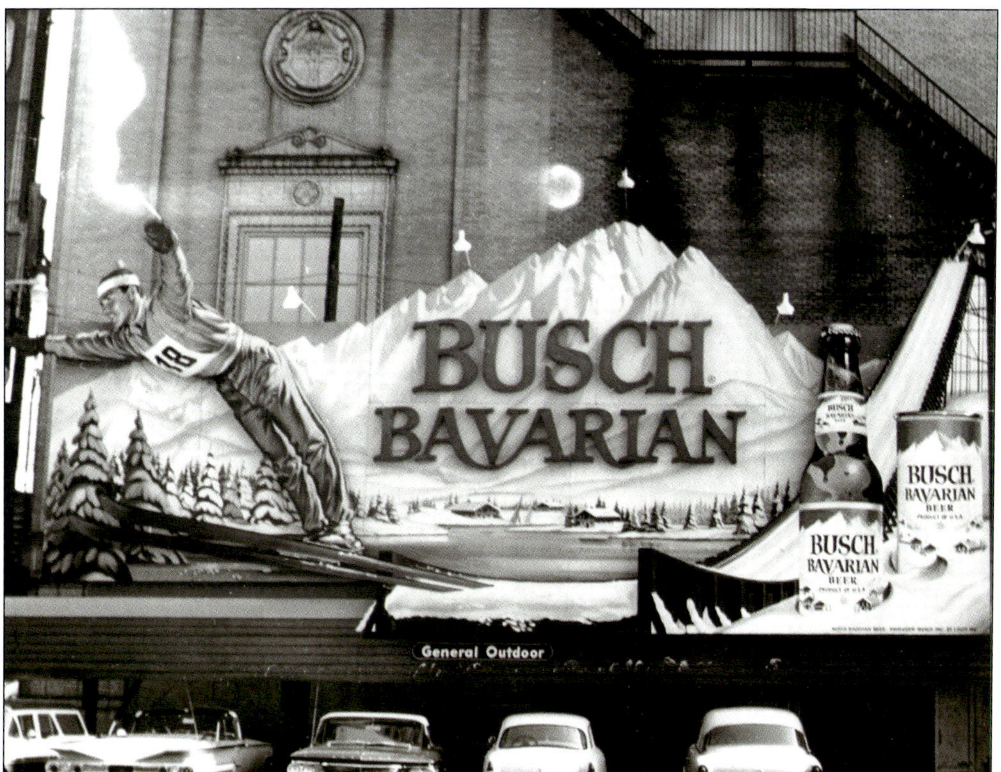

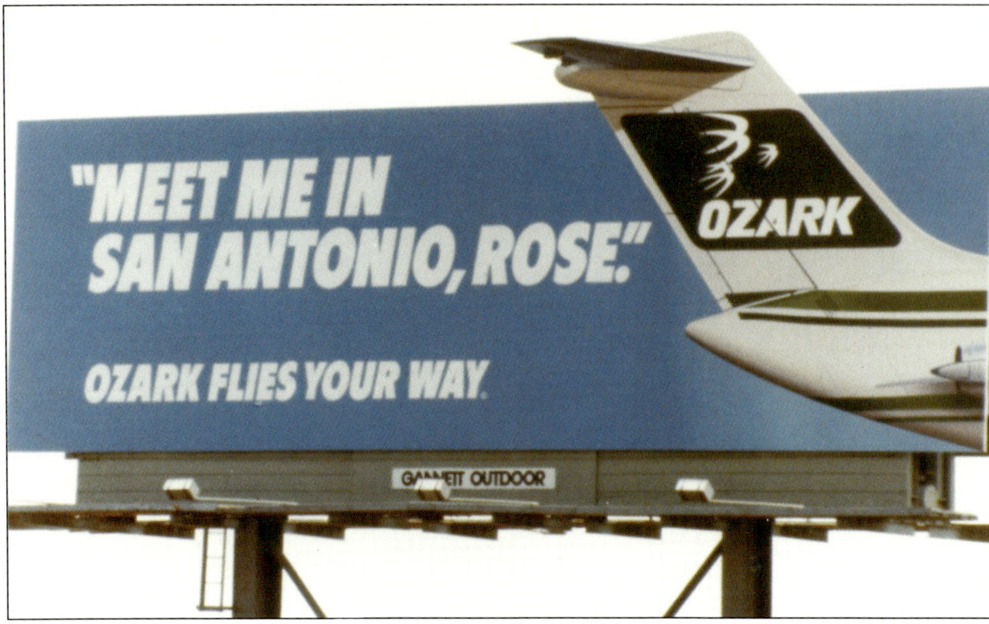
"MEET ME IN
SAN ANTONIO, ROSE."
OZARK FLIES YOUR WAY.
OZARK

From 1950 until 1986, Ozark Airlines was based in St. Louis, and St. Louis–based D'Arcy Advertising handled the its account. The regional airline initially served the Midwest before branching out to Denver, Florida, and New York. Ozark merged with TWA in 1986. (St. Louis Media Archives.)

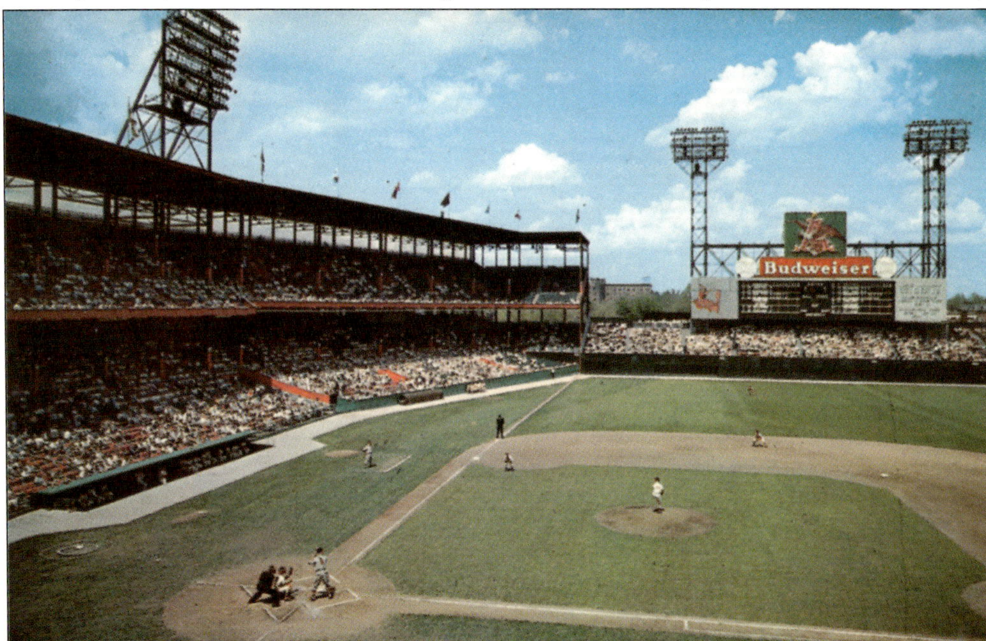
Budweiser

For many St. Louisans, including Dr. Kristy Tucciarone, baseball is a near-religious experience. Tucciarone says about this Sportsman's Park photograph, "Ah, the love of baseball! And the game is even better when no. 6 is at the plate, 'Stan the Man.' The massive Budweiser sign glows in left field as baseball lovers cheer on their favorite player. Under ownership in 1953 by Gussie Busch, it seems appropriate the beer giant's boss would want to display his brand here." (St. Louis Media Archives.)

Two

Trade Cards, Blotters, and Mail

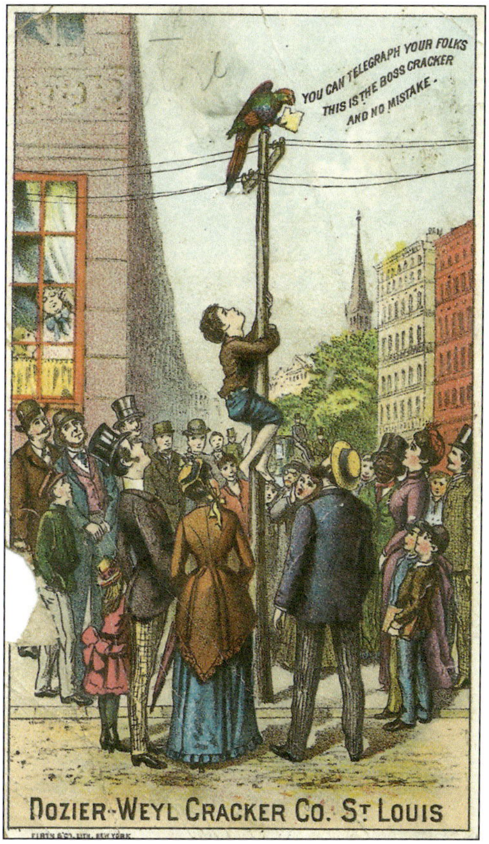
YOU CAN TELEGRAPH YOUR FOLKS
THIS IS THE BOSS CRACKER
AND NO MISTAKE.
DOZIER-WEYL CRACKER CO. ST LOUIS

As early as 1848, the Dozier baking facility was operating near the St. Louis riverfront at Third and Pine Streets. Within three decades, the company name had been changed to the Dozier-Wyle Company, and the plant had been expanded and was producing 1,500 barrels of crackers per day, along with cakes, pies, and bread, serving both retail and wholesale clients. By 1880, there were over 200 bakeries in St. Louis, so when the trading-card fad developed late in the 19th century, Dozier-Wyle put out a series of colorful ad trading cards, many of which featured a parrot in the art work. The company name became the Dozier-Wyle Cracker Company, and later, after a merger created the National Biscuit Company (Nabisco), it was instrumental in creating the iconic Animal Crackers. (St. Louis Media Archives.)

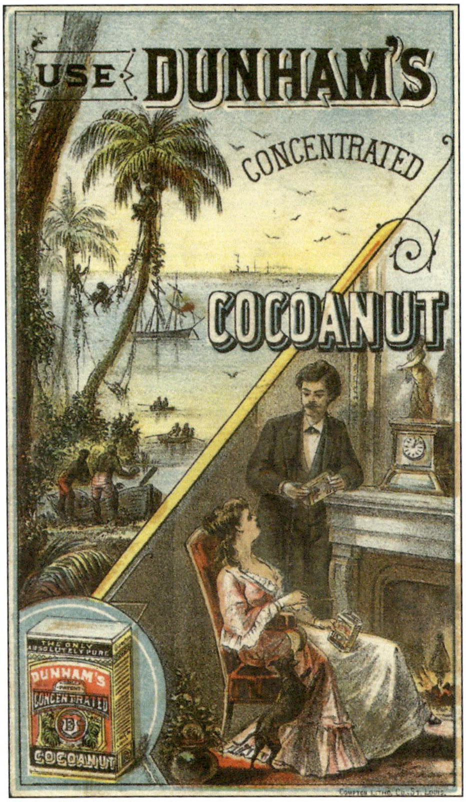
USE DUNHAM'S
CONCENTRATED
COCOANUT
DUNHAM'S
COCOANUT

Located at 9 Locust Street, near the edge of the Mississippi River, Dunham's relied heavily on trade cards for promotion. Owner John S. Dunham also sold kits that allowed people to turn the company's wooden shipping crates into dollhouses. (St. Louis Media Archives.)

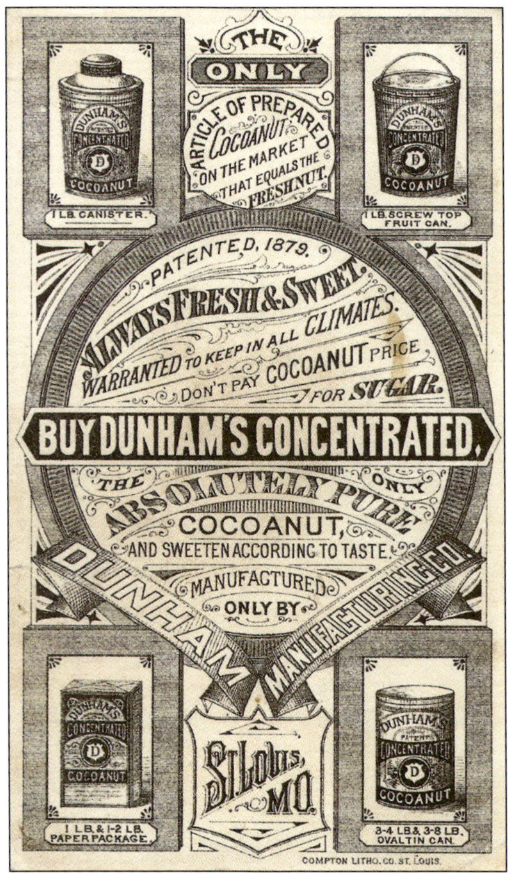
THE
ONLY
ARTICLE OF PREPARED
COCOANUT
ON THE MARKET
THAT EQUALS THE
FRESH NUT.
1 LB. CANISTER.
1 LB. SCREW TOP FRUIT CAN.
PATENTED, 1879.
ALWAYS FRESH & SWEET.
WARRANTED TO KEEP IN ALL CLIMATES.
DON'T PAY COCOANUT PRICE
FOR SUGAR.
BUY DUNHAM'S CONCENTRATED,
THE ONLY
ABSOLUTELY PURE
COCOANUT,
AND SWEETEN ACCORDING TO TASTE.
MANUFACTURED
ONLY BY
DUNHAM MANUFACTURING CO.
ST. LOUIS, MO.
1 LB. & 1-2 LB. PAPER PACKAGE.
3-4 LB. & 3-8 LB. OVALTIN CAN.
COMPTON LITHO. CO. ST. LOUIS.

This ad copy set the Dunham's product apart from other packaged coconut by telling consumers that the product was not weighted down with sugar, allowing users to sweeten it to individual tastes. (St. Louis Media Archives.)

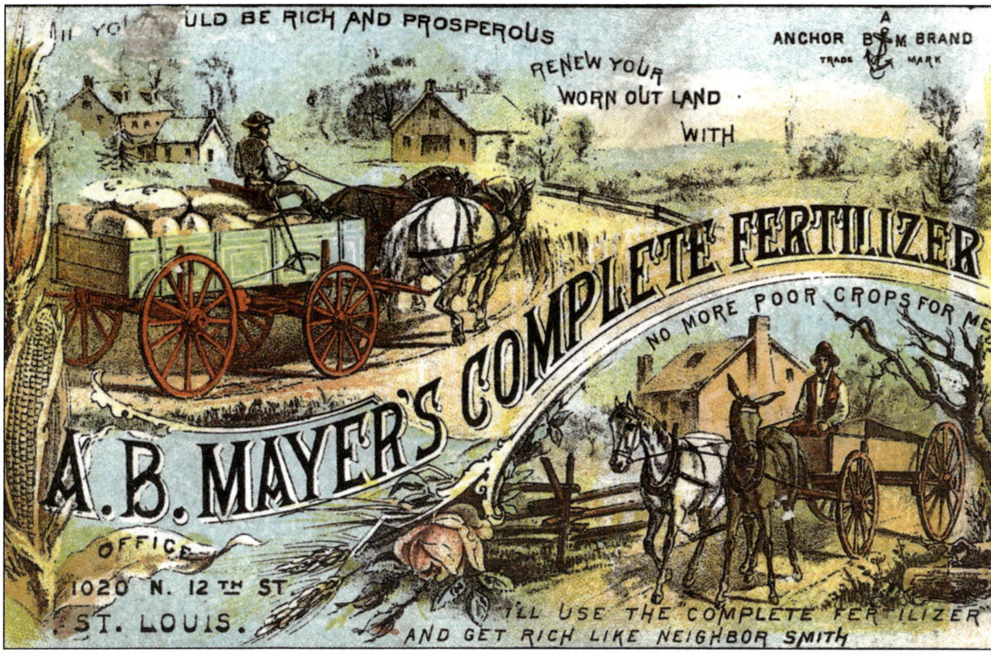
ULD BE RICH AND PROSPEROUS
RENEW YOUR WORN OUT LAND WITH
ANCHOR A B M BRAND
TRADE MARK
A. B. MAYER'S COMPLETE FERTILIZER
NO MORE POOR CROPS FOR ME
OFFICE
1020 N. 12TH ST.
ST. LOUIS.
I'LL USE THE "COMPLETE FERTILIZER"
AND GET RICH LIKE NEIGHBOR SMITH

This 1901 Mayer's trade-card advertising fertilizer is a perfect example of old-time ephemera, according to commercial artist R.J. Shay. The art was all done by hand, including the typeface created by the artist. (St. Louis Media Archives.)

ANALYSIS OF MAYER'S "ANCHOR BRAND" COMPLETE FERTILIZER.

Moisture 212° Fah.	4.55.
Organic Matter, (Red Heat.)	34.33.
Yielding Nitrogen,	1.78.
" Ammonia,	2½ to 3

A. B. MAYER,

MANUFACTURER OF

THE "COMPLETE FERTILIZER,"

Prepared Especially for Wheat, Corn, Potatoes, and all Field and Garden Crops.

Above brand is made from strictly "dissolved pure animal bone," and is guaranteed "free" from South Carolina Rock, or any other mineral phosphate deposit.

Farmers can always rely on an increased crop of one-third to one-half, early maturity, and an improved soil, by an application of 200 to 400 lbs. per acre, according to the quality of the land.

If anyone is skeptical regarding the value of "animal manures," let a simple experiment, one bag (200 lbs.) be made, and note the result.

My fertilizer, may be sown broadcast, or, as they are dry and ground fine, they may be drilled with ease and regularity. Put up in bags of 100 and 200 lbs.; full weight guaranteed. No charge for packages, and delivered to R. R. Depots, St. Louis, free of charge. I make and sell the simple and natural manures, dry and fine ground bone, meat, blood and potash.

For further information, address,

A. B. MAYER,

Anchor Bone Factory, Lowell Mo.
Anchor Fertilizing Works, *Foot of Harrison St.*

Office, 1020 N. 12th St., ST. LOUIS, MO.

Cash paid for paper stock, scrap iron, bones, &c.

FRED. MAYER, *Manager.*

The flip side of the Mayer's card was used for a detailed sales pitch. After touting the quality of the company's fertilizer, the writer added, almost as an afterthought, "Cash paid for paper stock, scrap iron, bones, &c." (St. Louis Media Archives.)

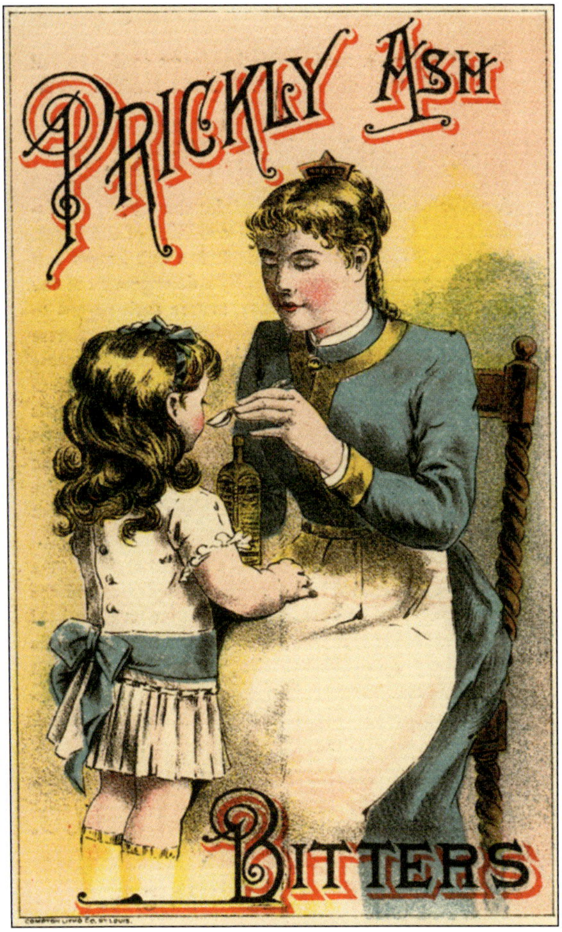

Prickly Ash Bitters was advertised as a "tonic for the kidneys, liver, stomach and bowels." Advertising professor Kristy Tucciarone says this ad "captures the essence of the role of women as the caretaker for the children." (St. Louis Media Archives.)

By 1892, St. Louis was the major manufacturing center for the nation's kitchen stoves, building over $2 million of stoves that year. Twenty years later, 2,500 people were employed in stove and range manufacturing in the St. Louis area, building 1.1 million stoves in 1912. (Shelly Donaho.)

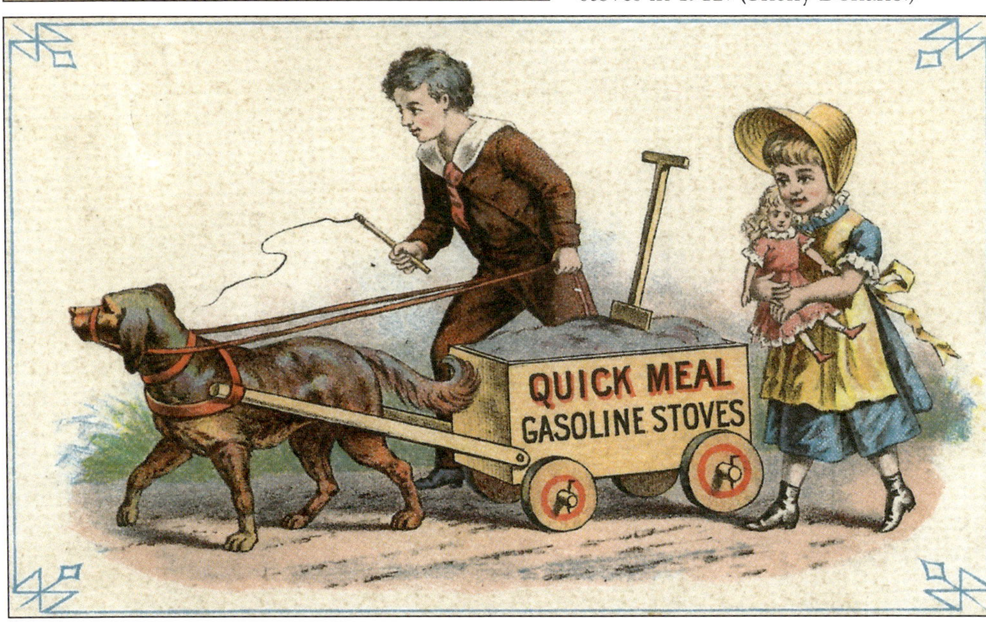

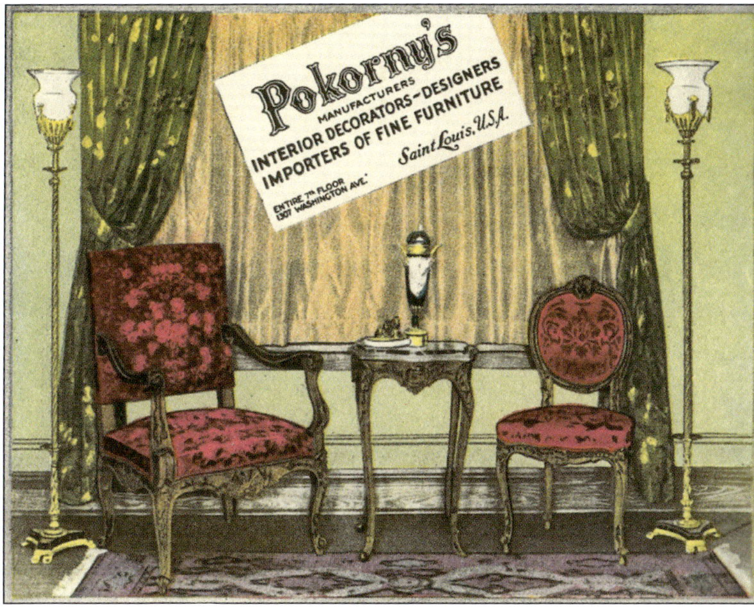

"Wow" was the reaction of commercial artist R.J. Shay when he saw this ad. The art, he said, is actually built atop a black-and-white photograph of the furniture setting, which then had brilliant colors painted over it. (Duane Marburger.)

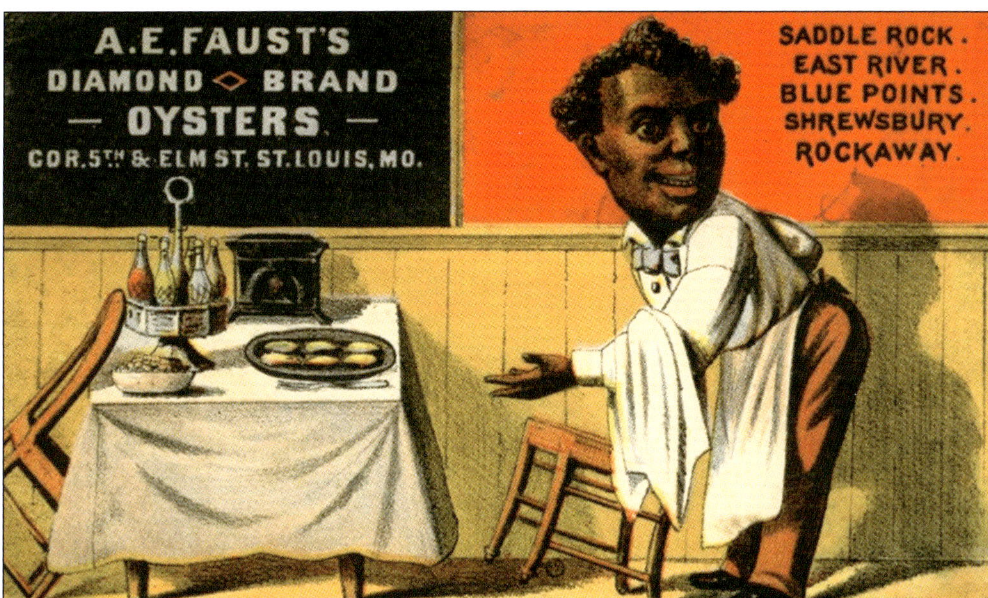

Tony Faust began his saloon in the 1860s in the Frenchtown neighborhood at Broadway and Elm Street. Faust's rooftop beer garden was reportedly the first in the nation. Retired ad man Gerry Mandel loves this advertisement: "It speaks to old St. Louis, old tastes, and attitudes. I'm fascinated by the idea of so many oyster choices in middle America in the days before speedy delivery of refrigerated items." (St. Louis Media Archives.)

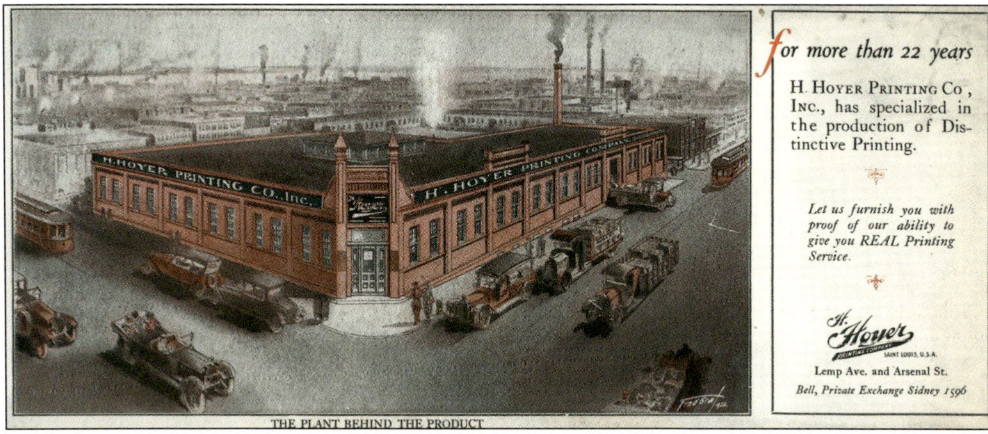
H. HOYER PRINTING CO., Inc.
H. HOYER PRINTING COMPANY
for more than 22 years
H. HOYER PRINTING CO., INC., has specialized in the production of Distinctive Printing.
Let us furnish you with proof of our ability to give you REAL Printing Service.
H. Hoyer
SAINT LOUIS, U.S.A.
Lemp Ave. and Arsenal St.
Bell, Private Exchange Sidney 1596
THE PLANT BEHIND THE PRODUCT

This ink blotter advertising a printing company impressed former ad man Gerry Mandel: "Interesting strategy to show the plant as proof of their printing expertise. I love the illustration, especially the elevation with other plants shown in the background and smoke rising from the stacks." (Duane Marburger.)

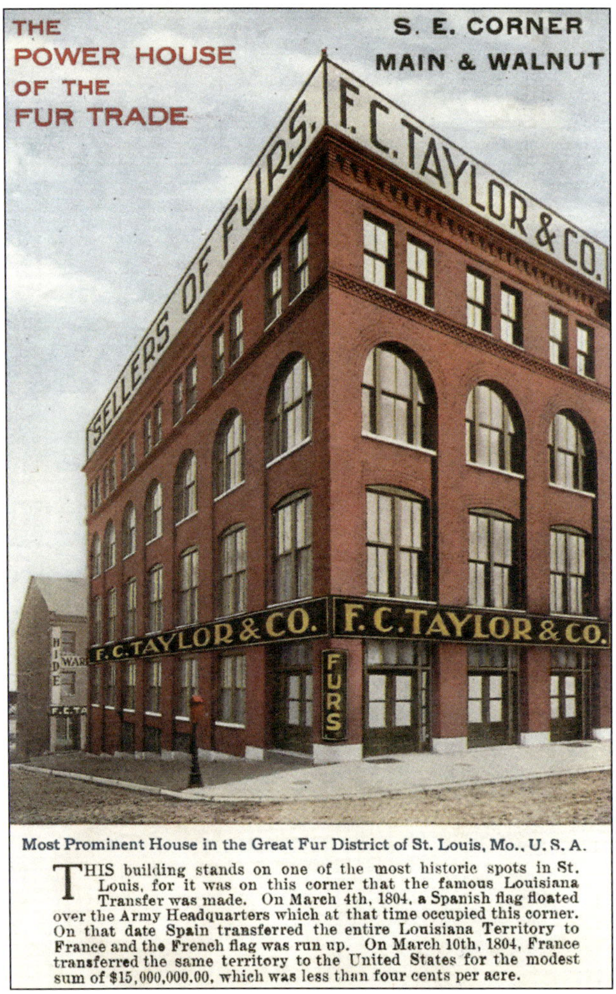
THE POWER HOUSE OF THE FUR TRADE
S. E. CORNER MAIN & WALNUT
SELLERS OF FURS.
F. C. TAYLOR & CO.
F. C. TAYLOR & CO.
F. C. TAYLOR & CO.
FURS
Most Prominent House in the Great Fur District of St. Louis, Mo., U. S. A.
THIS building stands on one of the most historic spots in St. Louis, for it was on this corner that the famous Louisiana Transfer was made. On March 4th, 1804, a Spanish flag floated over the Army Headquarters which at that time occupied this corner. On that date Spain transferred the entire Louisiana Territory to France and the French flag was run up. On March 10th, 1804, France transferred the same territory to the United States for the modest sum of $15,000,000.00, which was less than four cents per acre.

At the beginning of the 20th century, St. Louis had 40 fur houses. Most of the United States was rural, and residents could supplement their incomes with trapping. Huge fur houses like F.C. Taylor went after the trappers' business, sometimes using postcards. (St. Louis Media Archives.)

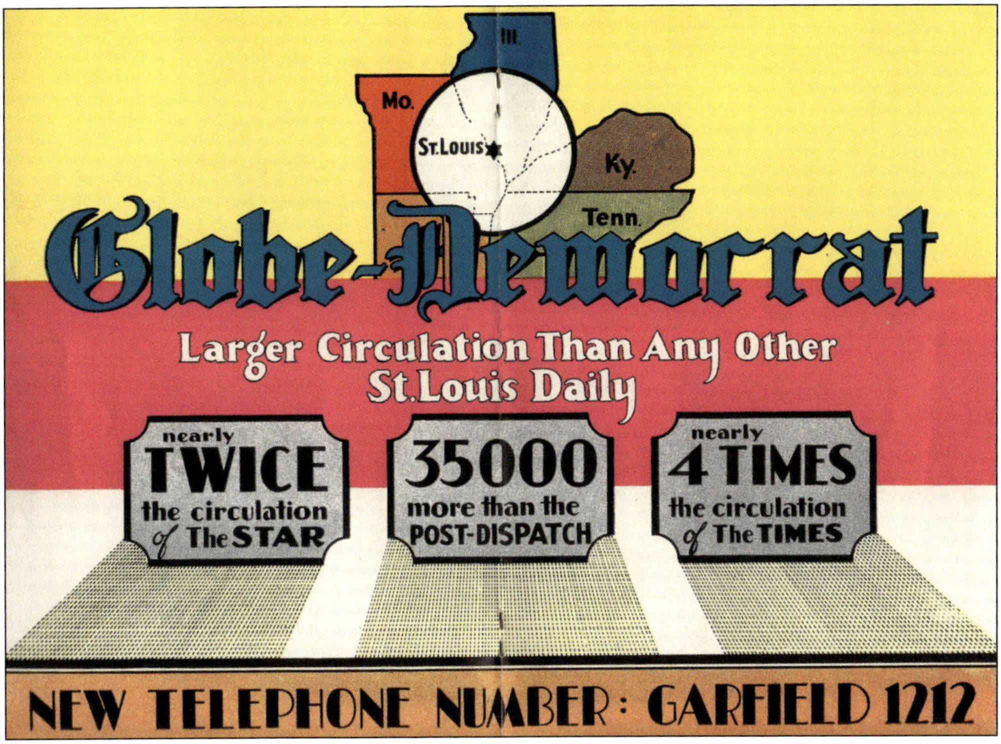
Ill.
Mo.
St.Louis
Ky.
Tenn.
Globe-Democrat
Larger Circulation Than Any Other St.Louis Daily
nearly TWICE the circulation of The STAR
35000 more than the POST-DISPATCH
nearly 4 TIMES the circulation of The TIMES
NEW TELEPHONE NUMBER: GARFIELD 1212

The *St. Louis Globe-Democrat*, which came into existence in 1875, was a major media player in St. Louis for 100 years. This 1929 ink blotter that favorably compares the *Globe-Democrat* to its competitors was part of a series provided for advertisers and potential advertisers. (St. Louis Media Archives.)

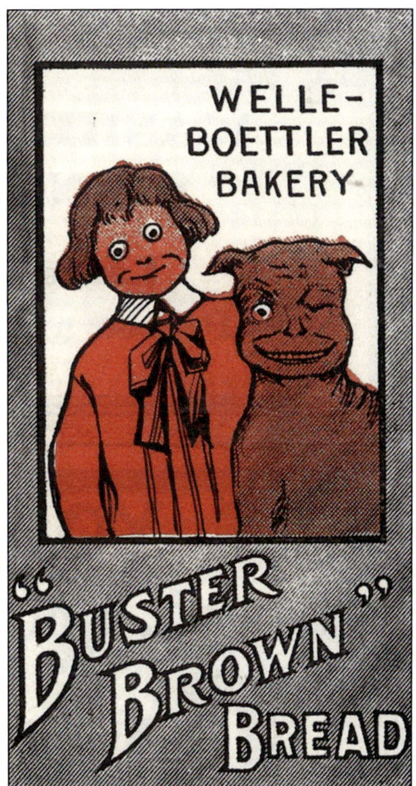
WELLE-BOETTLER BAKERY
"BUSTER BROWN" BREAD

It is likely that the Welle-Boettler Bakery simply appropriated the name and likeness of Buster Brown, a comic strip character often associated with the Brown Shoe Company, in an effort to promote its products in this 1910 advertisement. (St. Louis Media Archives.)

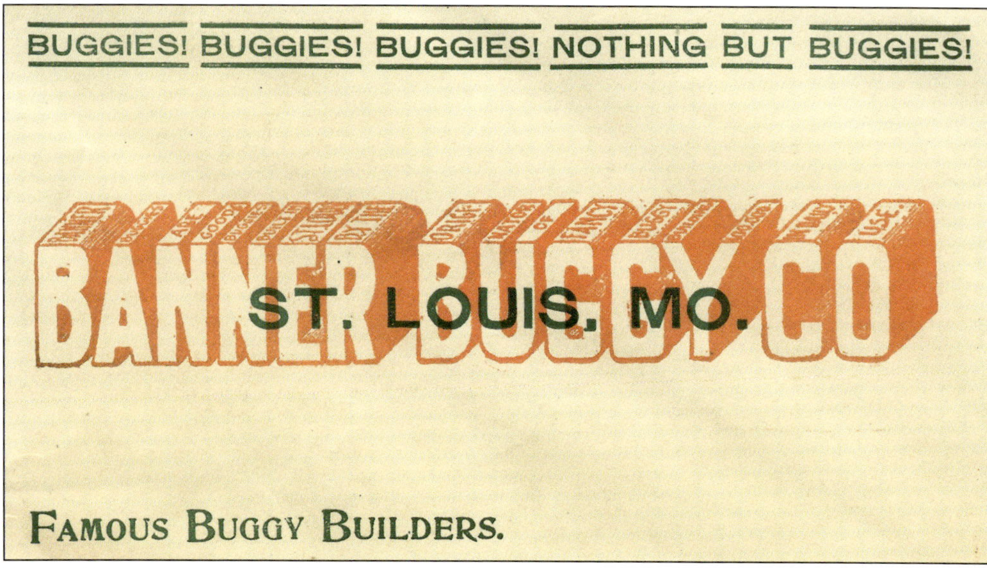
BUGGIES! BUGGIES! BUGGIES! NOTHING BUT BUGGIES!
BANNER BUGGY CO
ST. LOUIS, MO.
FAMOUS BUGGY BUILDERS.

Banner Buggy Company used this return envelope to advertise itself. As one of the nation's largest buggy manufacturers, the St. Louis–based corporation also produced detailed catalogues showing its various carriages and buggies. After World War 1, Banner established a local subsidiary that manufactured cars. (St. Louis Media Archives.)

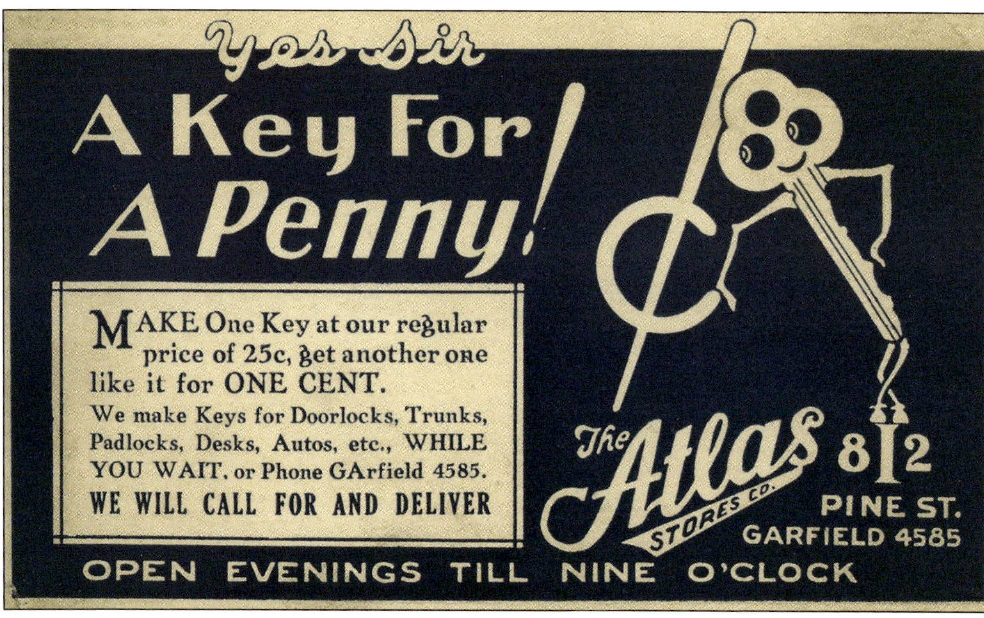
Yes Sir
A Key For A Penny!
MAKE One Key at our regular price of 25c, get another one like it for ONE CENT.
We make Keys for Doorlocks, Trunks, Padlocks, Desks, Autos, etc., WHILE YOU WAIT, or Phone GArfield 4585.
WE WILL CALL FOR AND DELIVER
The Atlas Stores Co.
812 PINE ST.
GARFIELD 4585
OPEN EVENINGS TILL NINE O'CLOCK

The artistic design of this postcard produced by the Atlas Stores Company in 1929 is, according to commercial artist R.J. Shay, a "horrible graphic, but it's indicative of the time period, when it was common to anthropomorphize objects." (St. Louis Media Archives.)

Bopp Funeral and Livery, founded in Kirkwood in 1902 to provide horse-drawn hearse service, later expanded into a funeral chapel with room for funeral services. In the days before air-conditioning, fans like this would have been found tucked in the slots next to hymnals in church. (St. Louis Media Archives.)

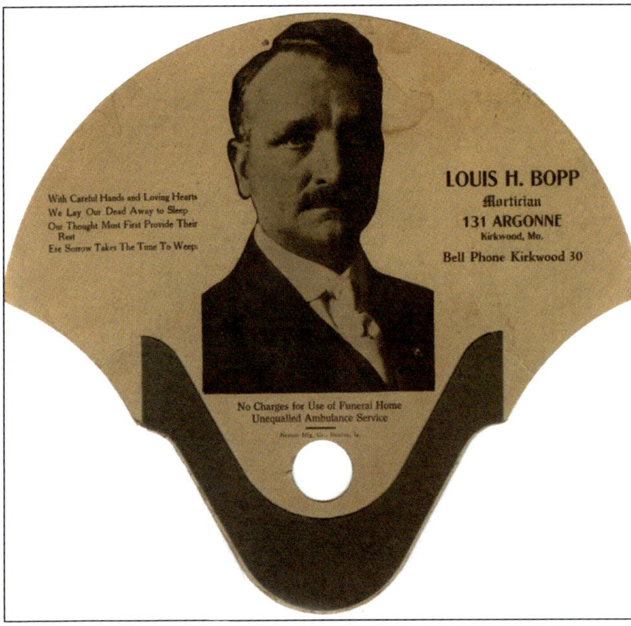
With Careful Hands and Loving Hearts
We Lay Our Dead Away to Sleep
Our Thought Must First Provide Their Rest
Ere Sorrow Takes The Time To Weep.
LOUIS H. BOPP
Mortician
131 ARGONNE
Kirkwood, Mo.
Bell Phone Kirkwood 30
No Charges for Use of Funeral Home
Unequalled Ambulance Service

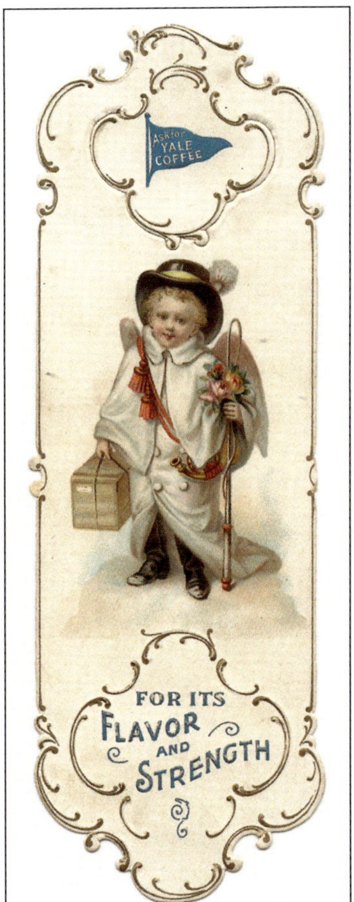
Ask for YALE COFFEE
FOR ITS
FLAVOR
AND
STRENGTH

Yale Coffee was made in St. Louis by the Steinwender Stoffregen Coffee Company. Founded in 1876, the company also sold spices. Its advertising for the Yale brand at the turn of the century included bookmarks (like this one) and trade cards. (St. Louis Media Archives.)

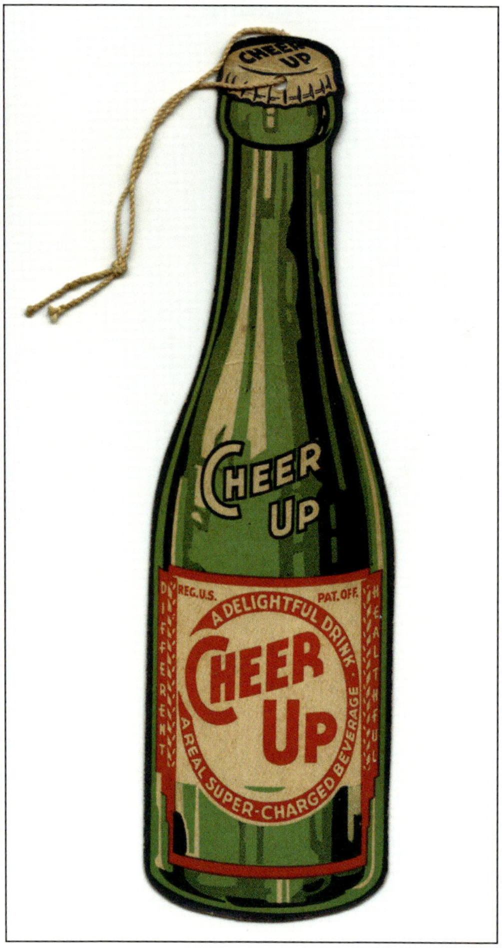

Cheer Up was a "lithiated lemon soda" licensed and produced by the Cheer Up Sales Company. At least five different bottling facilities in St. Louis produced Cheer Up in the late 1920s. The cardboard bottle shown was often tied to the pull chains of ceiling fans in the shops of retailers. (Duane Marburger.)

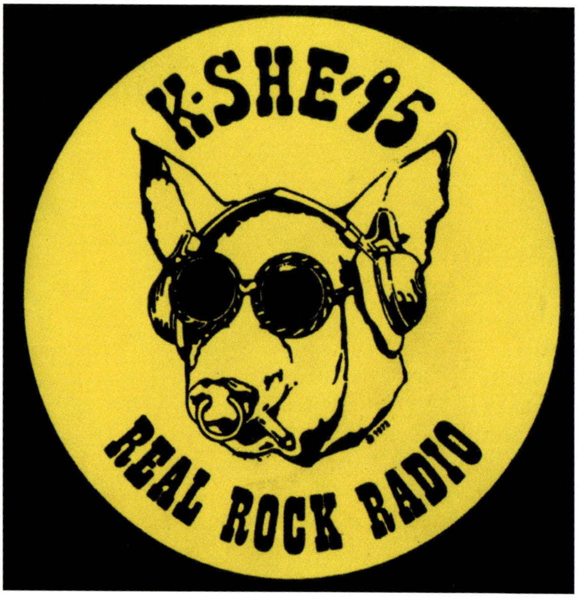

Professor Kristy Tucciarone celebrates the uniqueness of the porcine symbol of KSHE Radio: "What's not to love about 'Sweetmeat'?! Sweetmeat was effective at generating attention, both good and bad, because of the controversial 'joint' hanging from his mouth. The joint disappeared in the 1980s." (St. Louis Media Archives.)

Three

STUFF TO WEAR

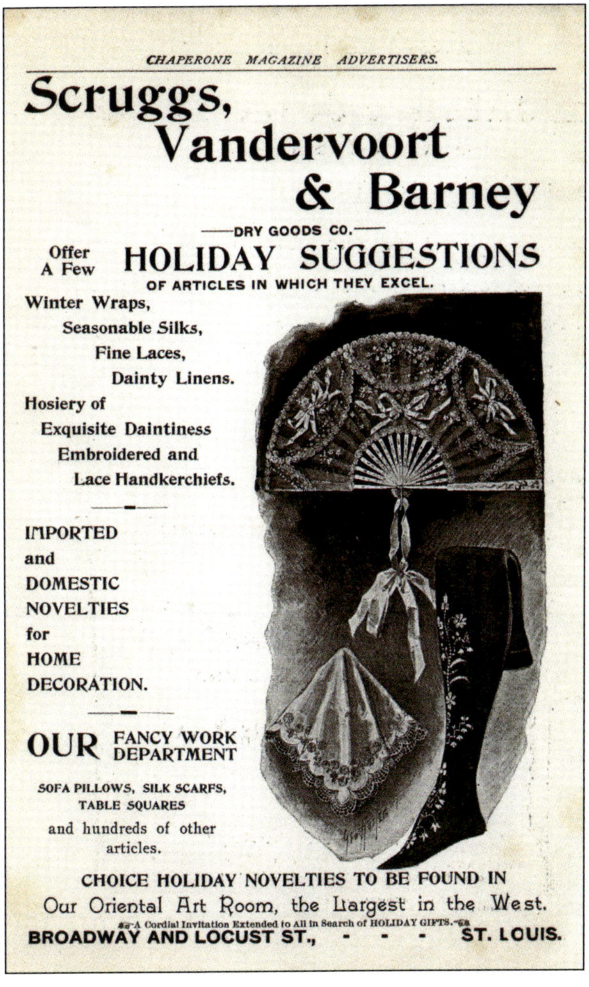
CHAPERONE MAGAZINE ADVERTISERS.
Scruggs, Vandervoort & Barney
DRY GOODS CO.
Offer A Few HOLIDAY SUGGESTIONS
OF ARTICLES IN WHICH THEY EXCEL.
Winter Wraps,
Seasonable Silks,
Fine Laces,
Dainty Linens.
Hosiery of Exquisite Daintiness
Embroidered and Lace Handkerchiefs.
IMPORTED and DOMESTIC NOVELTIES for HOME DECORATION.
OUR FANCY WORK DEPARTMENT
SOFA PILLOWS, SILK SCARFS, TABLE SQUARES
and hundreds of other articles.
CHOICE HOLIDAY NOVELTIES TO BE FOUND IN
Our Oriental Art Room, the Largest in the West.
A Cordial Invitation Extended to All in Search of HOLIDAY GIFTS.
BROADWAY AND LOCUST ST., - - - ST. LOUIS.

Scruggs, Vandervoort & Barney ran this ad during the Christmas holiday season in 1895, capitalizing on the store's size and large variety of dry goods available to shoppers. Since women were the most likely customers, the ad tempted them with "winter wraps, seasonal silks" and even "hosiery of exquisite daintiness," certainly ad copy that bordered on the edge of being explicit in those days. (St. Louis Media Archives.)

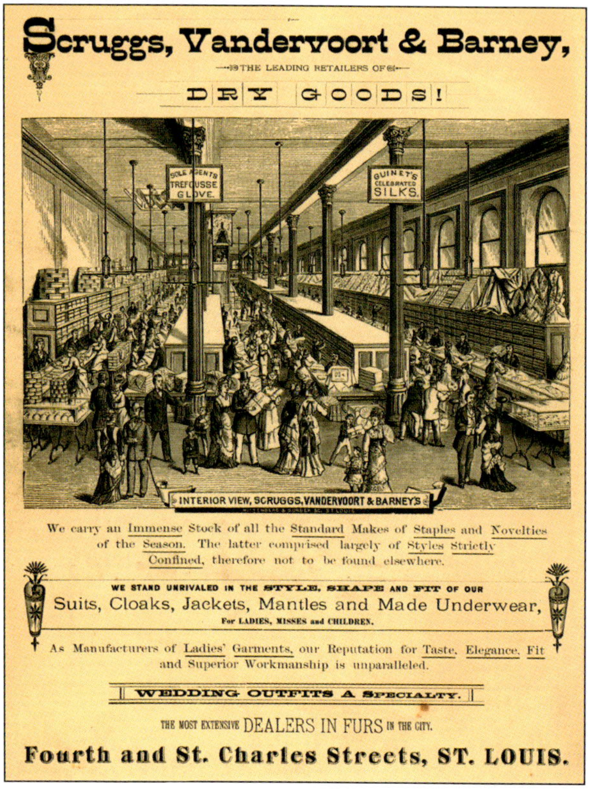
Scruggs, Vandervoort & Barney,
THE LEADING RETAILERS OF
DRY GOODS!
SOLE AGENTS TREFOUSSE GLOVE.
GUINET'S CELEBRATED SILKS.
INTERIOR VIEW, SCRUGGS, VANDERVOORT & BARNEY'S
We carry an Immense Stock of all the Standard Makes of Staples and Novelties of the Season. The latter comprised largely of Styles Strictly Confined, therefore not to be found elsewhere.
WE STAND UNRIVALED IN THE STYLE, SHAPE AND FIT OF OUR
Suits, Cloaks, Jackets, Mantles and Made Underwear,
For LADIES, MISSES and CHILDREN.
As Manufacturers of Ladies' Garments, our Reputation for Taste, Elegance, Fit and Superior Workmanship is unparalleled.
WEDDING OUTFITS A SPECIALTY.
THE MOST EXTENSIVE DEALERS IN FURS IN THE CITY.
Fourth and St. Charles Streets, ST. LOUIS.

Of this 1879 ad, Gerry Mandel says, "This illustration blows me away! The underlining in the copy is wonderful—just to make sure no one misses all those convincing sales points." And Don Stork adds, "Scruggs, Vandervoort & Barney looks to be trying to convey the image of its 'full service' department store in this ad. It was known as upscale, catering to the style-conscious and well-to-do shopper." (St. Louis Media Archives.)

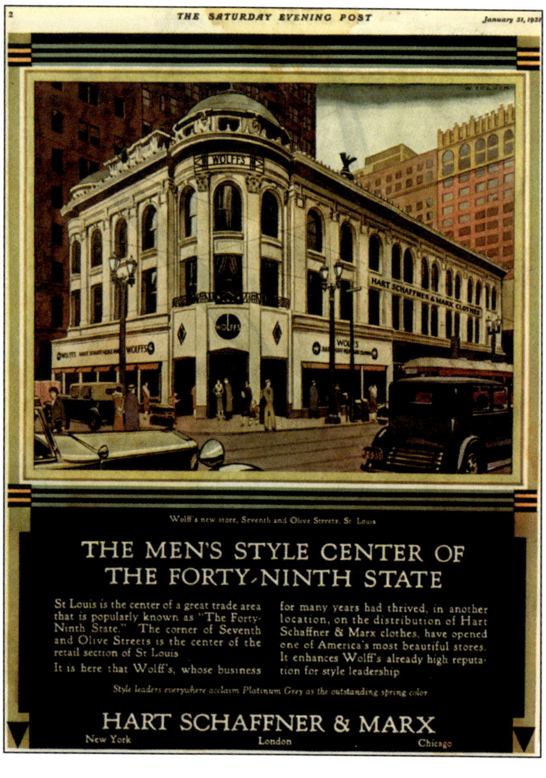
2
THE SATURDAY EVENING POST
WOLFF'S
Wolff's new store, Seventh and Olive Streets, St Louis
THE MEN'S STYLE CENTER OF THE FORTY-NINTH STATE
St Louis is the center of a great trade area that is popularly known as "The Forty-Ninth State." The corner of Seventh and Olive Streets is the center of the retail section of St Louis
It is here that Wolff's, whose business for many years had thrived, in another location, on the distribution of Hart Schaffner & Marx clothes, have opened one of America's most beautiful stores. It enhances Wolff's already high reputation for style leadership
Style leaders everywhere acclaim Platinum Grey as the outstanding spring color
HART SCHAFFNER & MARX
New York
London
Chicago

Wolff's, one of the finer downtown men's clothing shops, was located at Seventh and Olive Streets and catered to the discriminating businessman with brand names like Hart Schaffner and Marx. Placement for this type of ad, often called a co-op, was partially paid for by the brand that was prominently featured, with the local store paying the remainder. (St. Louis Media Archives.)

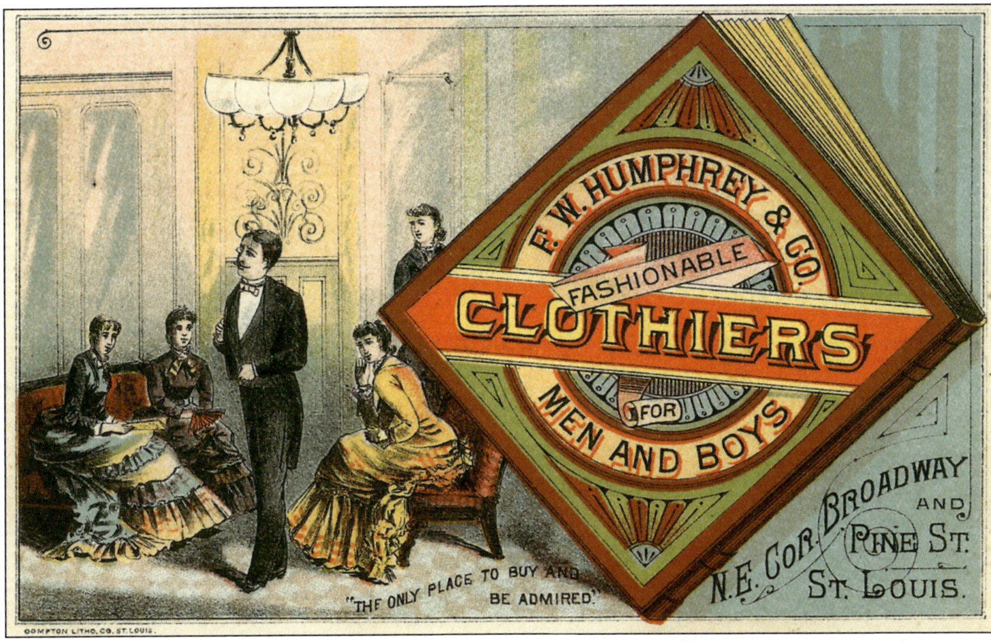
F. W. HUMPHREY & CO.
FASHIONABLE
CLOTHIERS
FOR
MEN AND BOYS
N.E. COR. BROADWAY AND PINE ST.
ST. LOUIS.
"THE ONLY PLACE TO BUY AND BE ADMIRED."
COMPTON LITHO. CO. ST. LOUIS.

Humphrey Clothiers occupied a four-story building downtown, selling clothes for men, boys, and children. At one point, the store gave away a ping-pong set with every purchase of a boy's suit or overcoat that cost more than $5. Humphrey was a longtime, regular user of trade cards to promote the business. (St. Louis Media Archives.)

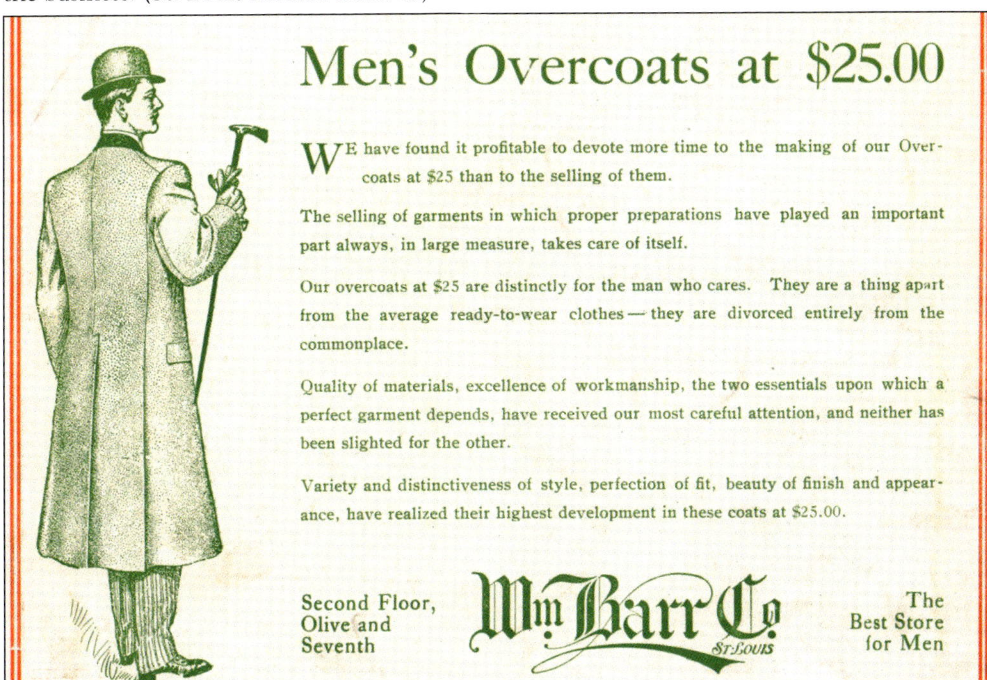
Men's Overcoats at $25.00
WE have found it profitable to devote more time to the making of our Overcoats at $25 than to the selling of them.
The selling of garments in which proper preparations have played an important part always, in large measure, takes care of itself.
Our overcoats at $25 are distinctly for the man who cares. They are a thing apart from the average ready-to-wear clothes — they are divorced entirely from the commonplace.
Quality of materials, excellence of workmanship, the two essentials upon which a perfect garment depends, have received our most careful attention, and neither has been slighted for the other.
Variety and distinctiveness of style, perfection of fit, beauty of finish and appearance, have realized their highest development in these coats at $25.00.
Second Floor, Olive and Seventh
Wm. Barr Co.
St. Louis
The Best Store for Men

The William Barr department store, which eventually evolved into Famous Barr, ran this ad in 1906. Heavy on copy, the ad strives to convey the quality of the coats the company manufactured while using only a minimal illustration of the product. (Missouri History Museum.)

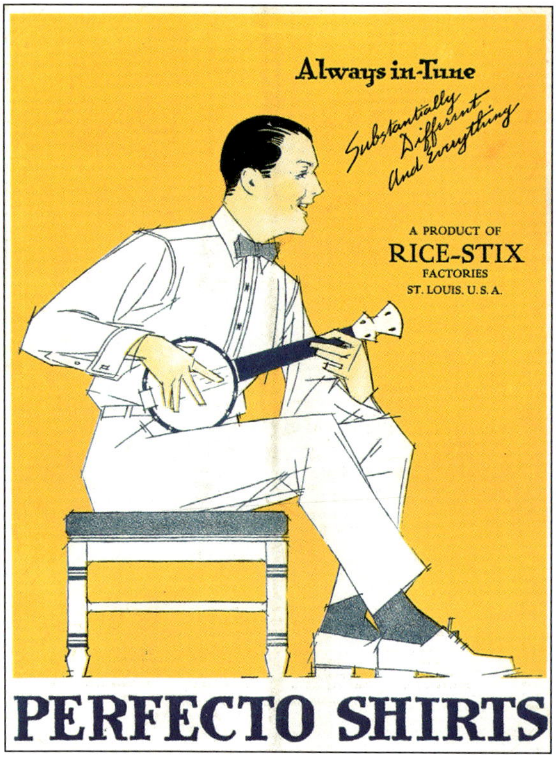
Always in-Tune
Substantially Different And Everything
A PRODUCT OF
RICE-STIX
FACTORIES
ST. LOUIS, U.S.A.
PERFECTO SHIRTS

Begun in St. Louis in 1879, Rice-Stix Dry Goods made and sold clothing. After a short time in a building at 410 North Broadway, Rice-Stix took over the city's largest retail space in the Merchandise Mart, which later underwent two expansions. In response to this 1924 ad selling the company's shirts, Gerry Mandel says, "The illustration looks like a rough draft in some ways, but I like it." (St. Louis Media Archives.)

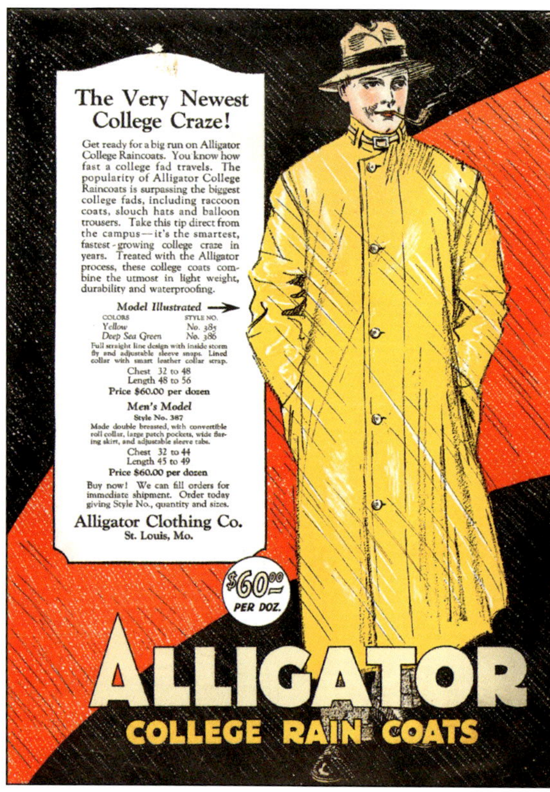
The Very Newest College Craze!
Get ready for a big run on Alligator College Raincoats. You know how fast a college fad travels. The popularity of Alligator College Raincoats is surpassing the biggest college fads, including raccoon coats, slouch hats and balloon trousers. Take this tip direct from the campus—it's the smartest, fastest-growing college craze in years. Treated with the Alligator process, these college coats combine the utmost in light weight, durability and waterproofing.
Model Illustrated
COLORS STYLE NO.
Yellow No. 385
Deep Sea Green No. 386
Full straight line design with inside storm fly and adjustable sleeve snaps. Lined collar with smart leather collar strap.
Chest 32 to 48
Length 48 to 56
Price $60.00 per dozen
Men's Model
Style No. 387
Made double breasted, with convertible roll collar, large patch pockets, wide flaring skirt, and adjustable sleeve tabs.
Chest 32 to 44
Length 45 to 49
Price $60.00 per dozen
Buy now! We can fill orders for immediate shipment. Order today giving Style No., quantity and sizes.
Alligator Clothing Co.
St. Louis, Mo.
$60.00 PER DOZ.
ALLIGATOR
COLLEGE RAIN COATS

This is an example of a trade ad aimed at getting other businesses to buy (and in this case sell) a company's products. Alligator coats were made in the company's factory at 4171 Bingham Avenue. The parent company began as the Ferguson Waterproof Company in the early 1900s and was renamed Alligator Clothing Company in 1916. (St. Louis Media Archives.)

The Gauss-Langenberg Hat Company was one of the market's most successful purveyors of men's hats. It underwent a few name changes after its founding in 1860 and also managed to acquire the assets of one major competitor. The company eventually occupied two multistory buildings on the 400 block of North Twelfth Street. In addition to manufacturing hats, the company produced gloves, umbrellas, and caps. (St. Louis Media Archives.)

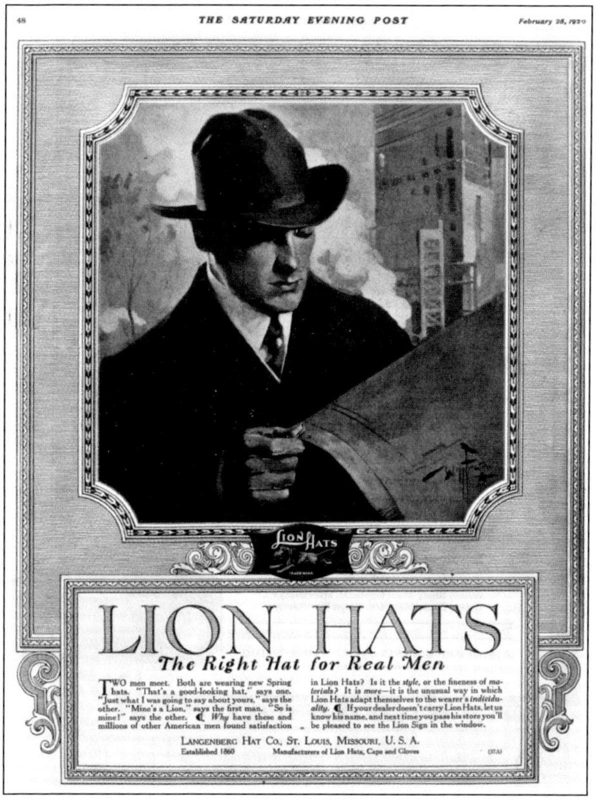
48
THE SATURDAY EVENING POST
February 28, 1920
LION HATS
LION HATS
The Right Hat for Real Men
TWO men meet. Both are wearing new Spring hats. "That's a good-looking hat," says one. "Just what I was going to say about yours," says the other. "Mine's a Lion," says the first man. "So is mine!" says the other. Why have these and millions of other American men found satisfaction in Lion Hats? Is it the style, or the fineness of materials? It is more—it is the unusual way in which Lion Hats adapt themselves to the wearer's individuality. If your dealer doesn't carry Lion Hats, let us know his name, and next time you pass his store you'll be pleased to see the Lion Sign in the window.
LANGENBERG HAT CO., ST. LOUIS, MISSOURI, U. S. A.
Established 1860
Manufacturers of Lion Hats, Caps and Gloves

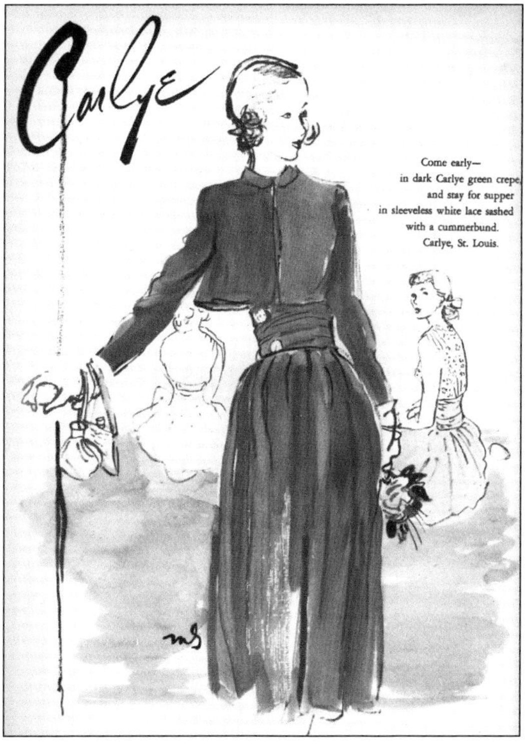
Carlye
Come early—
in dark Carlye green crepe
and stay for supper
in sleeveless white lace sashed
with a cummerbund.
Carlye, St. Louis.

In the 1930s, St. Louis was known nationally for its women's junior fashions. The Carlye Dress Corporation was established in 1938, and its success continued for nearly three decades. In 1967, the Leslie Faye company bought the business and merged it into its product line. (Duane Marburger.)

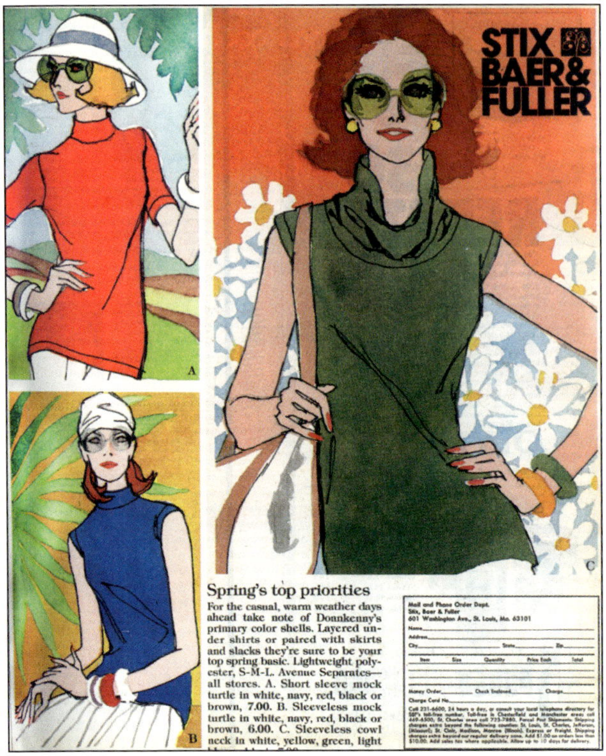
STIX BAER & FULLER
A
B
C
Spring's top priorities
For the casual, warm weather days ahead take note of Donnkenny's primary color shells. Layered under shirts or paired with skirts and slacks they're sure to be your top spring basic. Lightweight polyester, S-M-L. Avenue Separates—all stores. A. Short sleeve mock turtle in white, navy, red, black or brown, 7.00. B. Sleeveless mock turtle in white, navy, red, black or brown, 6.00. C. Sleeveless cowl neck in white, yellow, green, light
Mail and Phone Order Dept.
Stix, Baer & Fuller
601 Washington Ave., St. Louis, Mo. 63101
Name
Address
City State Zip
Item Size Quantity Price Each Total
Money Order Check Enclosed Charge
Charge Card No.

Stix, Baer & Fuller began in St. Louis as a manufacturer and retailer of clothing under the name Rice-Stix. The company later evolved into a department store chain. This ad, and the other one on this page from competitor Famous-Barr, ran in the Sunday magazine section of the *St. Louis Globe-Democrat* in 1977. (Del Schwinke.)

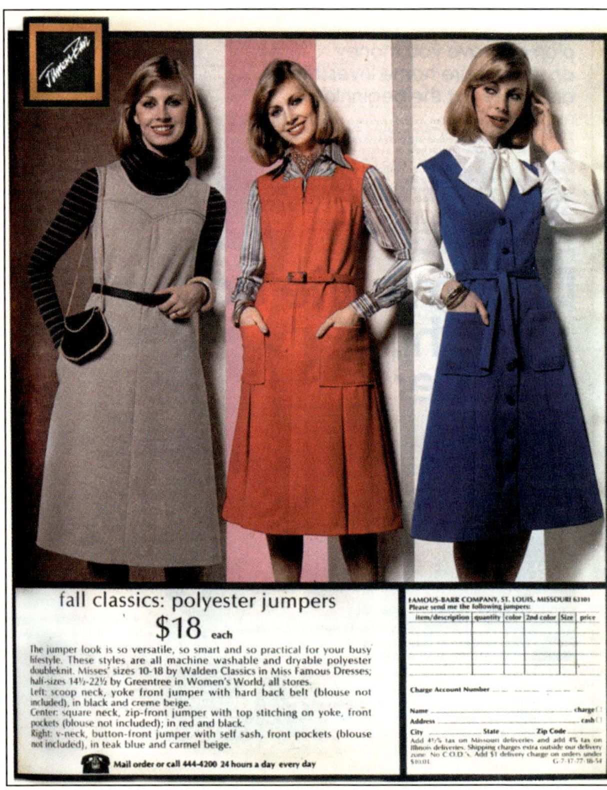
fall classics: polyester jumpers
$18 each
The jumper look is so versatile, so smart and so practical for your busy lifestyle. These styles are all machine washable and dryable polyester doubleknit. Misses' sizes 10-18 by Walden Classics in Miss Famous Dresses; half-sizes 14½-22½ by Greentree in Women's World, all stores.
Left: scoop neck, yoke front jumper with hard back belt (blouse not included), in black and creme beige.
Center: square neck, zip-front jumper with top stitching on yoke, front pockets (blouse not included); in red and black.
Right: v-neck, button-front jumper with self sash, front pockets (blouse not included), in teak blue and carmel beige.
Mail order or call 444-4200 24 hours a day every day
FAMOUS-BARR COMPANY, ST. LOUIS, MISSOURI 63101
Please send me the following jumpers:
item/description quantity color 2nd color Size price
Charge Account Number
Name charge
Address cash
City State Zip Code

The purpose of an advertisement like this one from Famous Barr was to offer the wide product range of a big department store to those who may not be able to visit the store in person. Both Famous Barr and Stix, Baer & Fuller both had mail-order departments that were promoted through ads in the Sunday papers, which had wide regional circulation. (Del Schwinke.)

Four

WHEELS

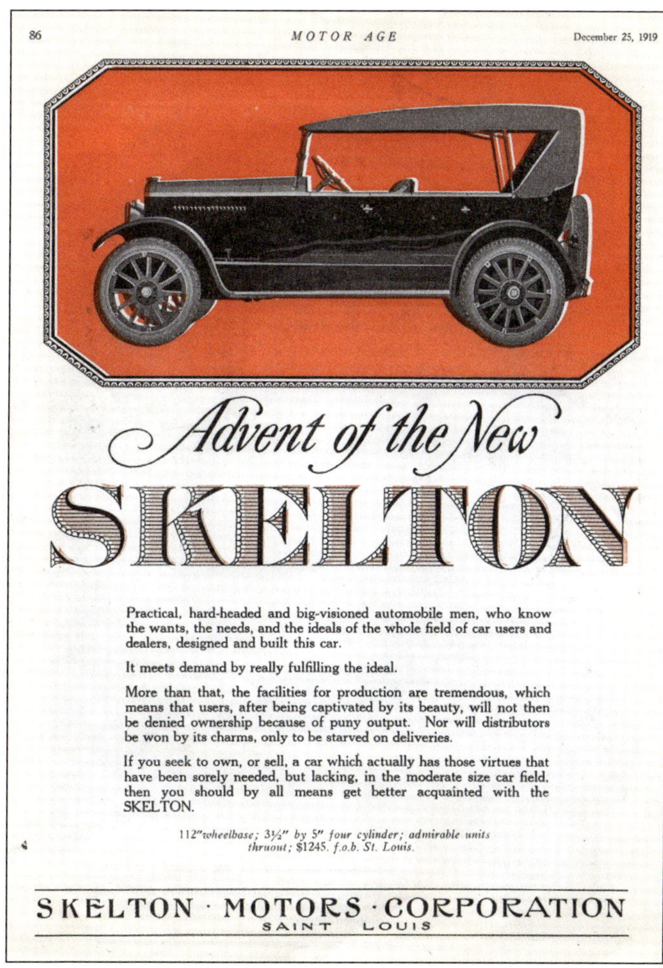
86
MOTOR AGE
December 25, 1919
Advent of the New
SKELTON
Practical, hard-headed and big-visioned automobile men, who know the wants, the needs, and the ideals of the whole field of car users and dealers, designed and built this car.
It meets demand by really fulfilling the ideal.
More than that, the facilities for production are tremendous, which means that users, after being captivated by its beauty, will not then be denied ownership because of puny output. Nor will distributors be won by its charms, only to be starved on deliveries.
If you seek to own, or sell, a car which actually has those virtues that have been sorely needed, but lacking, in the moderate size car field, then you should by all means get better acquainted with the SKELTON.
112" wheelbase; 3½" by 5" four cylinder; admirable units thruout; $1245. f.o.b. St. Louis.
SKELTON · MOTORS · CORPORATION
SAINT LOUIS

The Skelton auto has been described as a mid-priced car produced by the St. Louis Car Company at its Baden Street plant from 1919 to 1921. The car's body was built by another local company, Meuck Auto Body. It was all part of a dream financed by Dr. L. Sherman Skelton, a wealthy Oklahoma millionaire, but when he died unexpectedly in 1921, the dream vanished and the St. Louis Car Company was forced to shut down the car's assembly and take a $2 million loss. (St. Louis Media Archives.)

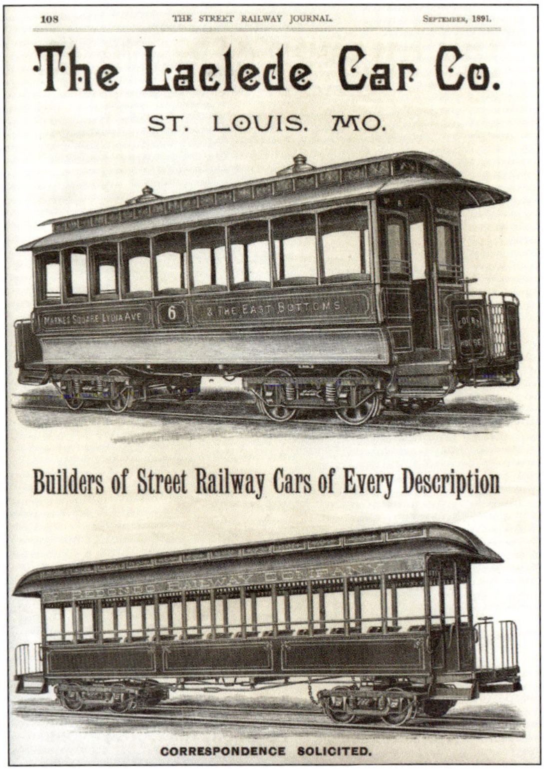
108 THE STREET RAILWAY JOURNAL. September, 1891.
The Laclede Car Co.
ST. LOUIS. MO.
Builders of Street Railway Cars of Every Description
CORRESPONDENCE SOLICITED.

William Sutton and Emil Alexander founded Laclede Car Company in 1883. This ad ran in 1891 shortly after the company recovered from severe businesses losses. The factory, located near the riverfront, was bounded by May, North First, Douglas, and North Second Streets. (St. Louis Media Archives.)

American Mors was originally a French-designed car licensed to be made in St. Louis by the St. Louis Car Company. Within three years, the St. Louis Car Company had created its own design and began manufacturing it under the same nameplate. The Mors engines were among the first to be designed with the pistons in a V-formation. (Missouri History Museum.)

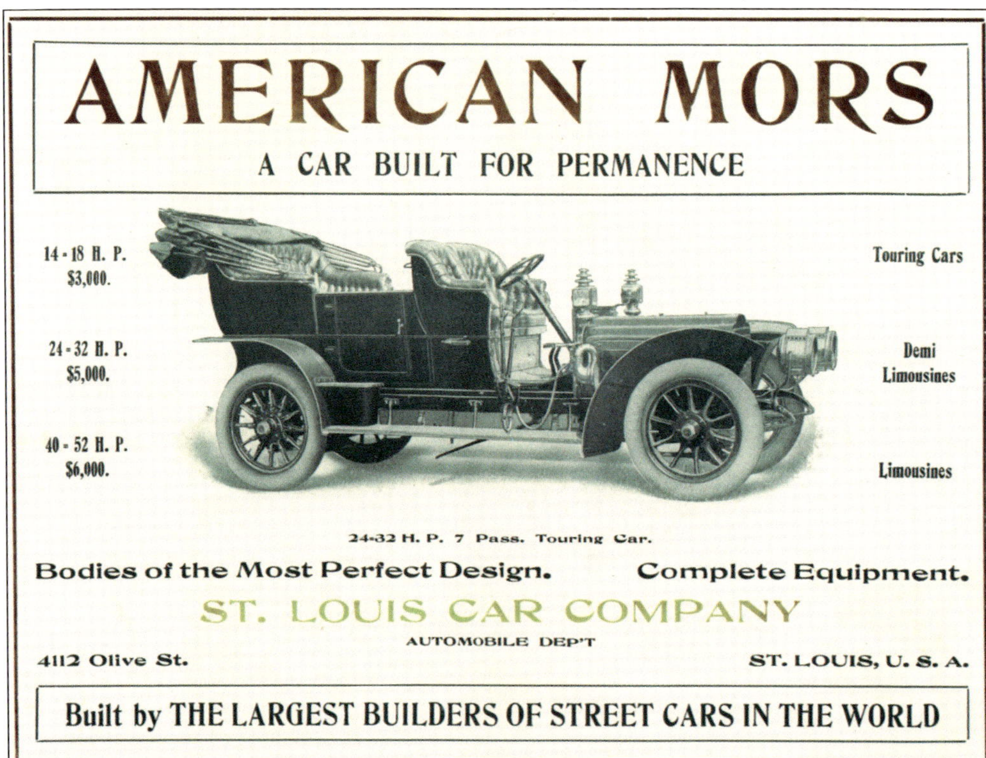
AMERICAN MORS
A CAR BUILT FOR PERMANENCE
14-18 H. P. $3,000.
24-32 H. P. $5,000.
40-52 H. P. $6,000.
Touring Cars
Demi Limousines
Limousines
24-32 H. P. 7 Pass. Touring Car.
Bodies of the Most Perfect Design.
Complete Equipment.
ST. LOUIS CAR COMPANY
AUTOMOBILE DEP'T
4112 Olive St.
ST. LOUIS, U. S. A.
Built by THE LARGEST BUILDERS OF STREET CARS IN THE WORLD

From 1917 to 1929, Traffic Motor Truck Corporation produced vehicles from its assembly plant at 5200 North Second Street. It was, for a time, reportedly the largest assembler of trucks in the world. (St. Louis Media Archives.)

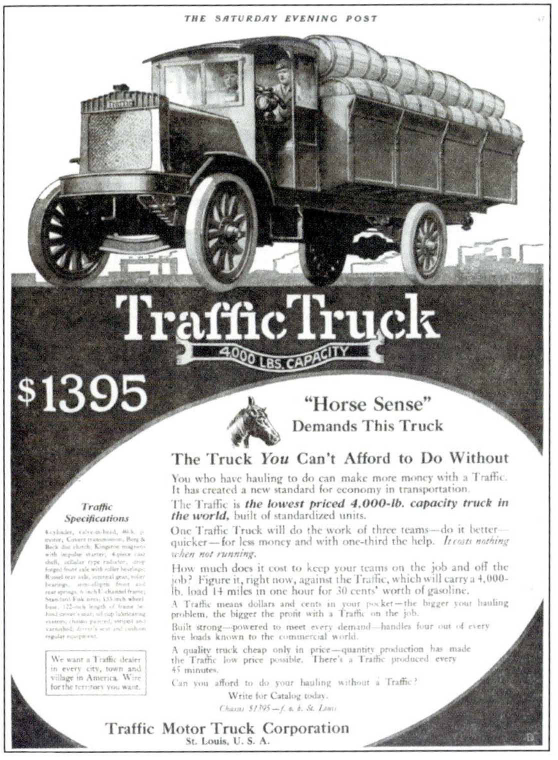
THE SATURDAY EVENING POST
Traffic Truck
4,000 LBS. CAPACITY
$1395
"Horse Sense"
Demands This Truck
The Truck You Can't Afford to Do Without
You who have hauling to do can make more money with a Traffic. It has created a new standard for economy in transportation.
The Traffic is the lowest priced 4,000-lb. capacity truck in the world, built of standardized units.
One Traffic Truck will do the work of three teams—do it better—quicker—for less money and with one-third the help. It costs nothing when not running.
How much does it cost to keep your teams on the job and off the job? Figure it, right now, against the Traffic, which will carry a 4,000-lb. load 14 miles in one hour for 30 cents' worth of gasoline.
A Traffic means dollars and cents in your pocket—the bigger your hauling problem, the bigger the profit with a Traffic on the job.
Built strong—powered to meet every demand—handles four out of every five loads known to the commercial world.
A quality truck cheap only in price—quantity production has made the Traffic low price possible. There's a Traffic produced every 45 minutes.
Can you afford to do your hauling without a Traffic?
Write for Catalog today.
Chassis $1395—f. o. b. St. Louis
Traffic Specifications
We want a Traffic dealer in every city, town and village in America. Wire for the territory you want.
Traffic Motor Truck Corporation
St. Louis, U. S. A.

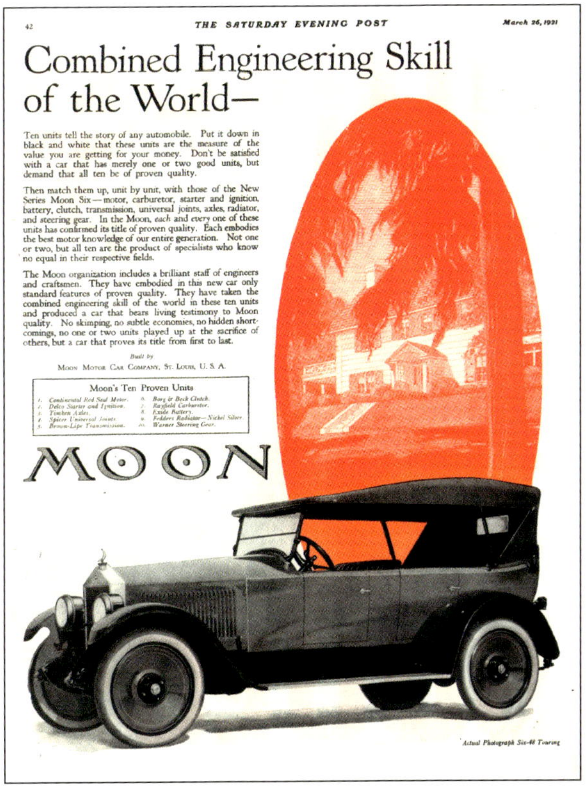
42
THE SATURDAY EVENING POST
March 26, 1921
Combined Engineering Skill of the World—
Ten units tell the story of any automobile. Put it down in black and white that these units are the measure of the value you are getting for your money. Don't be satisfied with a car that has merely one or two good units, but demand that all ten be of proven quality.
Then match them up, unit by unit, with those of the New Series Moon Six—motor, carburetor, starter and ignition, battery, clutch, transmission, universal joints, axles, radiator, and steering gear. In the Moon, each and every one of these units has confirmed its title of proven quality. Each embodies the best motor knowledge of our entire generation. Not one or two, but all ten are the product of specialists who know no equal in their respective fields.
The Moon organization includes a brilliant staff of engineers and craftsmen. They have embodied in this new car only standard features of proven quality. They have taken the combined engineering skill of the world in these ten units and produced a car that bears living testimony to Moon quality. No skimping, no subtle economies, no hidden shortcomings, no one or two units played up at the sacrifice of others, but a car that proves its title from first to last.
Built by
Moon Motor Car Company, St. Louis, U. S. A.
Moon's Ten Proven Units
1. Continental Red Seal Motor.
2. Delco Starter and Ignition.
3. Timken Axles.
4. Spicer Universal Joints.
5. Brown-Lipe Transmission.
6. Borg & Beck Clutch.
7. Rayfield Carburetor.
8. Exide Battery.
9. Fedders Radiator—Nickel Silver.
10. Warner Steering Gear.
MOON
Actual Photograph Six-48 Touring

The first Moon was built in St. Louis in 1905 and cost $3,000. Later Moons sold for $2,000 or less. By 1924, the company could not meet the dealers' demand for cars. Over 13,000 Moon automobiles were reportedly sold in 1925. Ad man Gerry Mandel says of this 1921 ad, "I like the layout and copy in this ad. Hardworking, of interest to anyone in the market for a new car. Good use of two colors." Moon was driven out of business during the Depression. (St. Louis Media Archives.)

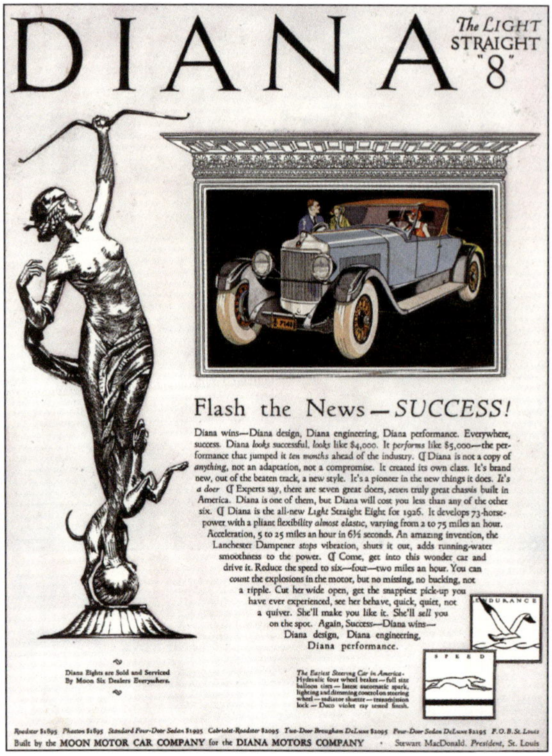
DIANA
The LIGHT STRAIGHT "8"
Flash the News—SUCCESS!
Diana wins—Diana design, Diana engineering, Diana performance. Everywhere, success. Diana looks successful, looks like $4,000. It performs like $5,000—the performance that jumped it ten months ahead of the industry. Diana is not a copy of anything, not an adaptation, not a compromise. It created its own class. It's brand new, out of the beaten track, a new style. It's a pioneer in the new things it does. It's a doer. Experts say, there are seven great doers, seven truly great chassis built in America. Diana is one of them, but Diana will cost you less than any of the other six. Diana is the all-new Light Straight Eight for 1926. It develops 73-horsepower with a pliant flexibility almost elastic, varying from 2 to 75 miles an hour. Acceleration, 5 to 25 miles an hour in 6½ seconds. An amazing invention, the Lanchester Dampener stops vibration, shuts it out, adds running-water smoothness to the power. Come, get into this wonder car and drive it. Reduce the speed to six—four—two miles an hour. You can count the explosions in the motor, but no missing, no bucking, not a ripple. Cut her wide open, get the snappiest pick-up you have ever experienced, see her behave, quick, quiet, not a quiver. She'll make you like it. She'll sell you on the spot. Again, Success—Diana wins—Diana design, Diana engineering, Diana performance.
ENDURANCE
SPEED
Diana Eights are Sold and Serviced By Moon Six Dealers Everywhere.
The Easiest Steering Car in America. Hydraulic four wheel brakes—full size balloon tires—latest automatic spark, lighting and dimming control on steering wheel—radiator shutter—transmission lock—Duco violet ray tested finish.
Roadster $1895 Phaeton $1895 Standard Four-Door Sedan $1995 Cabriolet-Roadster $2095 Two-Door Brougham DeLuxe $2095 Four-Door Sedan DeLuxe $2195 F.O.B. St. Louis
Built by the MOON MOTOR CAR COMPANY for the DIANA MOTORS COMPANY · Stewart MacDonald, President, St. Louis

The Diana, made in St. Louis from 1925 to 1928, was built by a Moon Motor Car Company subsidiary that offered six different models. This ad ran in 1926, five years later than the Moon ad on the previous page, and it was in full color as opposed to using only one color for accent (spot color). Using full color creates a high-quality image of the product. (St. Louis Media Archives.)

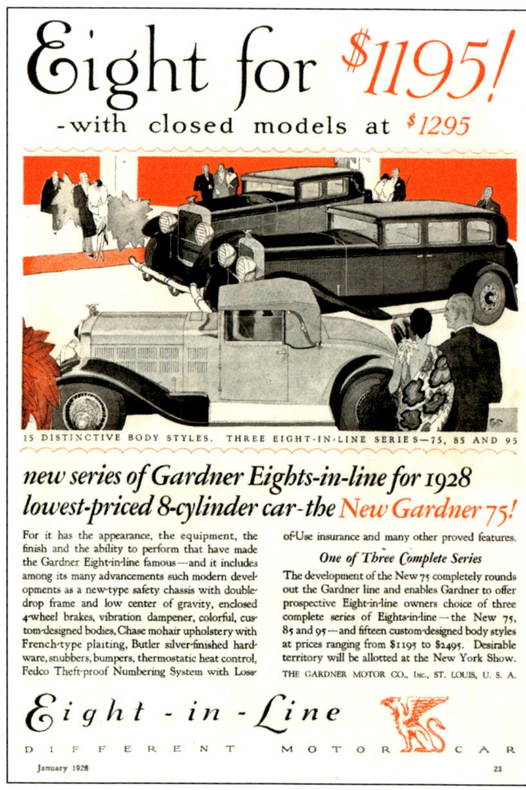
Eight for $1195!
-with closed models at $1295
15 DISTINCTIVE BODY STYLES. THREE EIGHT-IN-LINE SERIES—75, 85 AND 95
new series of Gardner Eights-in-line for 1928
lowest-priced 8-cylinder car-the New Gardner 75!
For it has the appearance, the equipment, the finish and the ability to perform that have made the Gardner Eight-in-line famous—and it includes among its many advancements such modern developments as a new-type safety chassis with double-drop frame and low center of gravity, enclosed 4-wheel brakes, vibration dampener, colorful, custom-designed bodies, Chase mohair upholstery with French-type plaiting, Butler silver-finished hardware, snubbers, bumpers, thermostatic heat control, Fedco Theft-proof Numbering System with Loss-of-Use insurance and many other proved features.
One of Three Complete Series
The development of the New 75 completely rounds out the Gardner line and enables Gardner to offer prospective Eight-in-line owners choice of three complete series of Eights-in-line—the New 75, 85 and 95—and fifteen custom-designed body styles at prices ranging from $1195 to $2495. Desirable territory will be allotted at the New York Show.
THE GARDNER MOTOR CO., Inc., ST. LOUIS, U. S. A.
Eight-in-Line
DIFFERENT MOTOR CAR
January 1928
23

The St. Louis–built Gardner was a short-lived automobile nameplate, but it holds a very important place in automotive history. The Banner Buggy Company, the largest in the country and owned by Russell Gardner, began building automobile bodies for General Motors' Chevrolets, but that soon expanded to assembling the entire car in 1915. The plant was later bought out by General Motors. Banner then developed and manufactured the Gardner automobile. The last model was built in 1932. (St. Louis Media Archives.)

Former ad man Gerry Mandel calls this 1927 Yellow Cab ad a "terrific piece of advertising. Clean, good use of color [yellow], gets the sales points across, even tells folks that 1-2-3-4 are the first four numbers on the dial." (St. Louis Public Library.)

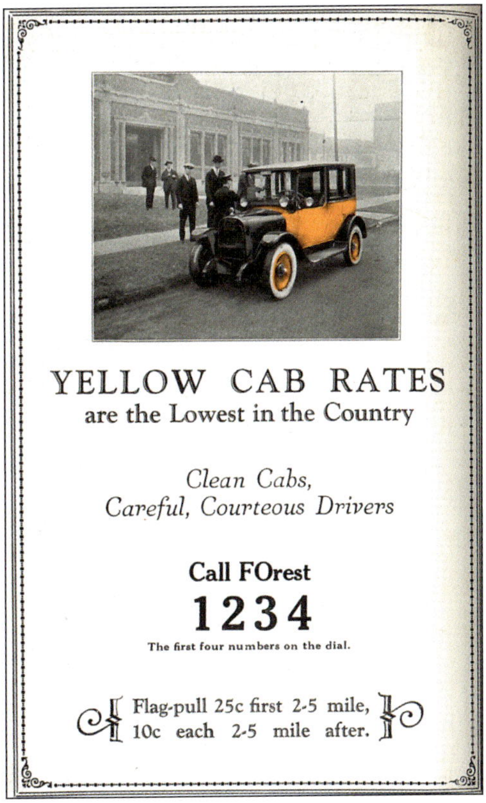

YELLOW CAB RATES
are the Lowest in the Country
Clean Cabs,
Careful, Courteous Drivers
Call FOrest
1234
The first four numbers on the dial.
Flag-pull 25c first 2-5 mile,
10c each 2-5 mile after.

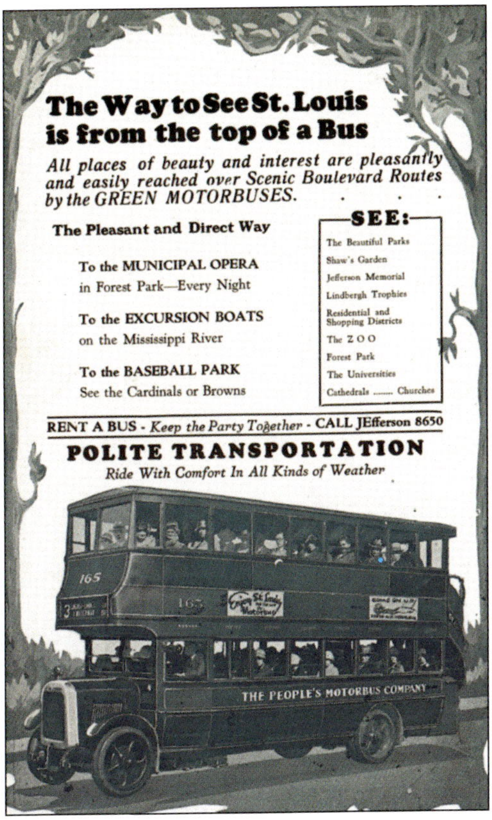

The Way to See St. Louis is from the top of a Bus
All places of beauty and interest are pleasantly and easily reached over Scenic Boulevard Routes by the GREEN MOTORBUSES.
The Pleasant and Direct Way
To the MUNICIPAL OPERA in Forest Park—Every Night
To the EXCURSION BOATS on the Mississippi River
To the BASEBALL PARK See the Cardinals or Browns
SEE:
The Beautiful Parks
Shaw's Garden
Jefferson Memorial
Lindbergh Trophies
Residential and Shopping Districts
The ZOO
Forest Park
The Universities
Cathedrals ...... Churches
RENT A BUS - Keep the Party Together - CALL JEfferson 8650
POLITE TRANSPORTATION
Ride With Comfort In All Kinds of Weather
165
THE PEOPLE'S MOTORBUS COMPANY

People's Motorbuses were the first buses to operate in St. Louis, beginning in 1923, and they provided direct competition to existing streetcar services. The company's ads, like this one from 1928, extolled the virtues of being able to travel in comfort to places where there were no streetcar tracks. The bus company was taken over by St. Louis Public Service in 1934. (St. Louis Public Library.)

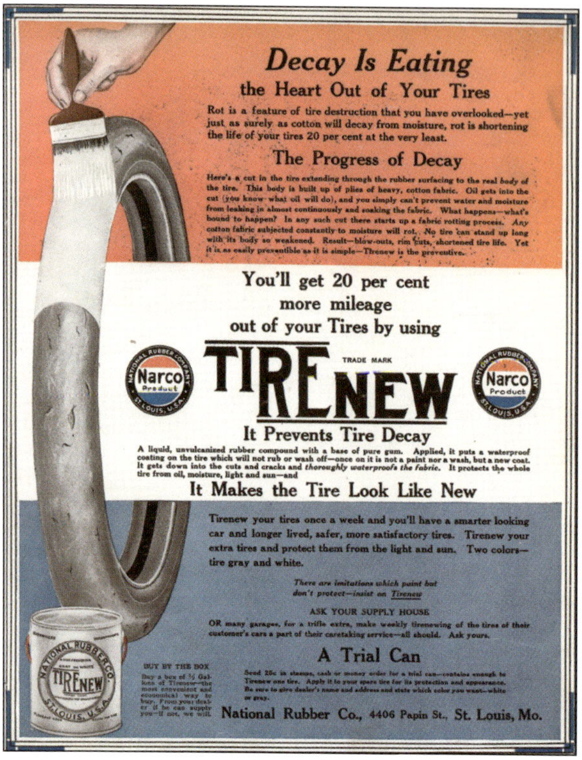
Decay Is Eating
the Heart Out of Your Tires
Rot is a feature of tire destruction that you have overlooked—yet just as surely as cotton will decay from moisture, rot is shortening the life of your tires 20 per cent at the very least.
The Progress of Decay
Here's a cut in the tire extending through the rubber surfacing to the real body of the tire. This body is built up of plies of heavy, cotton fabric. Oil gets into the cut (you know what oil will do), and you simply can't prevent water and moisture from leaking in almost continuously and soaking the fabric. What happens—what's bound to happen? In any such cut there starts up a fabric rotting process. Any cotton fabric subjected constantly to moisture will rot. No tire can stand up long with its body so weakened. Result—blow-outs, rim cuts, shortened tire life. Yet it is as easily preventible as it is simple—Tirenew is the preventive.
You'll get 20 per cent
more mileage
out of your Tires by using
Narco Product
TIRENEW
TRADE MARK
It Prevents Tire Decay
A liquid, unvulcanized rubber compound with a base of pure gum. Applied, it puts a waterproof coating on the tire which will not rub or wash off—once on it is not a paint nor a wash, but a new coat. It gets down into the cuts and cracks and thoroughly waterproofs the fabric. It protects the whole tire from oil, moisture, light and sun—and
It Makes the Tire Look Like New
Tirenew your tires once a week and you'll have a smarter looking car and longer lived, safer, more satisfactory tires. Tirenew your extra tires and protect them from the light and sun. Two colors—tire gray and white.
There are imitations which paint but don't protect—insist on Tirenew
ASK YOUR SUPPLY HOUSE
OR many garages, for a trifle extra, make weekly tirenewing of the tires of their customer's cars a part of their caretaking service—all should. Ask yours.
A Trial Can
BUY BY THE BOX
Buy a box of ½ Gallons of Tirenew—the most convenient and economical way to buy. From your dealer if he can supply you—if not, we will.
Send 25c in stamps, cash or money order for a trial can—contains enough to Tirenew one tire. Apply it to your spare tire for its protection and appearance. Be sure to give dealer's name and address and state which color you want—white or gray.
National Rubber Co., 4406 Papin St., St. Louis, Mo.

TiRenew was developed and marketed by the National Rubber Company (or Narco) in St. Louis. This 1912 advertisement promised a restoration of the rubber in consumers' tires after application of the product. Within two years of this ad's appearance, all Narco products were acquired by the Johns-Manville Company. (St. Louis Media Archives.)

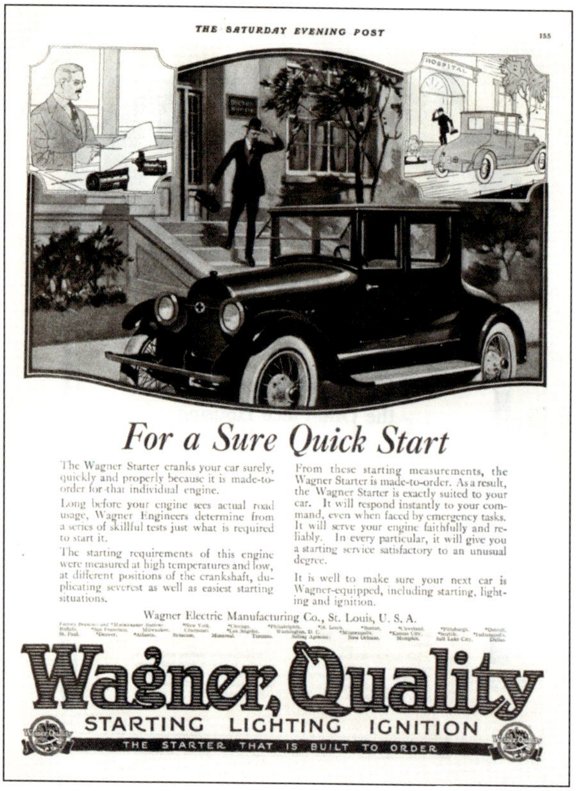
THE SATURDAY EVENING POST
155
HOSPITAL
For a Sure Quick Start
The Wagner Starter cranks your car surely, quickly and properly because it is made-to-order for that individual engine.
Long before your engine sees actual road usage, Wagner Engineers determine from a series of skillful tests just what is required to start it.
The starting requirements of this engine were measured at high temperatures and low, at different positions of the crankshaft, duplicating severest as well as easiest starting situations.
From these starting measurements, the Wagner Starter is made-to-order. As a result, the Wagner Starter is exactly suited to your car. It will respond instantly to your command, even when faced by emergency tasks. It will serve your engine faithfully and reliably. In every particular, it will give you a starting service satisfactory to an unusual degree.
It is well to make sure your next car is Wagner-equipped, including starting, lighting and ignition.
Wagner Electric Manufacturing Co., St. Louis, U. S. A.
Wagner Quality
STARTING LIGHTING IGNITION
THE STARTER THAT IS BUILT TO ORDER

Wagner Electric Manufacturing Company started in downtown St. Louis in 1891, but business expansion necessitated a move to the suburb of Wellston on Plymouth Avenue in 1906, and the company encouraged plant workers to build their homes around the factory. The factory eventually took up an entire block there and, during its peak times during the war, employed over 5,000 people. (St. Louis Media Archives.)

In 1927, St. Louis–based Lubrite Gasoline ran ads with humorous dialogue that assured consumers that the Lubrite product was a step above "ordinary gasoline." The company also operated a chain of automotive lubrication centers. (St. Louis Media Archives.)

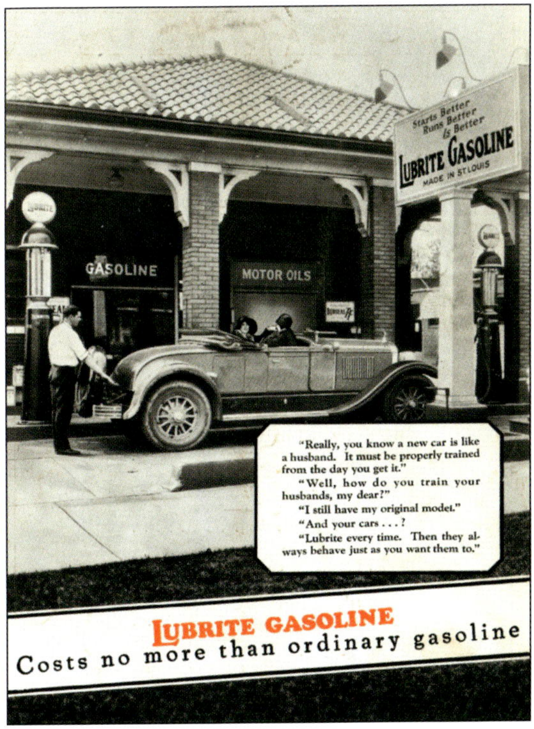
Starts Better Runs Better & Better
LUBRITE GASOLINE
MADE IN ST. LOUIS
GASOLINE
MOTOR OILS
"Really, you know a new car is like a husband. It must be properly trained from the day you get it."
"Well, how do you train your husbands, my dear?"
"I still have my original model."
"And your cars . . . ?
"Lubrite every time. Then they always behave just as you want them to."
LUBRITE GASOLINE
Costs no more than ordinary gasoline

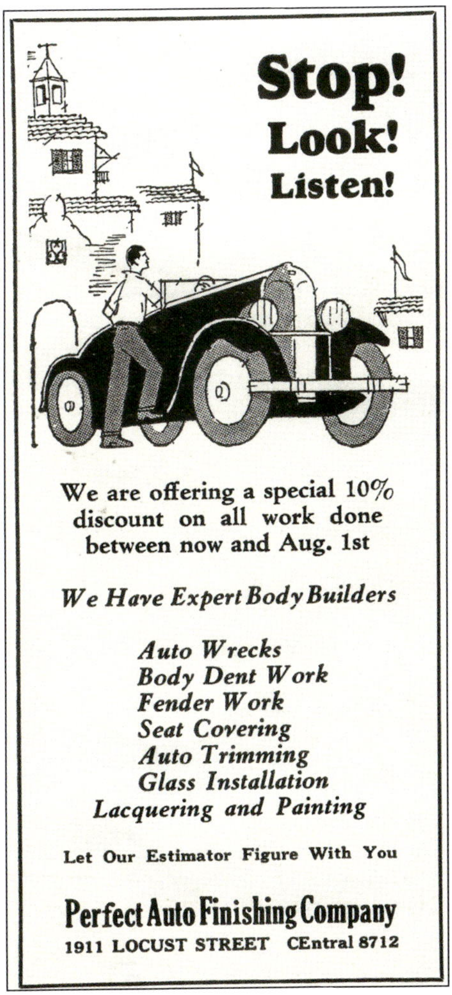
Stop!
Look!
Listen!
We are offering a special 10% discount on all work done between now and Aug. 1st
We Have Expert Body Builders
Auto Wrecks
Body Dent Work
Fender Work
Seat Covering
Auto Trimming
Glass Installation
Lacquering and Painting
Let Our Estimator Figure With You
Perfect Auto Finishing Company
1911 LOCUST STREET CEntral 8712

From the perspective of artist R.J. Shay, everything about this 1929 ad for Perfect Auto Finishing Company is wrong. Shay says the layout is not correct, the lines of the car lead the reader's eyes in the wrong direction, and the typesetting is basic at best. (St. Louis Public Library.)

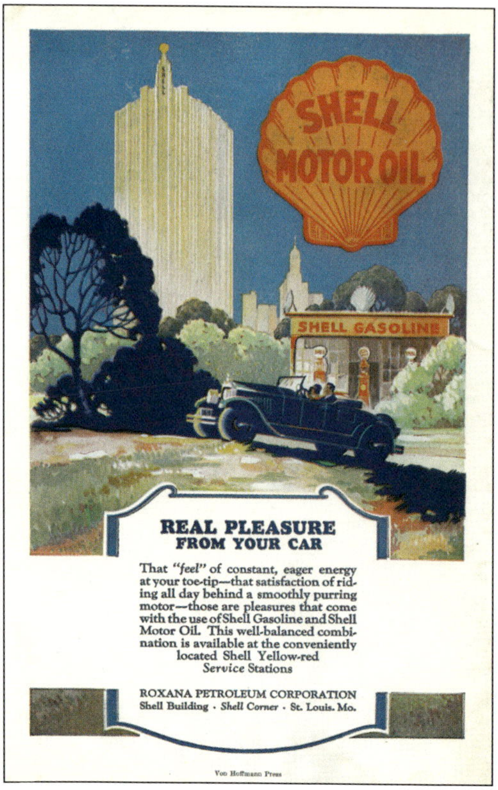
SHELL
MOTOR OIL
SHELL GASOLINE
REAL PLEASURE
FROM YOUR CAR
That "feel" of constant, eager energy at your toe-tip—that satisfaction of riding all day behind a smoothly purring motor—those are pleasures that come with the use of Shell Gasoline and Shell Motor Oil. This well-balanced combination is available at the conveniently located Shell Yellow-red Service Stations
ROXANA PETROLEUM CORPORATION
Shell Building · Shell Corner · St. Louis. Mo.

The Roxana Petroleum Corporation, better known as Shell Oil, ran this ad in 1927. It shows a stylized rendition of its corporate headquarters in the background; the building in downtown St. Louis is still known as the Shell Building but is no longer associated with the oil company. (Duane Marburger.)

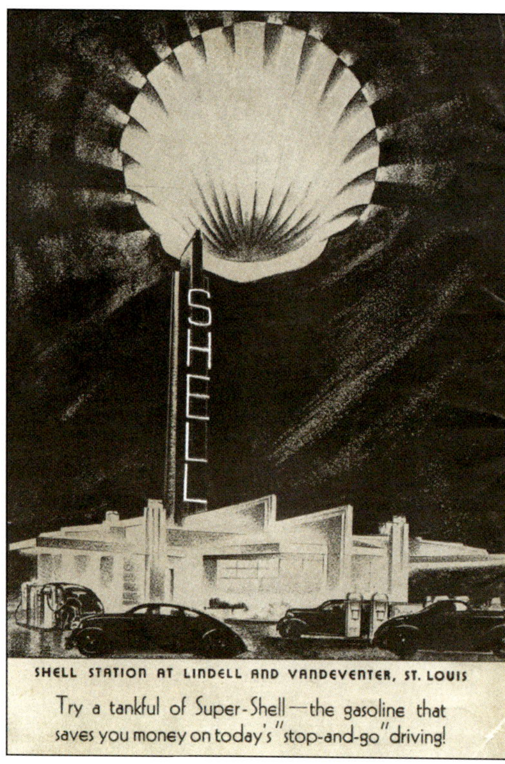
SHELL
SHELL STATION AT LINDELL AND VANDEVENTER, ST. LOUIS
Try a tankful of Super-Shell—the gasoline that saves you money on today's "stop-and-go" driving!

Shell Oil's very effective use of art and architecture continued in this 1935 ad showing the Shell station at Lindell Boulevard and Vandeventer Avenue in Midtown. Minimal ad copy extols the virtue of using Shell gas to save money when driving in the city. (St. Louis Media Archives.)

Five

Booze, Shoes, and the American League

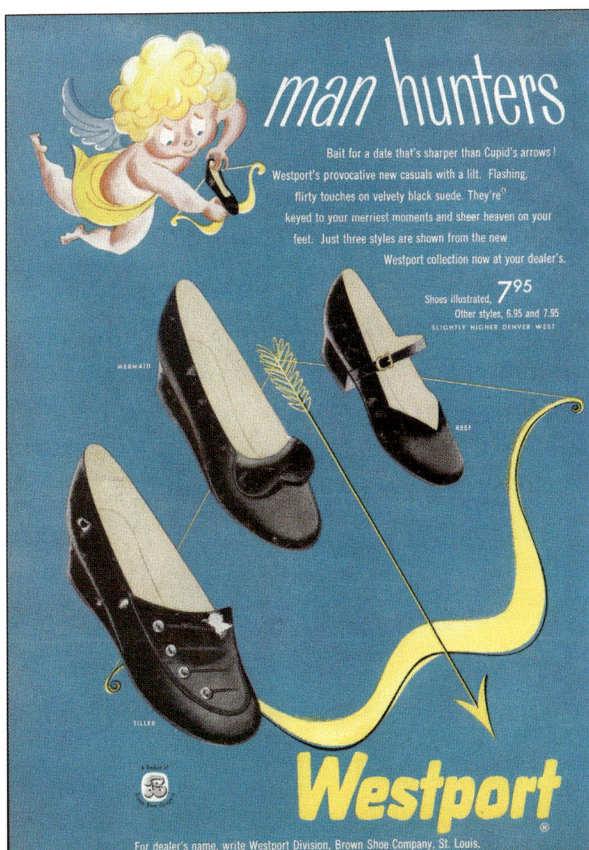

man hunters
Bait for a date that's sharper than Cupid's arrows!
Westport's provocative new casuals with a lilt. Flashing, flirty touches on velvety black suede. They're keyed to your merriest moments and sheer heaven on your feet. Just three styles are shown from the new Westport collection now at your dealer's.
Shoes illustrated, 7.95
Other styles, 6.95 and 7.95
SLIGHTLY HIGHER DENVER WEST
MERMAID
REEF
TILLER
Westport
For dealer's name, write Westport Division, Brown Shoe Company, St. Louis.

It might have been a safe assumption that men do not pay nearly as much attention to shoes as do members of the fairer sex. St. Louis–based Brown Shoe Company begged to differ in this 1949 ad aimed at young women. Cupid is at-the-ready with "velvety black suede" to capture the eyes of all those men home from the war to end all wars and eying the eligible women. (St. Louis Media Archives.)

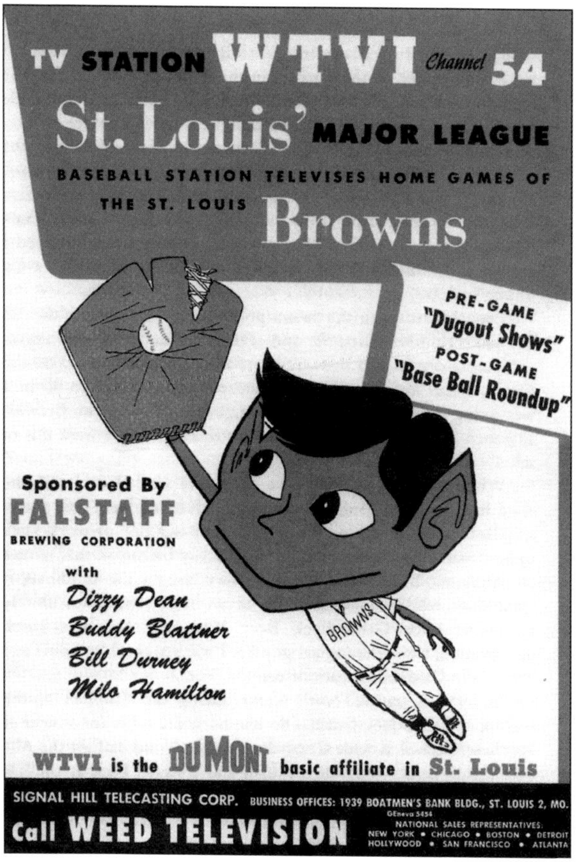
TV STATION WTVI Channel 54
St. Louis' MAJOR LEAGUE
BASEBALL STATION TELEVISES HOME GAMES OF
THE ST. LOUIS Browns
PRE-GAME
"Dugout Shows"
POST-GAME
"Base Ball Roundup"
Sponsored By
FALSTAFF
BREWING CORPORATION
with
Dizzy Dean
Buddy Blattner
Bill Durney
Milo Hamilton
BROWNS
WTVI is the DUMONT basic affiliate in St. Louis
SIGNAL HILL TELECASTING CORP. BUSINESS OFFICES: 1939 BOATMEN'S BANK BLDG., ST. LOUIS 2, MO.
Call WEED TELEVISION
NATIONAL SALES REPRESENTATIVES:
NEW YORK • CHICAGO • BOSTON • DETROIT
HOLLYWOOD • SAN FRANCISCO • ATLANTA

The St. Louis Browns American League baseball franchise was the team directly referenced in the famous "first in booze, first in shoes, and last in the American League" quote. The team saw little success in its time here (1902–1953). St. Louis's two national baseball teams shared Sportsman's Park, located at Grand Boulevard and Dodier Street, and the stadium was sold by Browns' owner Bill Veeck to the St. Louis Cardinals in 1953 after Anheuser-Busch bought the team and the Browns fell on hard financial times. (St. Louis Public Library.)

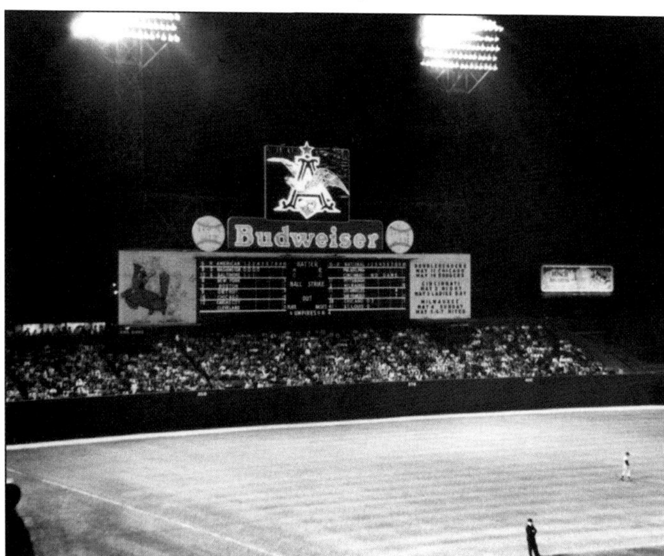
Budweiser

After the Browns left town in 1953, the Cardinals became the sole tenants of Sportsman's Park. This scoreboard, with its massive Budweiser advertisement, is etched in the memories of those who saw it in action. When the Cardinals scored a home run, the bird on the left would swing a bat and then fly all over the board, and the big eagle inside the "A" at the top would flap its wings. (Copyright © Anheuser-Busch, LLC. Used with permission of Anheuser-Busch, LLC. All rights reserved.)

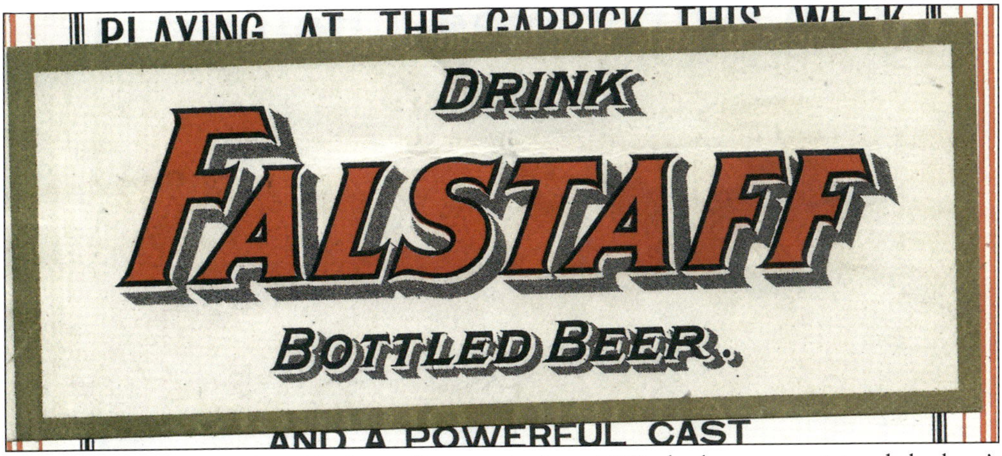
PLAYING AT THE GARRICK THIS WEEK
DRINK
FALSTAFF
BOTTLED BEER..
AND A POWERFUL CAST
Falstaff Beer was introduced by Lemp Brewery in June 1899; the brewery registered the beer's trademark in 1902. This ad ran as a color insert in a local theater program in 1910. The Falstaff trademark was bought by Joe Griesedieck in 1920, and the label finally disappeared in 2005 after steady declines in sales. (St. Louis Public Library.)

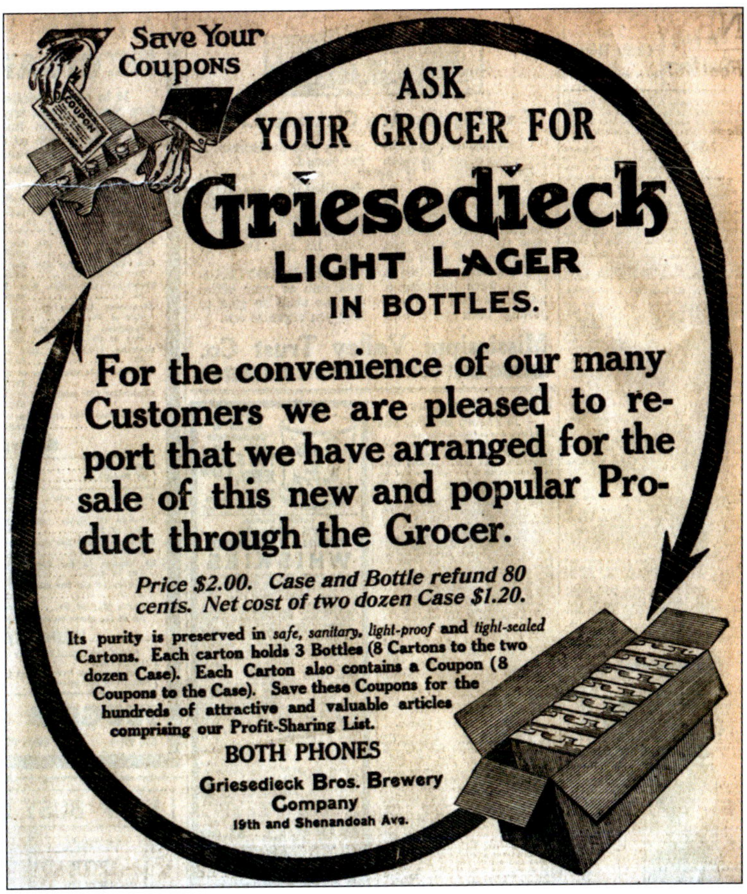
Save Your Coupons
ASK YOUR GROCER FOR
Griesedieck
LIGHT LAGER
IN BOTTLES.
For the convenience of our many Customers we are pleased to report that we have arranged for the sale of this new and popular Product through the Grocer.
Price $2.00. Case and Bottle refund 80 cents. Net cost of two dozen Case $1.20.
Its purity is preserved in safe, sanitary, light-proof and tight-sealed Cartons. Each carton holds 3 Bottles (8 Cartons to the two dozen Case). Each Carton also contains a Coupon (8 Coupons to the Case). Save these Coupons for the hundreds of attractive and valuable articles comprising our Profit-Sharing List.
BOTH PHONES
Griesedieck Bros. Brewery Company
19th and Shenandoah Ave.
In this 1912 newspaper ad, Griesedieck Brothers Brewery attempts to deliver many varied sales messages to consumers: glass bottles available at the grocer, coupons, saving points for premiums, and refundable bottle deposits. (St. Louis Media Archives.)

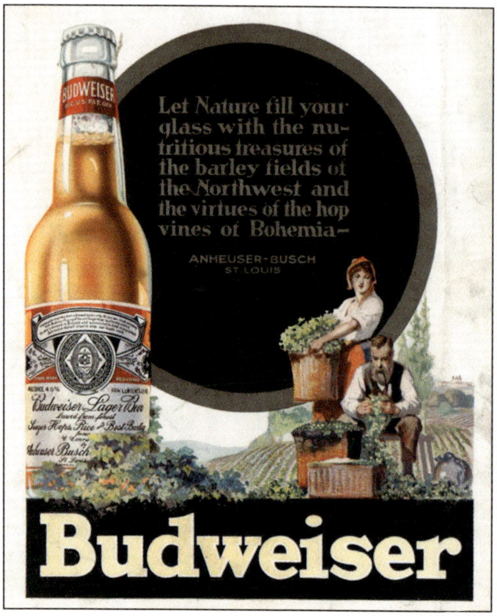
Let Nature fill your glass with the nutritious treasures of the barley fields of the Northwest and the virtues of the hop vines of Bohemia—
ANHEUSER-BUSCH
ST LOUIS
Budweiser

Prohibition was three years away when this ad for Budweiser ran in 1917. (Copyright © Anheuser-Busch, LLC. Used with permission of Anheuser-Busch, LLC. All rights reserved.)

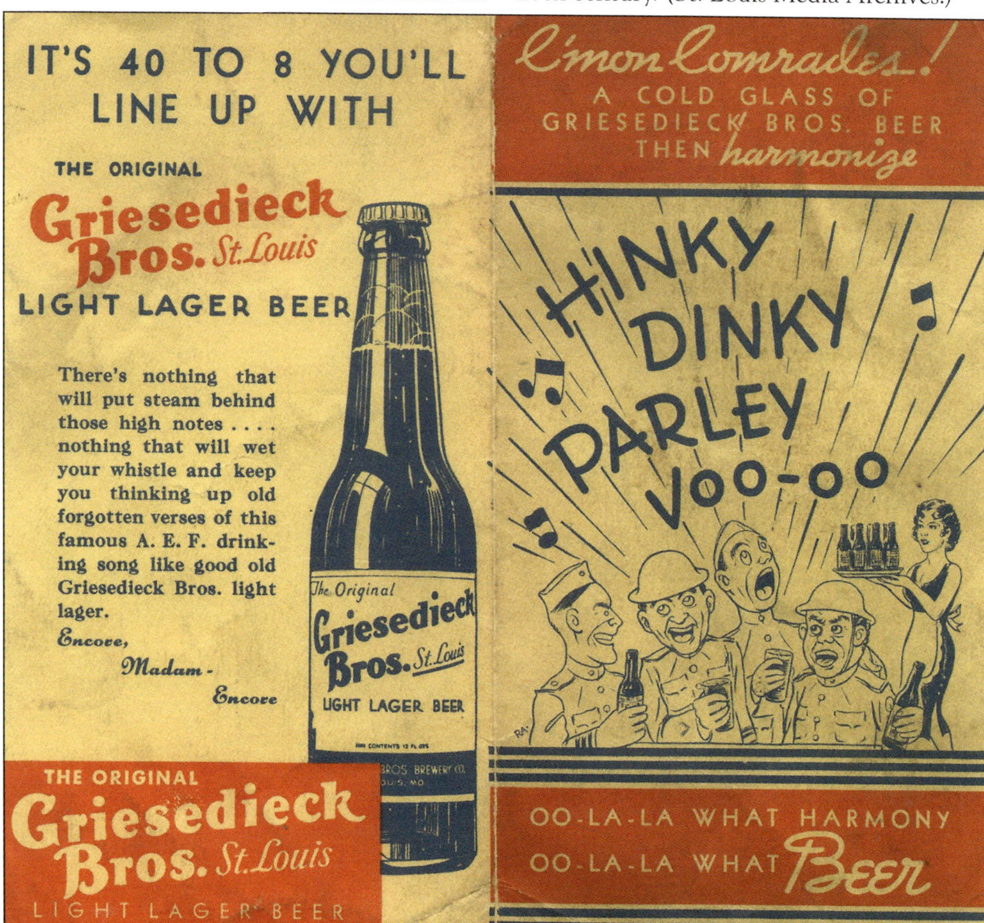
IT'S 40 TO 8 YOU'LL LINE UP WITH
THE ORIGINAL
Griesedieck Bros. St. Louis
LIGHT LAGER BEER
There's nothing that will put steam behind those high notes . . . . nothing that will wet your whistle and keep you thinking up old forgotten verses of this famous A. E. F. drinking song like good old Griesedieck Bros. light lager.
Encore,
Madam -
Encore
The Original
Griesedieck Bros. St. Louis
LIGHT LAGER BEER
THE ORIGINAL
Griesedieck Bros. St. Louis
LIGHT LAGER BEER
C'mon Comrades!
A COLD GLASS OF GRIESEDIECK BROS. BEER THEN harmonize
HINKY DINKY PARLEY VOO-OO
OO-LA-LA WHAT HARMONY
OO-LA-LA WHAT BEER

In this 1918 promotion, which ran during the World War I, Griesedieck Brothers Brewery sought to capitalize on the camaraderie associated with drinking beer by providing a songbook. The Griesedieck beer brand was extremely popular in the first half of the 20th century. (St. Louis Media Archives.)

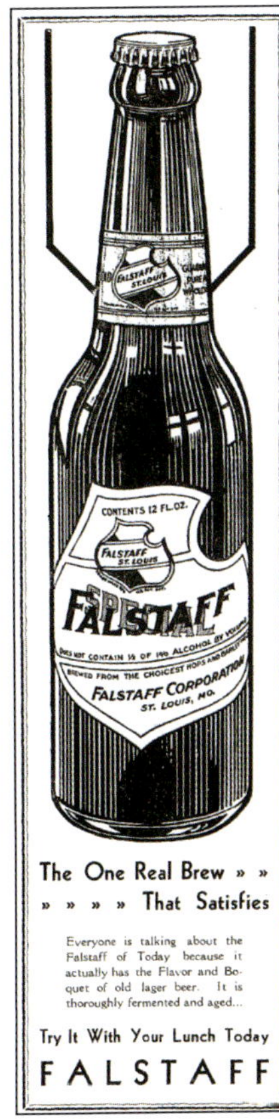
FALSTAFF
CONTENTS 12 FL. OZ.
FALSTAFF CORPORATION
ST. LOUIS, MO.
The One Real Brew » »
» » » » That Satisfies
Everyone is talking about the Falstaff of Today because it actually has the Flavor and Bo-quet of old lager beer. It is thoroughly fermented and aged...
Try It With Your Lunch Today
FALSTAFF

During Prohibition, breweries continued to market products such as the "near beer" beverage in this bottle. This was intended to perpetuate the brand name in consumers' minds until Prohibition was repealed. The logo is the same except for the overprinted "special" on the label. The label's fine print reads, "Does not contain one-half of one percent of alcohol by volume." (Missouri History Museum.)

In this ad, there is nothing on the Budweiser label that calls the product "beer." The alternative Busch Extra Dry ginger ale beverage, manufactured from 1921 until 1942, was described thusly: "Its delightful taste is due to the perfect blending of the best ginger and fruit juices obtainable, combined with the essence of a little shrub flowering in the tropics." (Copyright © Anheuser-Busch, LLC. Used with permission of Anheuser-Busch, LLC. All rights reserved.)

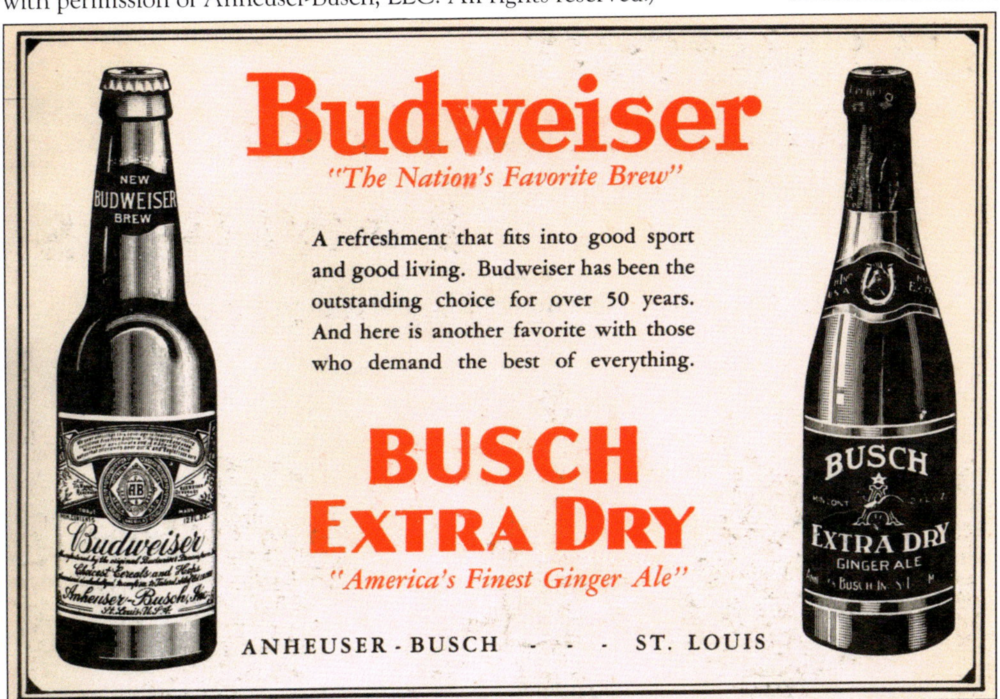
Budweiser
"The Nation's Favorite Brew"
A refreshment that fits into good sport and good living. Budweiser has been the outstanding choice for over 50 years. And here is another favorite with those who demand the best of everything.
BUSCH
EXTRA DRY
"America's Finest Ginger Ale"
ANHEUSER - BUSCH - - - ST. LOUIS
NEW BUDWEISER BREW
Budweiser
Anheuser-Busch, Inc.
St. Louis, U.S.A.
BUSCH
EXTRA DRY
GINGER ALE

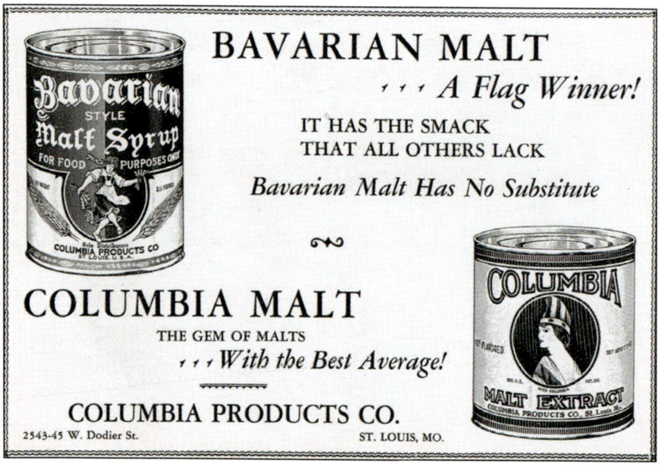

Columbia Malt Extract and Bavarian Malt Syrup were manufactured by Columbia Products Company, a division of the Columbia Weiss Beer Brewery that was located on West Dodier Street. Owners Walter Thoma and Otto Thoma Jr. marketed these products during Prohibition to keep some of their brewery workforce employed until the repeal of the 18th Amendment. (Missouri History Museum.)

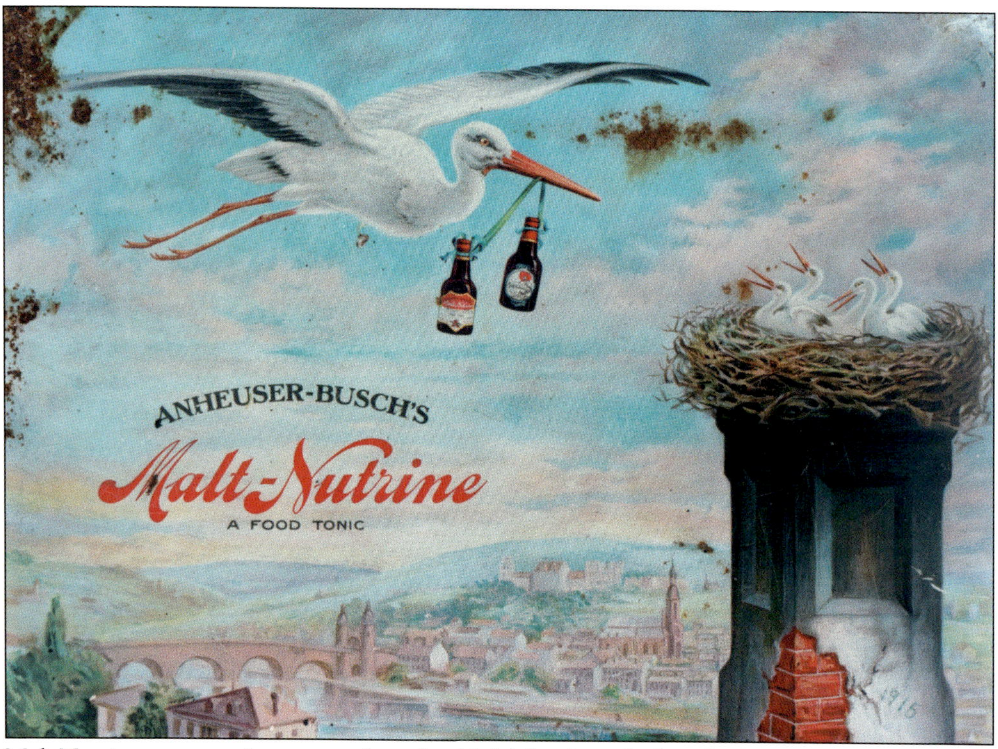

Malt-Nutrine was a tonic promoted as a healthful drink made from barley, malt, and hops. The drink was a favorite of the company's cofounder, Adolphus Busch, and was sold in drugstores from 1895 to 1942. Anheuser-Busch even created a separate sales department for the product. (Copyright © Anheuser-Busch, LLC. Used with permission of Anheuser-Busch, LLC. All rights reserved.)

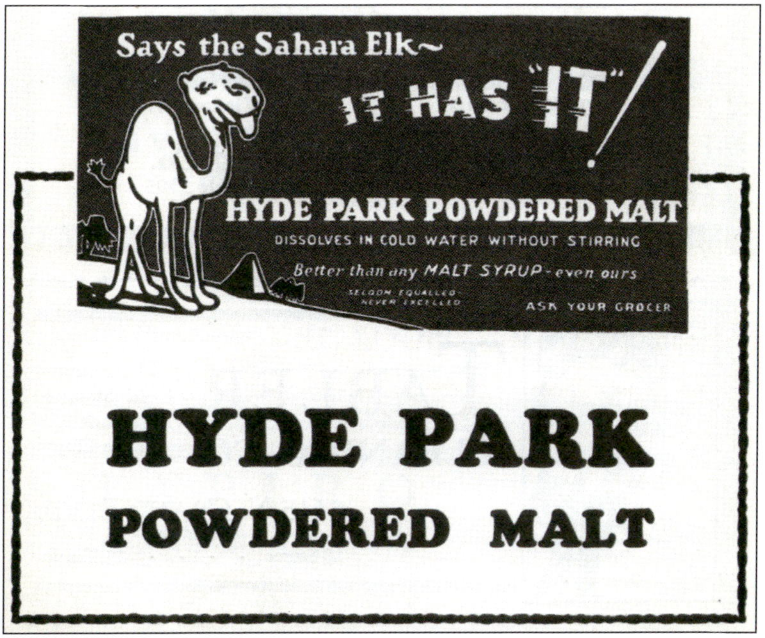
Says the Sahara Elk~
IT HAS "IT"!
HYDE PARK POWDERED MALT
DISSOLVES IN COLD WATER WITHOUT STIRRING
Better than any MALT SYRUP - even ours
SELDOM EQUALLED - NEVER EXCELLED
ASK YOUR GROCER
HYDE PARK
POWDERED MALT

Hyde Park Powdered Malt was one of many brands of malt powder sold by mothballed breweries during Prohibition. The malt was thought to aid in digestion, and it was also used in baking as a flavoring or to help make baked goods rise and give them a golden finish. (Duane Marburger.)

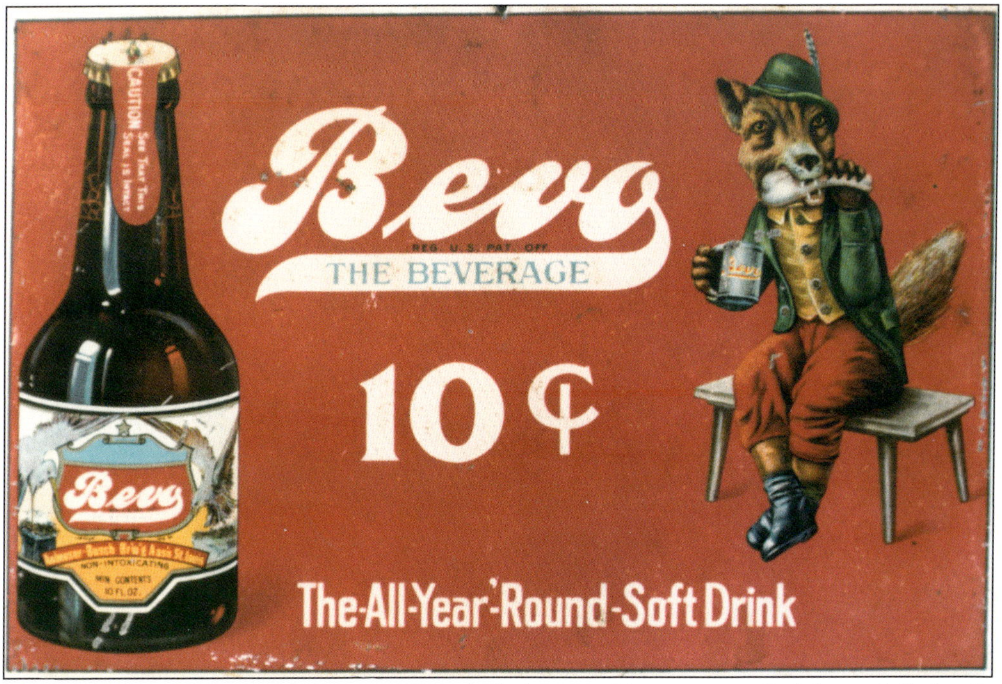
Bevo
REG. U.S. PAT. OFF.
THE BEVERAGE
10¢
The-All-Year-'Round-Soft Drink
CAUTION
Bevo
NON-INTOXICATING

Anheuser-Busch introduced the Bevo non-alcoholic cereal beverage in 1916. It was billed as "a strengthening, invigorating sedative." Within two years, demand was so great that Anheuser-Busch constructed one of the world's largest bottling plants to fulfill orders. As Prohibition progressed and bootleggers began to get a foothold, demand diminished, and the brand was discontinued in 1929. (Copyright © Anheuser-Busch, LLC. Used with permission of Anheuser-Busch, LLC. All rights reserved.)

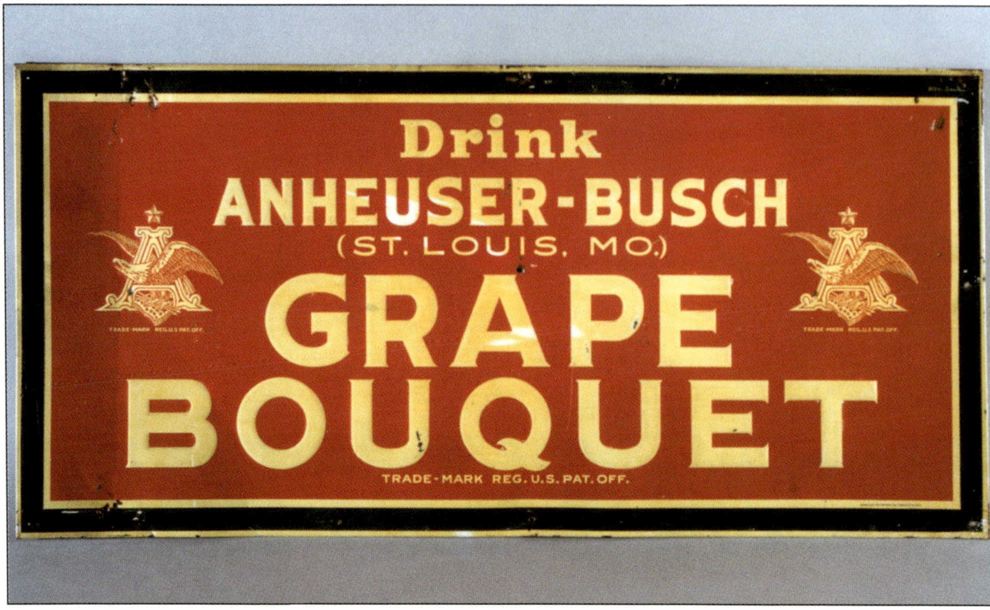

From 1922 to 1928, Anheuser-Busch sold this soft drink in bottles and as syrup to soda fountains. Consumers paid as little as 2¢ per bottle for it in 1922. Grape Bouquet was one of many non-alcoholic products manufactured by Anheuser-Busch during Prohibition.

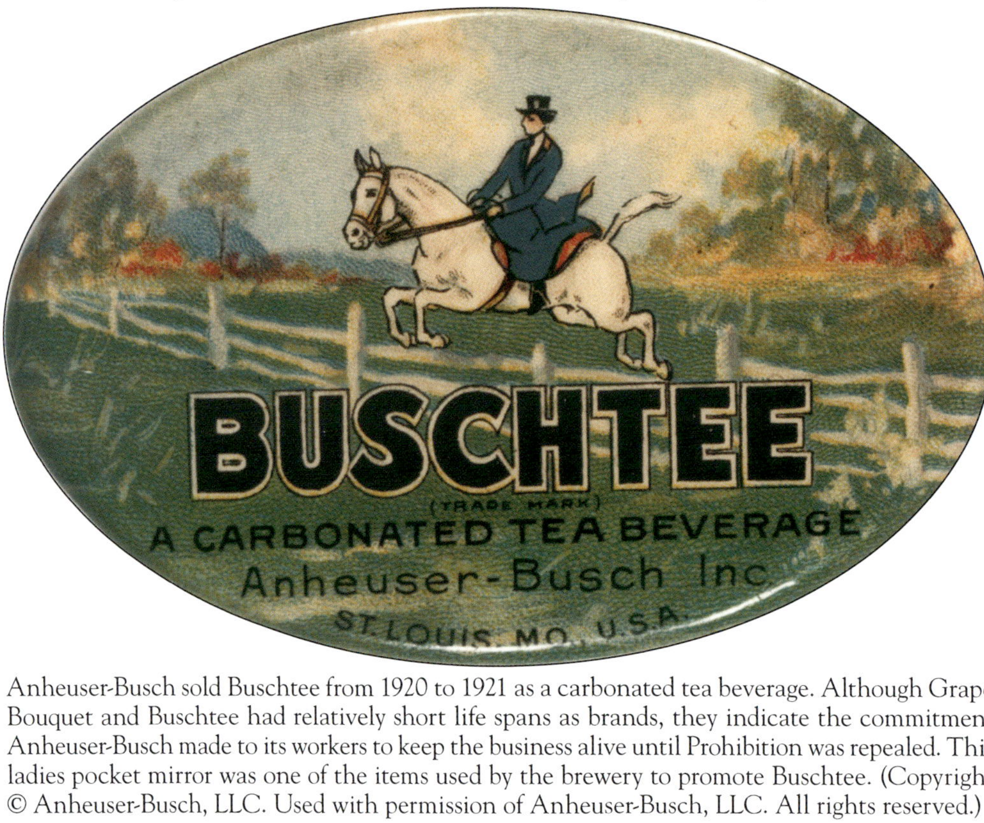

Anheuser-Busch sold Buschtee from 1920 to 1921 as a carbonated tea beverage. Although Grape Bouquet and Buschtee had relatively short life spans as brands, they indicate the commitment Anheuser-Busch made to its workers to keep the business alive until Prohibition was repealed. This ladies pocket mirror was one of the items used by the brewery to promote Buschtee.

Retired ad man Gerry Mandel says of this post-Prohibition ad, "It shows an early positioning of the brand as socially acceptable in high society. This feels more like a Michelob campaign that would come along later." (St. Louis Media Archives.)

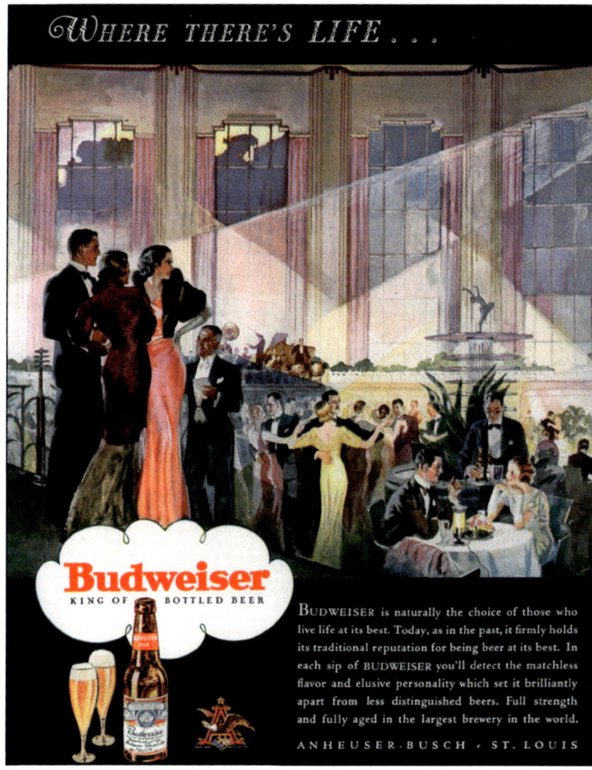

WHERE THERE'S LIFE . . .
Budweiser
KING OF BOTTLED BEER
BUDWEISER is naturally the choice of those who live life at its best. Today, as in the past, it firmly holds its traditional reputation for being beer at its best. In each sip of BUDWEISER you'll detect the matchless flavor and elusive personality which set it brilliantly apart from less distinguished beers. Full strength and fully aged in the largest brewery in the world.
ANHEUSER-BUSCH · ST. LOUIS

The huge Anheuser-Busch brewing complex in South St. Louis had its own rail transit system, known as the Manufacturers' Railway, from 1887 until 2011. It operated on a system that was less than 15 miles long, ferrying raw materials to the brewery and train cars full of packaged beer to various nearby shipping points. (Copyright © Anheuser-Busch, LLC. Used with permission of Anheuser-Busch, LLC. All rights reserved.)

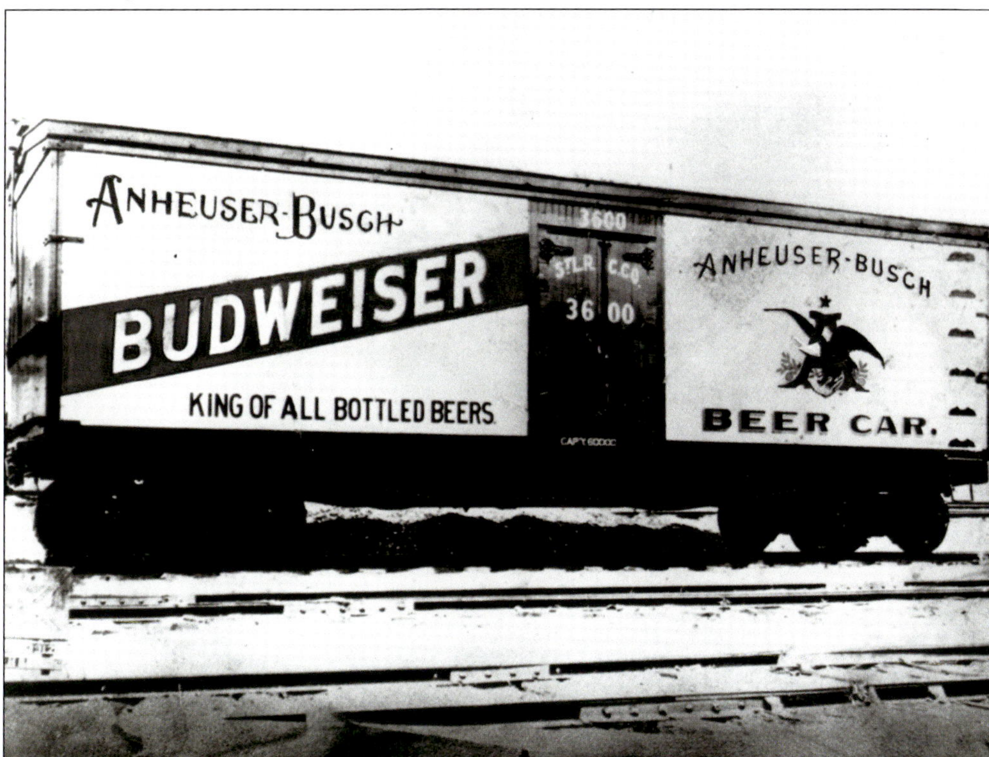

ANHEUSER-BUSCH
BUDWEISER
KING OF ALL BOTTLED BEERS
3600
STLR C.CO
36 00
ANHEUSER-BUSCH
BEER CAR.

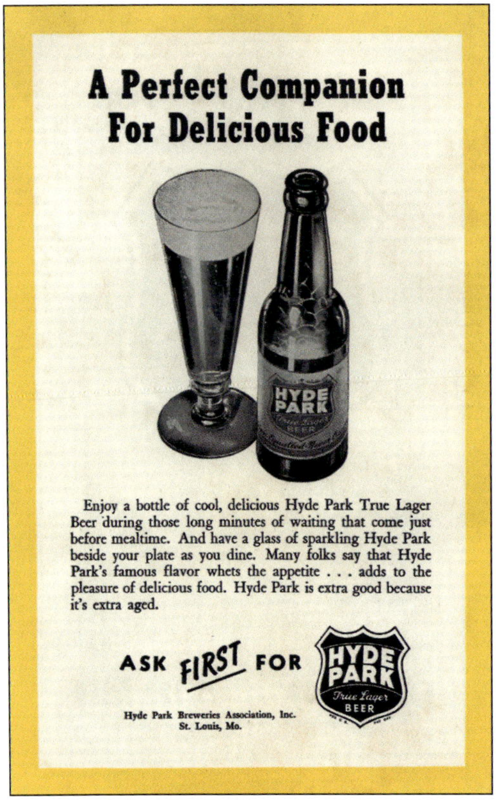
A Perfect Companion
For Delicious Food
HYDE PARK
True Lager
BEER
Enjoy a bottle of cool, delicious Hyde Park True Lager Beer during those long minutes of waiting that come just before mealtime. And have a glass of sparkling Hyde Park beside your plate as you dine. Many folks say that Hyde Park's famous flavor whets the appetite . . . adds to the pleasure of delicious food. Hyde Park is extra good because it's extra aged.
ASK FIRST FOR
HYDE PARK
True Lager
BEER
Hyde Park Breweries Association, Inc.
St. Louis, Mo.

Hyde Park Brewery was established in 1862 and incorporated in 1878. The brand died in 1954 after Carling bought out the company. Hyde Park is said to have produced the first beer commercials on television in February 1947, when the company sponsored *Meet Me in St. Louis* on KSD-TV. (Duane Marburger.)

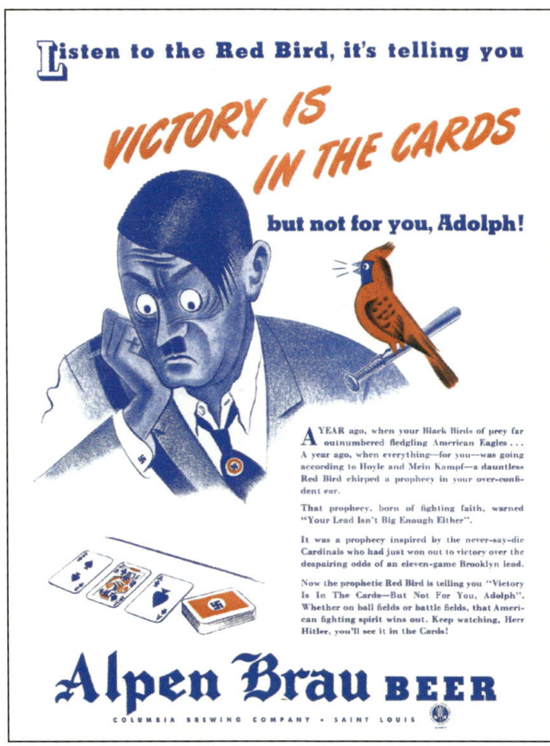
Listen to the Red Bird, it's telling you
VICTORY IS IN THE CARDS
but not for you, Adolph!
A YEAR ago, when your Black Birds of prey far outnumbered fledgling American Eagles . . . A year ago, when everything—for you—was going according to Hoyle and Mein Kampf—a dauntless Red Bird chirped a prophecy in your over-confident ear.
That prophecy, born of fighting faith, warned "Your Lead Isn't Big Enough Either".
It was a prophecy inspired by the never-say-die Cardinals who had just won out to victory over the despairing odds of an eleven-game Brooklyn lead.
Now the prophetic Red Bird is telling you "Victory Is In The Cards—But Not For You, Adolph". Whether on ball fields or battle fields, that American fighting spirit wins out. Keep watching, Herr Hitler, you'll see it in the Cards!
Alpen Brau BEER
COLUMBIA BREWING COMPANY • SAINT LOUIS

The Columbia Brewing Company introduced Alpen Brau at the 1904 World's Fair. Gerry Mandel thinks this ad, which ran during World War II, "seems a real stretch, selling this beer through patriotism. Wonder if it has something to do with the Germanic name of Alpen Brau?" Production of Alpen Brau ceased in 1948. (St. Louis Media Archives.)

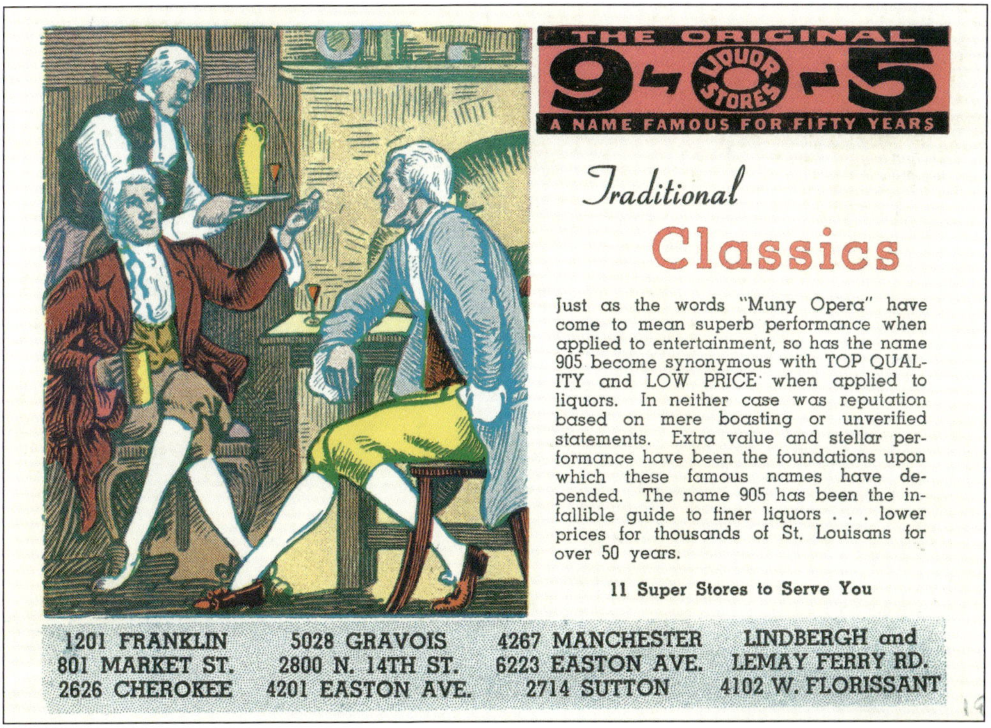
THE ORIGINAL
9-0-5
LIQUOR STORES
A NAME FAMOUS FOR FIFTY YEARS
Traditional
Classics
Just as the words "Muny Opera" have come to mean superb performance when applied to entertainment, so has the name 905 become synonymous with TOP QUALITY and LOW PRICE when applied to liquors. In neither case was reputation based on mere boasting or unverified statements. Extra value and stellar performance have been the foundations upon which these famous names have depended. The name 905 has been the infallible guide to finer liquors . . . lower prices for thousands of St. Louisans for over 50 years.
11 Super Stores to Serve You
1201 FRANKLIN
801 MARKET ST.
2626 CHEROKEE
5028 GRAVOIS
2800 N. 14TH ST.
4201 EASTON AVE.
4267 MANCHESTER
6223 EASTON AVE.
2714 SUTTON
LINDBERGH and
LEMAY FERRY RD.
4102 W. FLORISSANT

During its best years, 905 liquor stores had about 50 locations, making it one of the nation's largest chains of liquor stores. The late St. Louis historian Steve DeBellis noted that the retailer even had its own credit card. The 905 beer was actually brewed by Drewrys Brewery in Evansville, Indiana, and was selling over 900,000 cases a year at its peak. The company shut down in 1986. (Duane Marburger.)

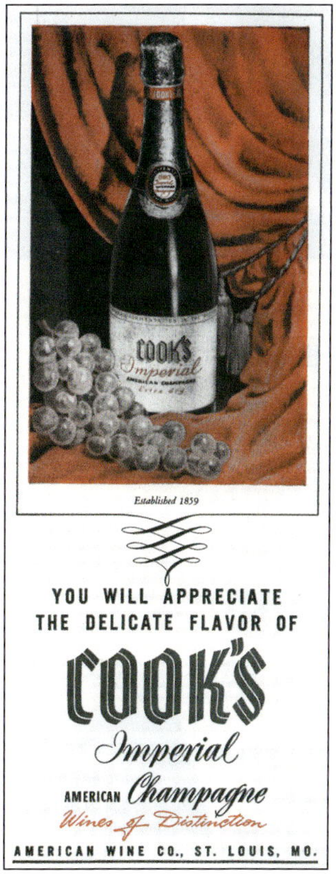
COOK'S
Imperial
Established 1859
YOU WILL APPRECIATE
THE DELICATE FLAVOR OF
COOK'S
Imperial
AMERICAN Champagne
Wines of Distinction
AMERICAN WINE CO., ST. LOUIS, MO.

Started by the Missouri Wine Company in 1859, Cook's champagne outlasted Prohibition and a federal shutdown during World War II. The winery's cellars were four stories below Cass Avenue near Grand Boulevard. The shutdown came when the feds took control of the winery after learning that a portion of the profits was being sent to Adolf Hitler's foreign minister, Joachim von Ribbentrop, who had invested in the winery. (St. Louis Media Archives.)

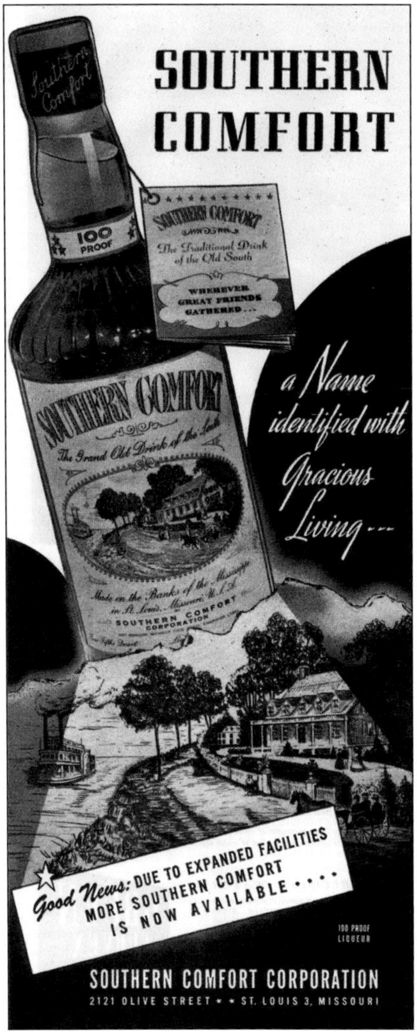

SOUTHERN COMFORT
a Name identified with Gracious Living . . .
Good News: DUE TO EXPANDED FACILITIES MORE SOUTHERN COMFORT IS NOW AVAILABLE . . . .
100 PROOF LIQUEUR
SOUTHERN COMFORT CORPORATION
2121 OLIVE STREET • • ST. LOUIS 3, MISSOURI

Southern Comfort was created by Martin Wilkes Heron in the New Orleans saloon where he worked as a bartender in 1874, but business developments brought him up the Mississippi to settle in St. Louis around 1900. Although Heron died in 1920, his business associate sold the formula to the Fowler family, who began producing and bottling the beverage after the end of Prohibition. It was bottled in St. Louis until the Brown-Forman Corporation bought the company in 1979. (Missouri Media Archives.)

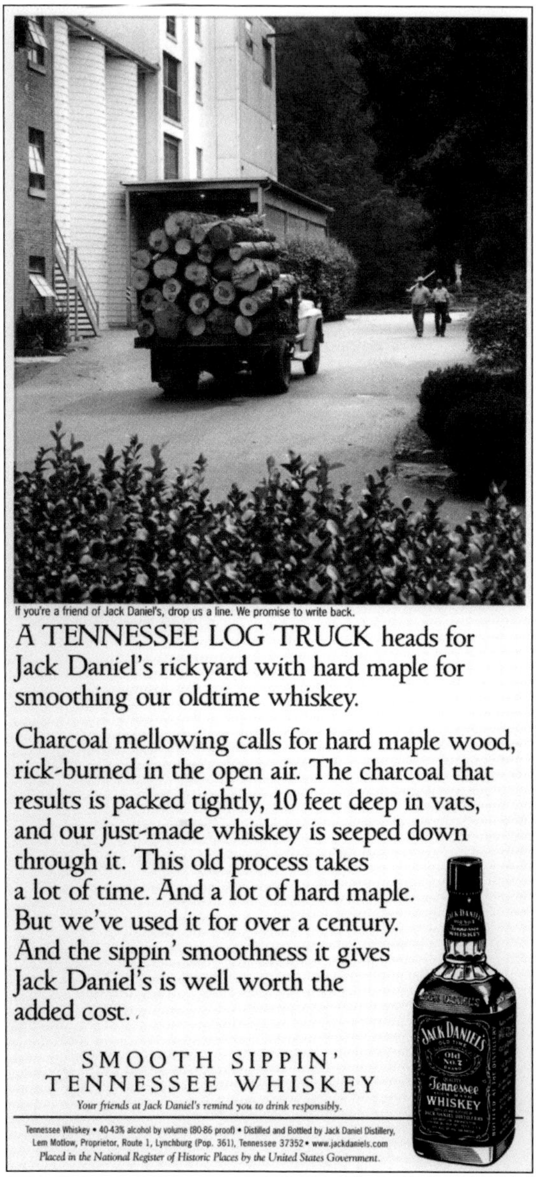

If you're a friend of Jack Daniel's, drop us a line. We promise to write back.
A TENNESSEE LOG TRUCK heads for Jack Daniel's rickyard with hard maple for smoothing our oldtime whiskey.
Charcoal mellowing calls for hard maple wood, rick-burned in the open air. The charcoal that results is packed tightly, 10 feet deep in vats, and our just-made whiskey is seeped down through it. This old process takes a lot of time. And a lot of hard maple. But we've used it for over a century. And the sippin' smoothness it gives Jack Daniel's is well worth the added cost.
SMOOTH SIPPIN' TENNESSEE WHISKEY
Your friends at Jack Daniel's remind you to drink responsibly.
Tennessee Whiskey • 40-43% alcohol by volume (80-86 proof) • Distilled and Bottled by Jack Daniel Distillery, Lem Motlow, Proprietor, Route 1, Lynchburg (Pop. 361), Tennessee 37352 • www.jackdaniels.com
Placed in the National Register of Historic Places by the United States Government.

Few people realize that the Jack Daniel's distillery and warehouse used to be in St. Louis (near Vandeventer and Forest Park Avenues at 3960 Duncan Avenue), and its award-winning ads were produced here. Retired ad man Don Stork explains the strategy behind this print ad: "The one column black/white ads were created and placed by Gardner Advertising. Gardner's media department conceived and successfully implemented the individual magazine negotiation guarantee that no other ad would run on the page." Fellow ad man Steve Kopcha says, "Ted Simmons's Jack Daniel ads were great when they were written and they're still great today." (Ted Simmons.)

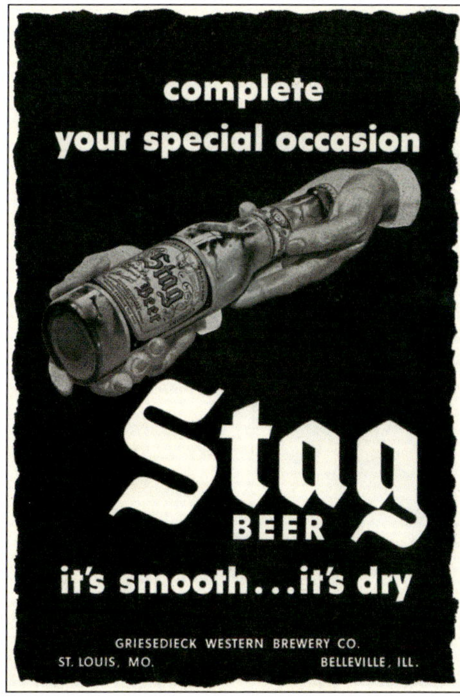
complete
your special occasion
Stag
BEER
it's smooth...it's dry
GRIESEDIECK WESTERN BREWERY CO.
ST. LOUIS, MO.
BELLEVILLE, ILL.

Stag was born at the Western Brewery in Belleville, Illinois, in the 1850s. The original name, Kaiser Beer, was changed in 1907 because of political developments in Germany. After being bought out by Griesedieck Brothers Brewery, the label's production was expanded to breweries in East St. Louis and St. Louis. (Missouri History Museum.)

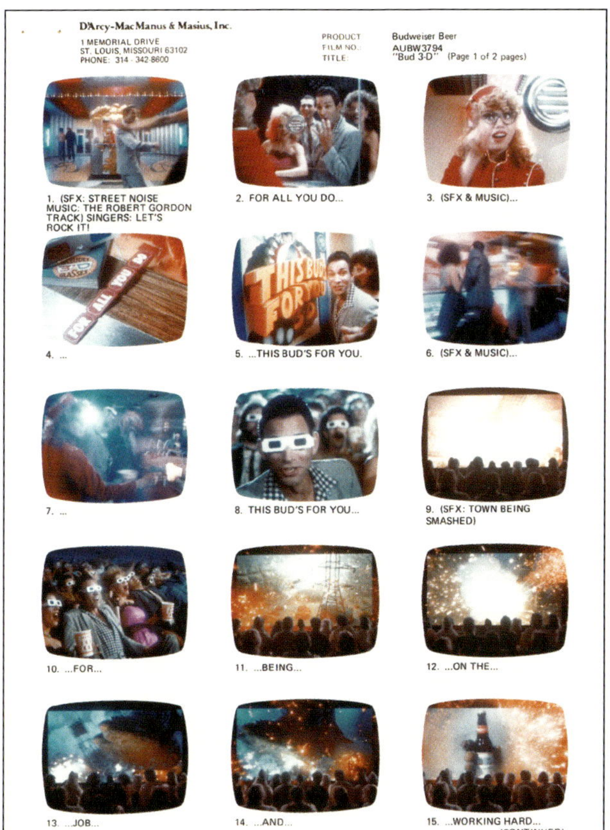
D'Arcy-MacManus & Masius, Inc.
1 MEMORIAL DRIVE
ST. LOUIS, MISSOURI 63102
PHONE: 314 - 342-8600
PRODUCT: Budweiser Beer
FILM NO.: AUBW3794
TITLE: "Bud 3-D" (Page 1 of 2 pages)
1. (SFX: STREET NOISE MUSIC: THE ROBERT GORDON TRACK) SINGERS: LET'S ROCK IT!
2. FOR ALL YOU DO...
3. (SFX & MUSIC)...
4. ...
5. ...THIS BUD'S FOR YOU.
6. (SFX & MUSIC)...
7. ...
8. THIS BUD'S FOR YOU...
9. (SFX: TOWN BEING SMASHED)
10. ...FOR...
11. ...BEING...
12. ...ON THE...
13. ...JOB...
14. ...AND...
15. ...WORKING HARD...
(CONTINUED)

The relationship between Anheuser-Busch and D'Arcy advertising produced some groundbreaking ad campaigns. Of this storyboard for a Budweiser TV commercial, Gerry Mandel writes, "I was creative director on Bud at D'Arcy when this spot was produced sometime during the early 1990s. It was shot in L.A. by one of the teams in my group." (St. Louis Media Archives.)

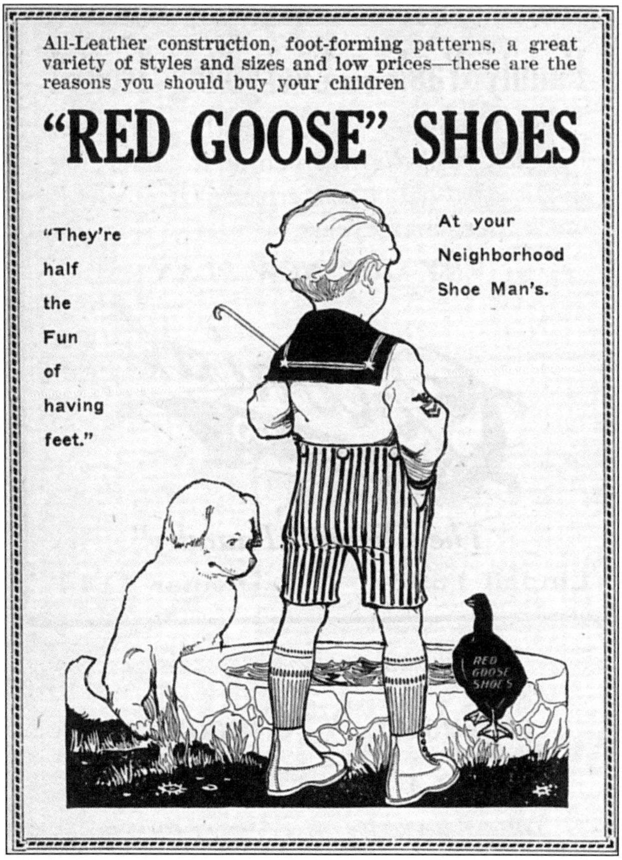
All-Leather construction, foot-forming patterns, a great variety of styles and sizes and low prices—these are the reasons you should buy your children
"RED GOOSE" SHOES
"They're half the Fun of having feet."
At your Neighborhood Shoe Man's.
RED GOOSE SHOES

The brilliant slogan that carried through most of the history of Red Goose shoes shows up in this 1922 ad: "They're half the fun of having feet." Any kid who shopped for Red Goose shoes with Mom will remember the goose-egg premium in the store, which involved getting a special golden plastic egg. Getting the kids to ask for Red Goose shoes may have been a parental headache, but it made for terrific advertising. (St. Louis Media Archives.)

Poll Parrot, like other brands of children's shoes, offered premiums such as trinkets, some of which turned into collectibles that can fetch a worthwhile price today. Poll Parrot and competitor Red Goose were both eventually purchased by the International Shoe Company. (St. Louis Media Archives.)

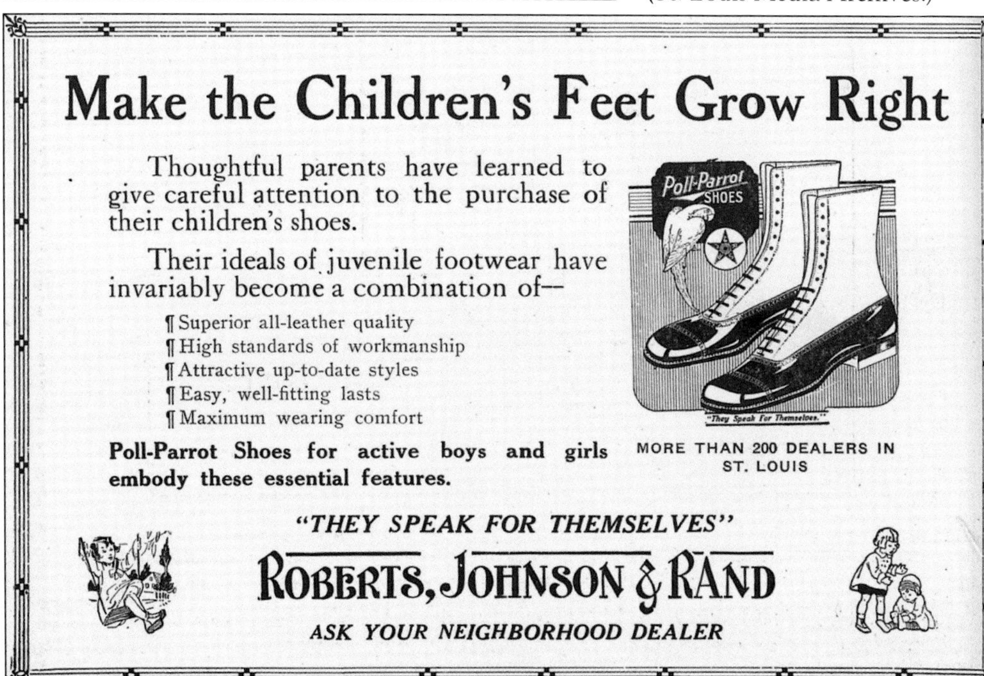
Make the Children's Feet Grow Right
Thoughtful parents have learned to give careful attention to the purchase of their children's shoes.
Their ideals of juvenile footwear have invariably become a combination of—
¶ Superior all-leather quality
¶ High standards of workmanship
¶ Attractive up-to-date styles
¶ Easy, well-fitting lasts
¶ Maximum wearing comfort
Poll-Parrot Shoes for active boys and girls embody these essential features.
Poll-Parrot SHOES
MORE THAN 200 DEALERS IN ST. LOUIS
"THEY SPEAK FOR THEMSELVES"
ROBERTS, JOHNSON & RAND
ASK YOUR NEIGHBORHOOD DEALER

McElroy-Sloan's Billiken shoes were made at its plant, located at 2101 Lucas Avenue on the western edge of downtown, until 1928. Advertising touted the company's scientific study of the special shoe requirements of children's feet, which led to rounded toes on the shoes. (St. Louis Media Archives.)

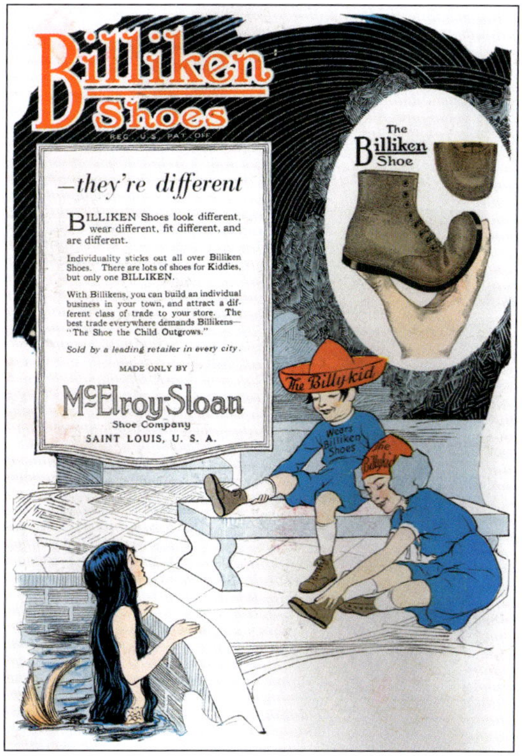
Billiken Shoes
REG. U.S. PAT. OFF.
—they're different
BILLIKEN Shoes look different, wear different, fit different, and are different.
Individuality sticks out all over Billiken Shoes. There are lots of shoes for Kiddies, but only one BILLIKEN.
With Billikens, you can build an individual business in your town, and attract a different class of trade to your store. The best trade everywhere demands Billikens—"The Shoe the Child Outgrows."
Sold by a leading retailer in every city.
MADE ONLY BY
McElroy-Sloan
Shoe Company
SAINT LOUIS, U. S. A.
The Billiken Shoe
The Billy kid
Wears Billiken Shoes

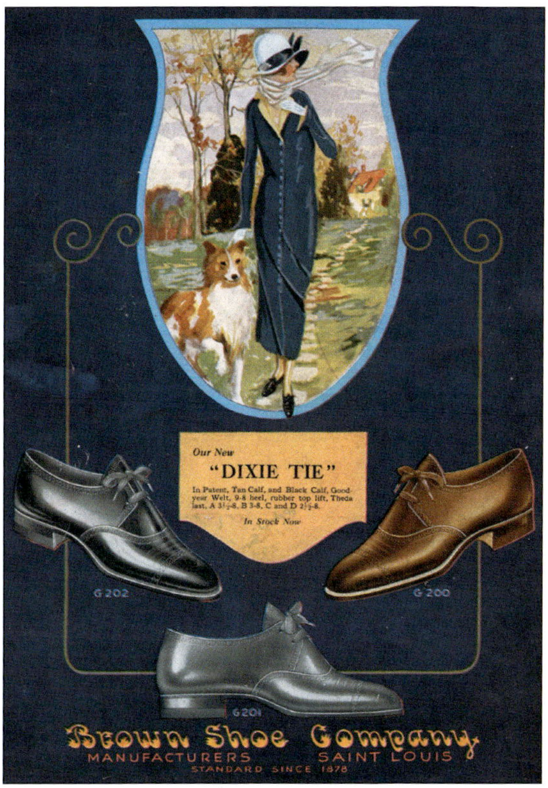
Our New
"DIXIE TIE"
In Stock Now
G 202
G 200
G 201
Brown Shoe Company
MANUFACTURERS
SAINT LOUIS
STANDARD SINCE 1878

Advertising veteran Gerry Mandel notes, "The ad reeks of 'elegance': the colors, the balanced layout, the shoes displayed, the fashionable woman with spoiled dog, the lovely home in the background." (St. Louis Media Archives.)

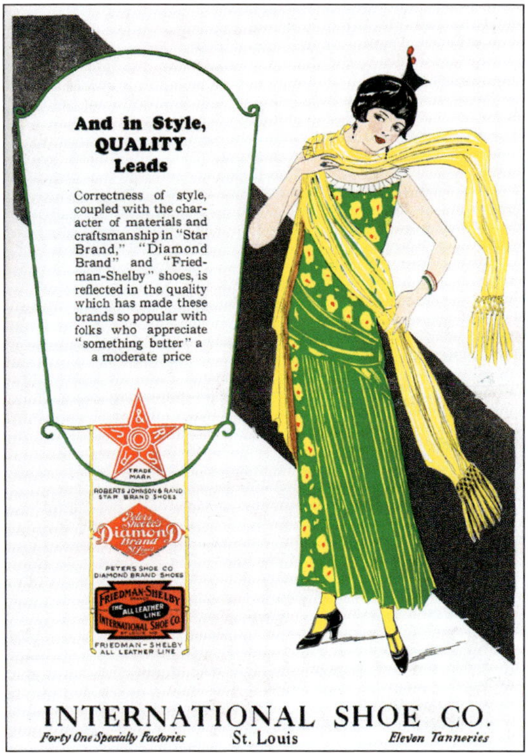
And in Style, QUALITY Leads
Correctness of style, coupled with the character of materials and craftsmanship in "Star Brand," "Diamond Brand" and "Friedman-Shelby" shoes, is reflected in the quality which has made these brands so popular with folks who appreciate "something better" a a moderate price
TRADE MARK
ROBERTS JOHNSON & RAND STAR BRAND SHOES
Diamond Brand
PETERS SHOE CO DIAMOND BRAND SHOES
FRIEDMAN-SHELBY THE ALL LEATHER LINE INTERNATIONAL SHOE CO.
FRIEDMAN-SHELBY ALL LEATHER LINE
INTERNATIONAL SHOE CO.
Forty One Specialty Factories
St. Louis
Eleven Tanneries

The International Shoe Company formed in St. Louis in 1911 following the merger of two large area shoe manufacturers. Its continued acquisitions made International the largest manufacturer of footwear in the United States. In the early 1960s, the company began acquiring clothing manufacturers, leading to a corporate name change in 1966, when it became Interco. (St. Louis Media Archives.)

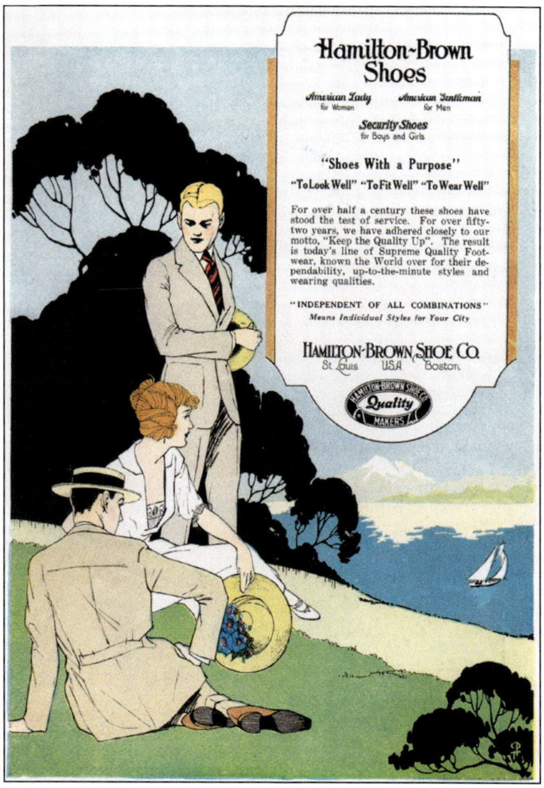
Hamilton-Brown Shoes
American Lady for Women
American Gentleman for Men
Security Shoes for Boys and Girls
"Shoes With a Purpose"
"To Look Well" "To Fit Well" "To Wear Well"
For over half a century these shoes have stood the test of service. For over fifty-two years, we have adhered closely to our motto, "Keep the Quality Up". The result is today's line of Supreme Quality Footwear, known the World over for their dependability, up-to-the-minute styles and wearing qualities.
"INDEPENDENT OF ALL COMBINATIONS"
Means Individual Styles for Your City
HAMILTON-BROWN SHOE CO.
St. Louis USA Boston
HAMILTON-BROWN SHOE CO. Quality MAKERS

This is probably an institutional business-to-business ad from 1924, although it is beautifully done with color artwork. The Hamilton-Brown nameplates are shown, along with a slogan in small print: "Means individual styles for your city." (St. Louis Media Archives.)

Vitality shoes were manufactured by the St. Louis–based International Shoe Company. It was mainly positioned as a women's brand, but Vitality ads from the 1940s showed kids' styles "twice as smart for children too." (St. Louis Media Archives.)

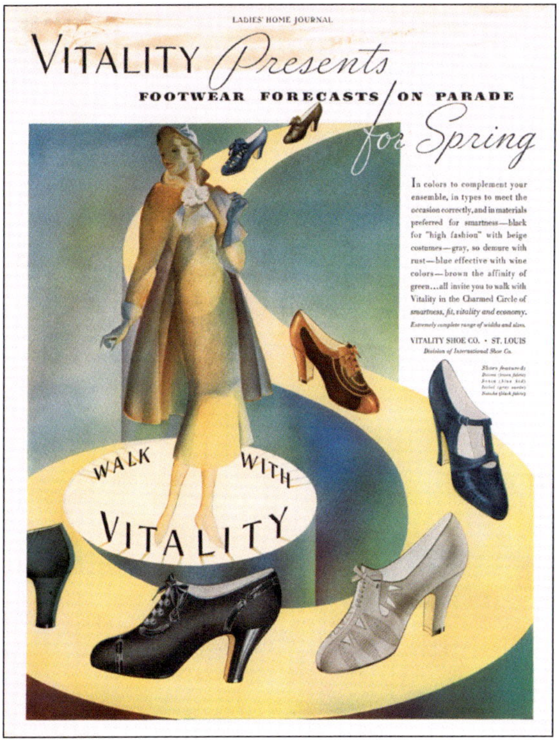
LADIES' HOME JOURNAL
VITALITY Presents
FOOTWEAR FORECASTS / ON PARADE
for Spring
In colors to complement your ensemble, in types to meet the occasion correctly, and in materials preferred for smartness—black for "high fashion" with beige costumes—gray, so demure with rust—blue effective with wine colors—brown the affinity of green…all invite you to walk with Vitality in the Charmed Circle of smartness, fit, vitality and economy.
Extremely complete range of widths and sizes.
VITALITY SHOE CO. • ST. LOUIS
Division of International Shoe Co.
WALK WITH VITALITY

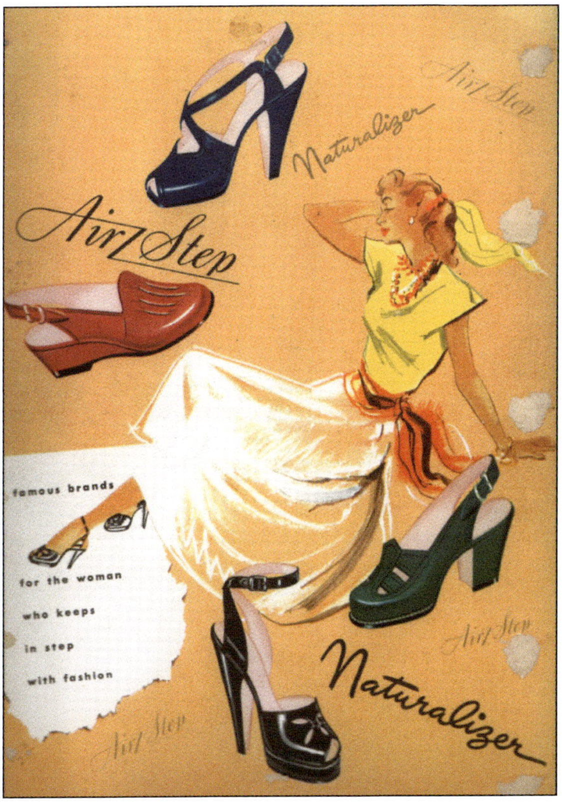
Naturalizer
Air Step
famous brands
for the woman
who keeps
in step
with fashion
Naturalizer

The Brown Shoe Company, originally named Bryan, Brown and Company when it formed in 1878, changed names in 1893. Its Naturalizer shoe line is positioned as a distinctively stylish brand. The brand, which began in 1927, has promoted comfort in its women's footwear, initially positioned as "the shoe with the beautiful fit." (Duane Marburger.)

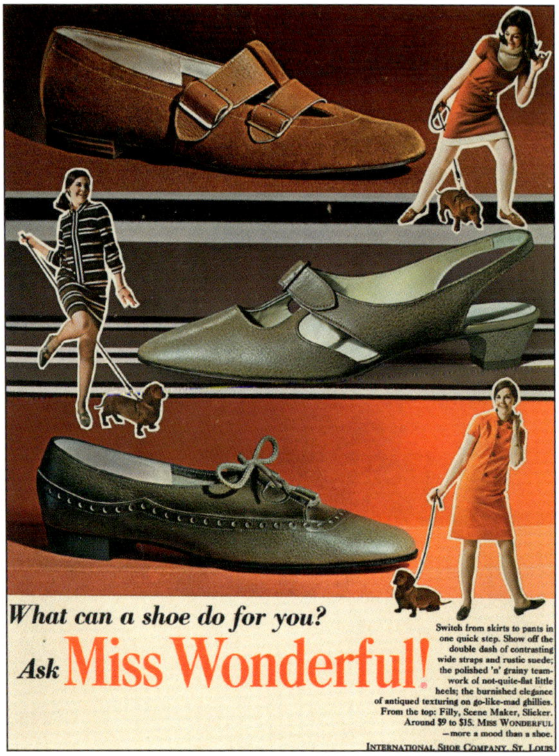
What can a shoe do for you?
Ask Miss Wonderful!
Switch from skirts to pants in one quick step. Show off the double dash of contrasting wide straps and rustic suede; the polished 'n' grainy teamwork of not-quite-flat little heels; the burnished elegance of antiqued texturing on go-like-mad ghillies. From the top: Filly, Scene Maker, Slicker. Around $9 to $15. Miss Wonderful —more a mood than a shoe.
International Shoe Company, St. Louis

The Miss Wonderful line, from International Shoe Company, is spotlighted in this ad from the 1960s. The brand shows consumers having fun while using the product. The copy even tries to express this idea by mimicking the speaking habits of the day, calling the leather "polished 'n' grainy." (St. Louis Media Archives.)

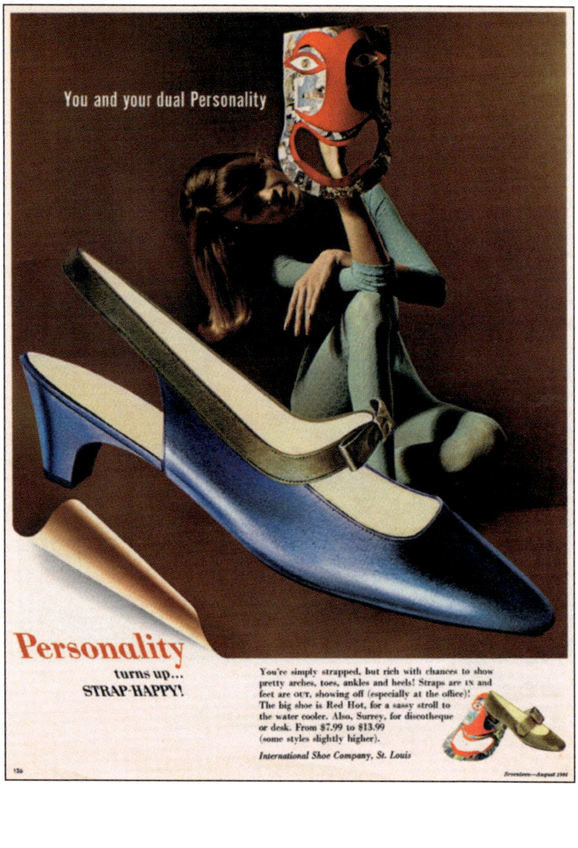
You and your dual Personality
Personality
turns up...
STRAP-HAPPY!
You're simply strapped, but rich with chances to show pretty arches, toes, ankles and heels! Straps are IN and feet are OUT, showing off (especially at the office)! The big shoe is Red Hot, for a sassy stroll to the water cooler. Also, Surrey, for discotheque or desk. From $7.99 to $13.99 (some styles slightly higher).
International Shoe Company, St. Louis

Advertising professor Kristy Tucciarone finds this 1966 ad confusing: "My eye does not know if I should focus on the shoe or the woman holding the creepy-looking mask. Straps are the 'big idea' in this ad, so that should be the highlight. The body copy turns feet into a negative, which is counterproductive to the message about shoes." (St. Louis Media Archives.)

Six

Print Advertising

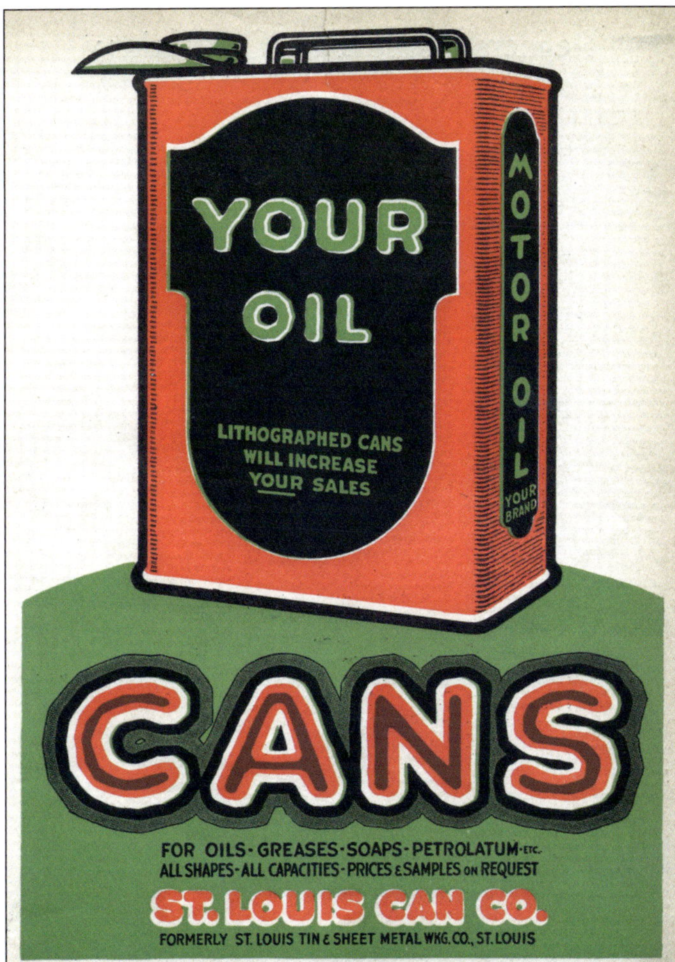

YOUR
OIL
LITHOGRAPHED CANS
WILL INCREASE
YOUR SALES
MOTOR OIL
YOUR BRAND
CANS
FOR OILS·GREASES·SOAPS·PETROLATUM·ETC.
ALL SHAPES·ALL CAPACITIES·PRICES & SAMPLES ON REQUEST
ST. LOUIS CAN CO.
FORMERLY ST. LOUIS TIN & SHEET METAL WKG. CO., ST. LOUIS

Cyrus F. Blanke was quite a businessman. His company's building still stands at the corner of Fourteenth Street and Chouteau Avenue. From there, he oversaw his tea and coffee company, spice packaging, and sheet metal company, the latter employing 350 people. During World War I, it produced 40,000 hard cans every day to be used to ship bread to the troops. The oilcan shown in this 1926 ad was manufactured for those companies selling lubricants to the growing population of auto owners. (St. Louis Media Archives.)

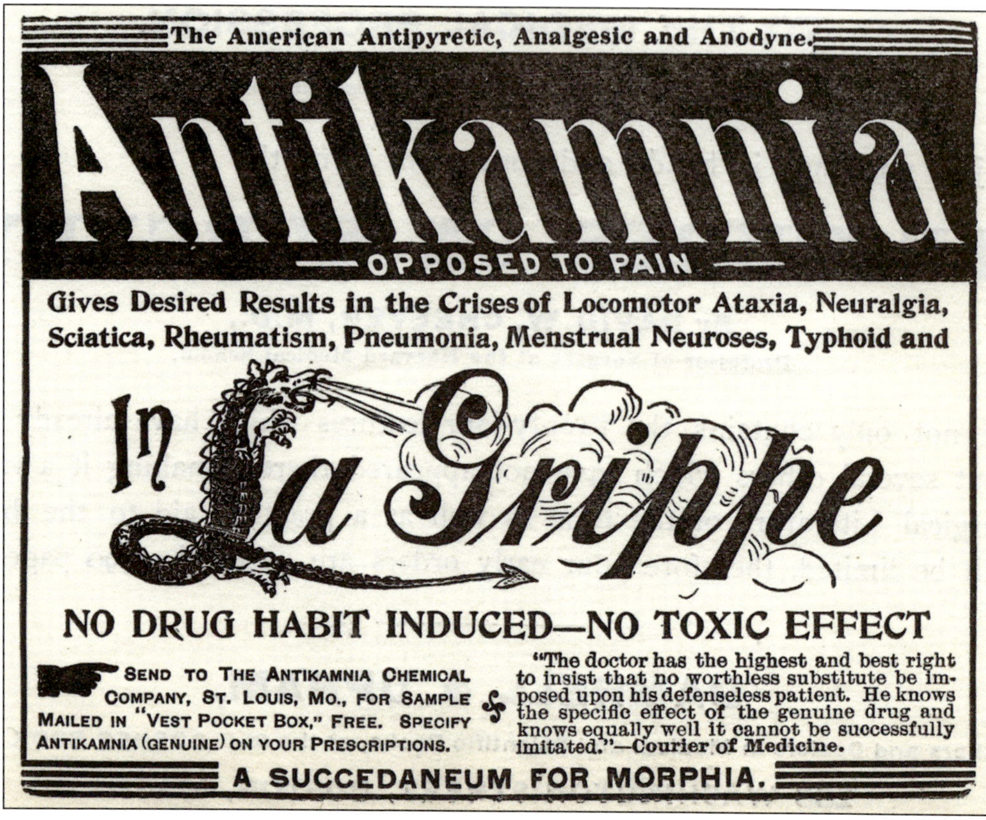
The American Antipyretic, Analgesic and Anodyne.
Antikamnia
OPPOSED TO PAIN
Gives Desired Results in the Crises of Locomotor Ataxia, Neuralgia, Sciatica, Rheumatism, Pneumonia, Menstrual Neuroses, Typhoid and
In La Grippe
NO DRUG HABIT INDUCED—NO TOXIC EFFECT
SEND TO THE ANTIKAMNIA CHEMICAL COMPANY, ST. LOUIS, MO., FOR SAMPLE MAILED IN "VEST POCKET BOX," FREE. SPECIFY ANTIKAMNIA (GENUINE) ON YOUR PRESCRIPTIONS.
"The doctor has the highest and best right to insist that no worthless substitute be imposed upon his defenseless patient. He knows the specific effect of the genuine drug and knows equally well it cannot be successfully imitated."—Courier of Medicine.
A SUCCEDANEUM FOR MORPHIA.

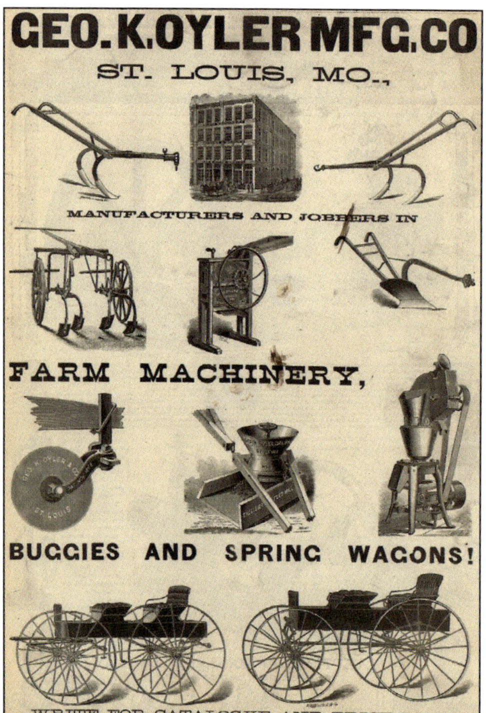
GEO. K. OYLER MFG. CO
ST. LOUIS, MO.,
MANUFACTURERS AND JOBBERS IN
FARM MACHINERY,
BUGGIES AND SPRING WAGONS!
WRITE FOR CATALOGUE AND PRICE LIST.

Although the Antikamnia Chemical Company began operating around 1890, it never patented the Antikamnia formula, which reportedly contained habit-forming compounds. The company's corporate offices were at 1723 Olive Street. Antikamnia relied on a junk-mail program to promote the product to potential customers, including doctors. The company shut down shortly after the Pure Food and Drug Act became law in 1906. Over a five-year period, the Antikamnia product was marketed to the medical community with odd calendars that portrayed skeletons dressed as people. (Missouri History Museum.)

George K. Oyler's company produced numerous types of farm equipment and carriages in St. Louis in the late 19th century. When a recession hit the agriculture sector in 1888, many farm-implement manufacturers closed, but the carriage trade kept Oyler's company afloat; farm implement production eventually made a comeback as well. (St. Louis Media Archives.)

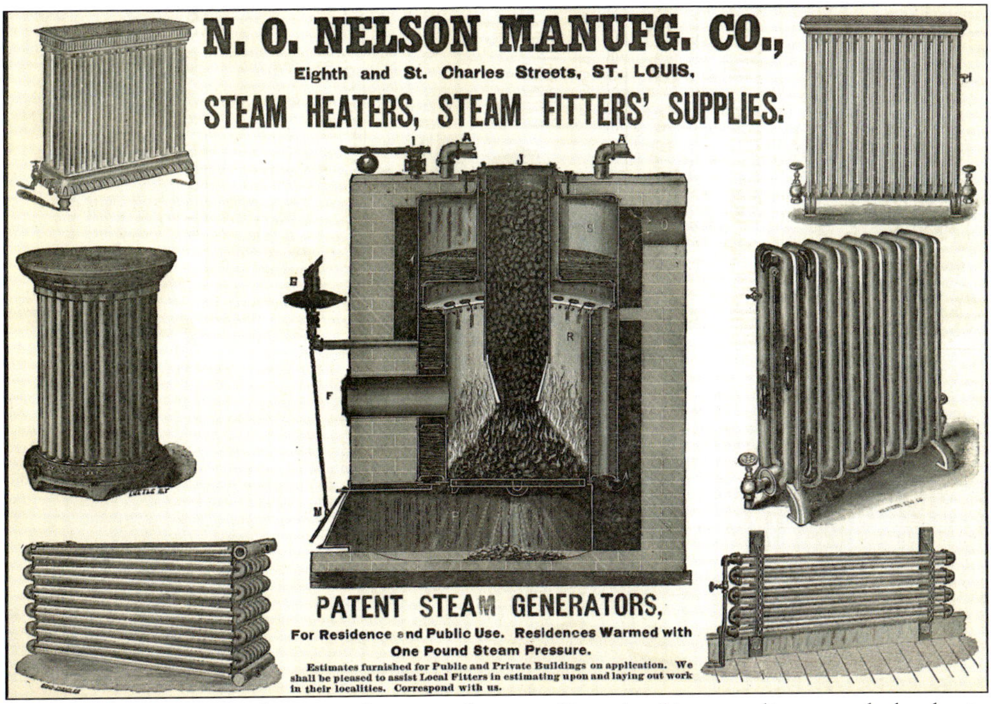
N. O. NELSON MANUFG. CO.,
Eighth and St. Charles Streets, ST. LOUIS,
STEAM HEATERS, STEAM FITTERS' SUPPLIES.
PATENT STEAM GENERATORS,
For Residence and Public Use. Residences Warmed with One Pound Steam Pressure.
Estimates furnished for Public and Private Buildings on application. We shall be pleased to assist Local Fitters in estimating upon and laying out work in their localities. Correspond with us.

The N.O. Nelson Manufacturing Company began selling plumbing supplies as a wholesaler in 1877 but soon got into manufacturing and distribution. When he needed to expand his factory, Nelson chose a rural site in Madison County, Illinois, and built a company town, which he named Leclaire, around it. (Missouri History Museum.)

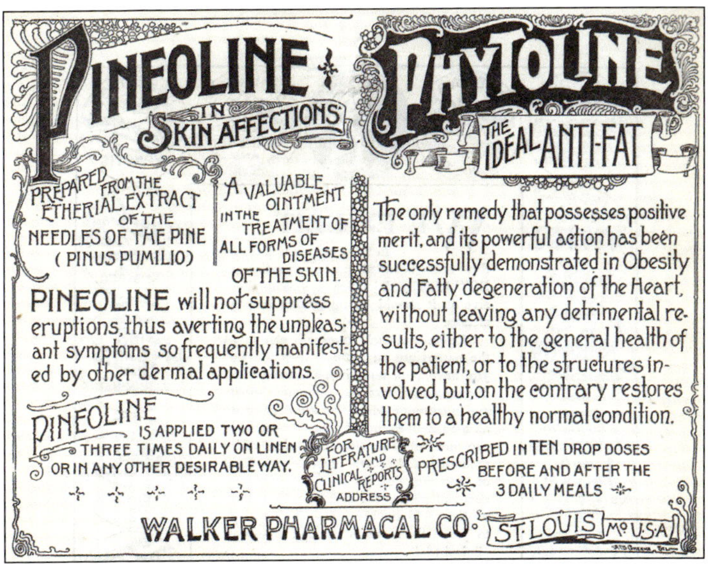
PINEOLINE IN SKIN AFFECTIONS
PHYTOLINE THE IDEAL ANTI-FAT
PREPARED FROM THE ETHERIAL EXTRACT OF THE NEEDLES OF THE PINE (PINUS PUMILIO)
A VALUABLE OINTMENT IN THE TREATMENT OF ALL FORMS OF DISEASES OF THE SKIN.
PINEOLINE will not suppress eruptions, thus averting the unpleasant symptoms so frequently manifested by other dermal applications.
PINEOLINE IS APPLIED TWO OR THREE TIMES DAILY ON LINEN OR IN ANY OTHER DESIRABLE WAY.
The only remedy that possesses positive merit, and its powerful action has been successfully demonstrated in Obesity and Fatty degeneration of the Heart, without leaving any detrimental results, either to the general health of the patient, or to the structures involved, but, on the contrary restores them to a healthy normal condition.
FOR LITERATURE AND CLINICAL REPORTS ADDRESS
PRESCRIBED IN TEN DROP DOSES BEFORE AND AFTER THE 3 DAILY MEALS
WALKER PHARMACAL CO. ST. LOUIS MO. U.S.A.

Walker Pharmacal Company also did business as Luyties Pharmacal, with offices and laboratories located in what was essentially a pharmaceutical specialties corridor on the 3800–4300 blocks of Laclede Avenue. Luyties promoted homeopathic products. (St. Louis Media Archives.)

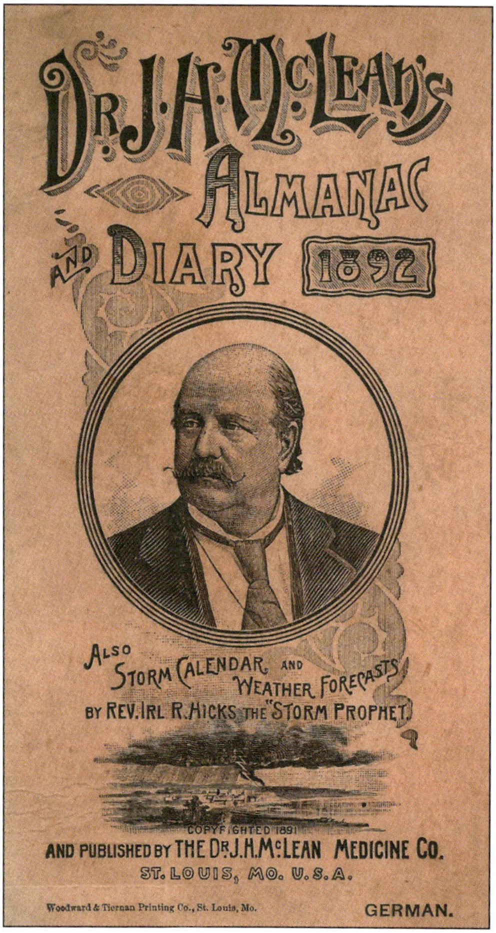
Dr. J. H. McLean's
Almanac
and Diary
1892
Also
Storm Calendar and
Weather Forecasts
by Rev. Irl R. Hicks the "Storm Prophet."
Copyrighted 1891
and published by The Dr. J. H. McLean Medicine Co.
St. Louis, Mo. U.S.A.
Woodward & Tiernan Printing Co., St. Louis, Mo.
GERMAN.

James Henry McLean used an annual almanac to promote his patent medicines, of which there were many, each promising miraculous cures for various infirmities. Although he referred to himself as "Dr." McLean, there is no evidence that he completed medical school; nonetheless, the dishonest use of the title was probably responsible for selling many oils, salves, and ointments. His plant was located on the 4100 block of Laclede Avenue. (Missouri History Museum.)

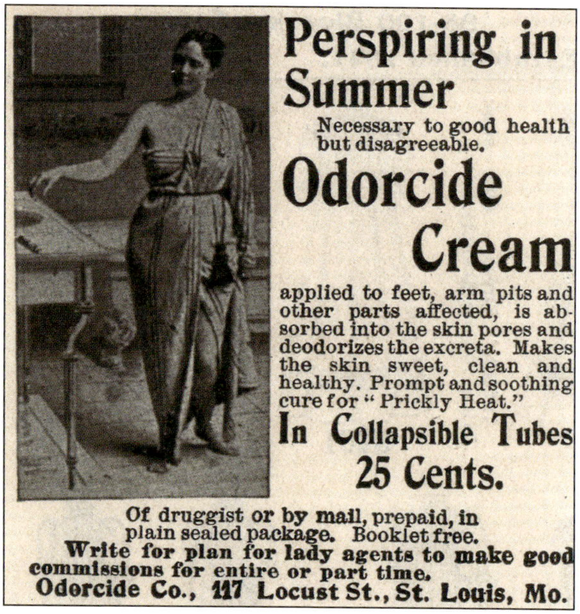
Perspiring in Summer
Necessary to good health but disagreeable.
Odorcide Cream
applied to feet, arm pits and other parts affected, is absorbed into the skin pores and deodorizes the excreta. Makes the skin sweet, clean and healthy. Prompt and soothing cure for "Prickly Heat."
In Collapsible Tubes
25 Cents.
Of druggist or by mail, prepaid, in plain sealed package. Booklet free.
Write for plan for lady agents to make good commissions for entire or part time.
Odorcide Co., 117 Locust St., St. Louis, Mo.

It appears this manufacturer failed to copyright or trademark the product name. Today, another Odorcide exists. Ad man Gerry Mandel comments on the advertisement, "This may be the only time in history when a copywriter wrote those magical words, 'deodorizes the excreta.'" (Missouri History Museum.)

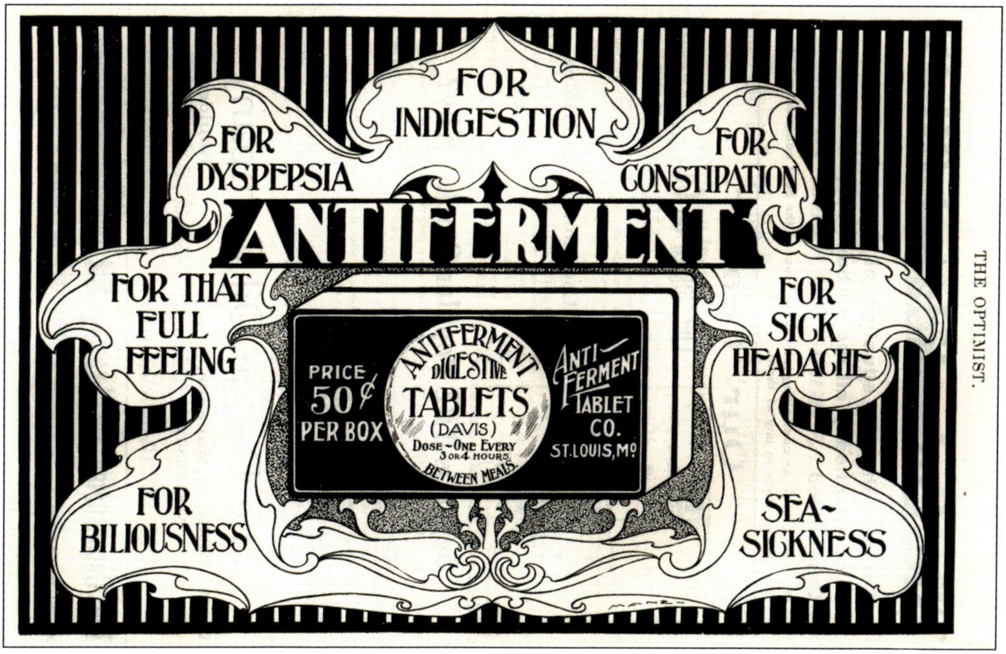
FOR INDIGESTION
FOR DYSPEPSIA
FOR CONSTIPATION
ANTIFERMENT
FOR THAT FULL FEELING
FOR SICK HEADACHE
PRICE 50¢ PER BOX
ANTIFERMENT DIGESTIVE TABLETS (DAVIS) DOSE - ONE EVERY 3 OR 4 HOURS BETWEEN MEALS.
ANTI-FERMENT TABLET CO. ST. LOUIS, MO
FOR BILIOUSNESS
SEA-SICKNESS
THE OPTIMIST.

People commonly used antiferment tablets at the beginning of the 20th century to treat digestive problems. Ingredients were basic, including bismuth and sodium bicarbonate, compounds that neutralize stomach acid. The tablets were available from many sources, including the Davis Company in St. Louis. (Missouri History Museum.)

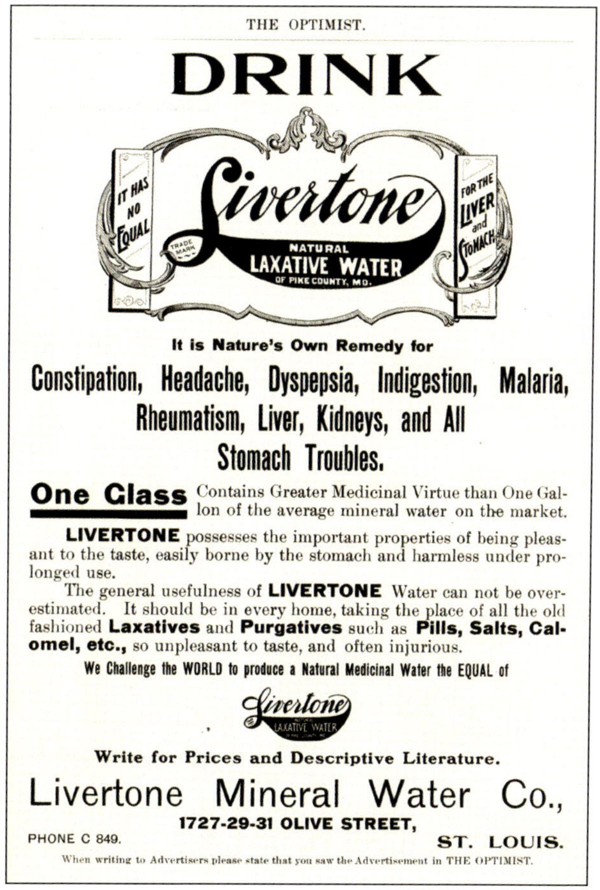
THE OPTIMIST.
DRINK
IT HAS NO EQUAL
Livertone
TRADE MARK
NATURAL LAXATIVE WATER OF PIKE COUNTY, MO.
FOR THE LIVER and STOMACH
It is Nature's Own Remedy for
Constipation, Headache, Dyspepsia, Indigestion, Malaria, Rheumatism, Liver, Kidneys, and All Stomach Troubles.
One Glass Contains Greater Medicinal Virtue than One Gallon of the average mineral water on the market.
LIVERTONE possesses the important properties of being pleasant to the taste, easily borne by the stomach and harmless under prolonged use.
The general usefulness of LIVERTONE Water can not be overestimated. It should be in every home, taking the place of all the old fashioned Laxatives and Purgatives such as Pills, Salts, Calomel, etc., so unpleasant to taste, and often injurious.
We Challenge the WORLD to produce a Natural Medicinal Water the EQUAL of
Livertone
Write for Prices and Descriptive Literature.
Livertone Mineral Water Co.,
1727-29-31 OLIVE STREET,
PHONE C 849.
ST. LOUIS.
When writing to Advertisers please state that you saw the Advertisement in THE OPTIMIST.

Livertone mineral water, imported from Pike County, Missouri, was sold as a digestive aid. There were many mineral springs and baths surrounding St. Louis, each boasting that its unique water could cure different ailments. Resorts were often built around these mineral wells to offer guests the opportunity to bathe in the "healing" waters. (Missouri History Museum.)

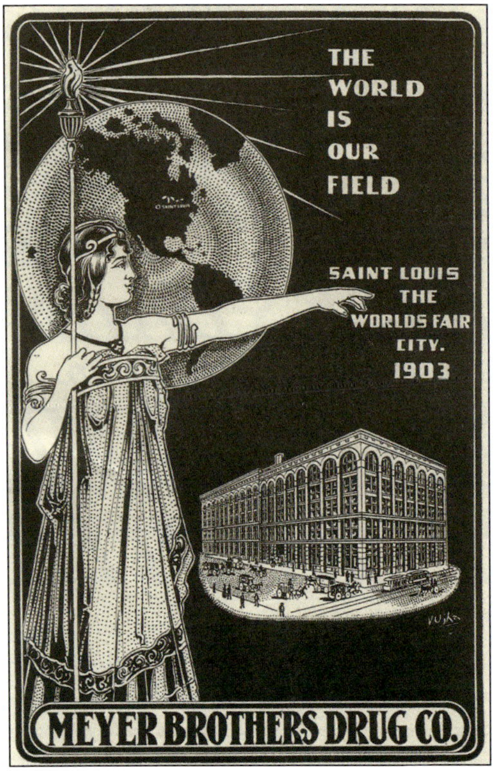
THE WORLD IS OUR FIELD
SAINT LOUIS THE WORLDS FAIR CITY. 1903
MEYER BROTHERS DRUG CO.

Meyer Brothers Drug Company began in Indiana in 1852. The company established a St. Louis facility in 1865, and by the time this ad was published, its headquarters had relocated to St. Louis, and Meyer Brothers, with an office at Second and Locust Streets, had become the country's largest drug and pharmaceutical distributor. A 1981 merger changed the company's name to FoxMeyer. The 1903 date in this ad for the local World's Fair is not a mistake; the original plan was to hold the fair then, but when it became apparent things would not be ready in time, it was delayed for a year. (Missouri History Museum.)

In the days before regulatory oversight of the medical profession and advertising, it was common to find advertisements for tonics, pills, and physicians that would cure just about any affliction, including, in Dr. W.A. Cook's case, a low level of "manhood." Cook claimed to have "the most perfect system of home treatment known to medical science." (Missouri History Museum.)

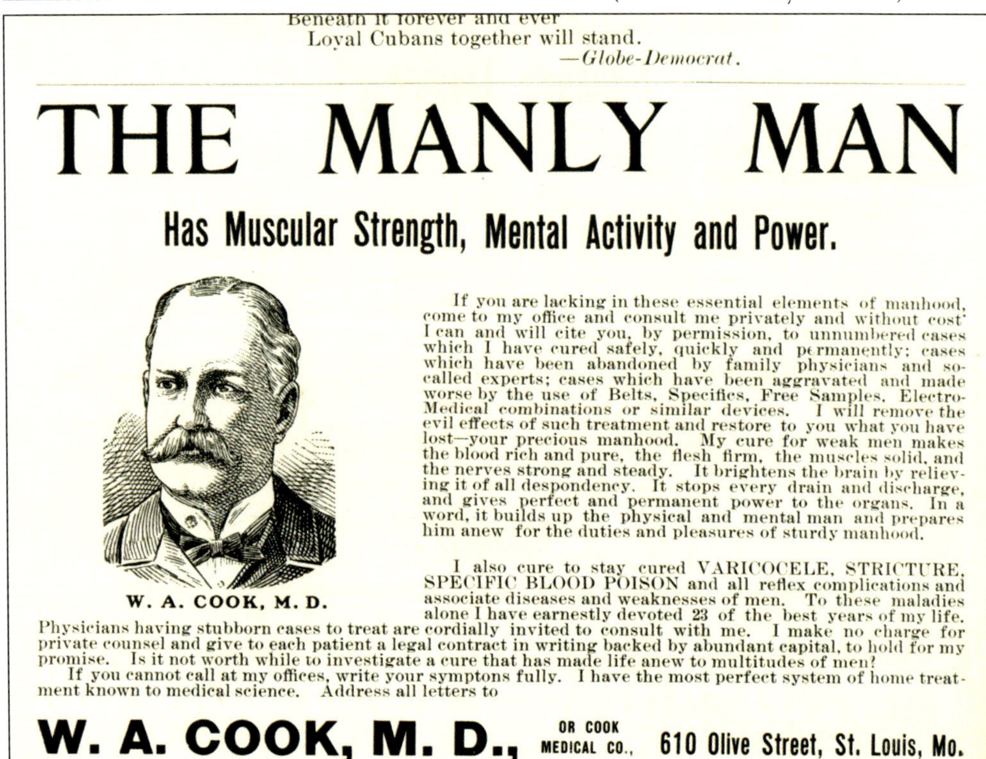
Beneath it forever and ever
Loyal Cubans together will stand.
—Globe-Democrat.
THE MANLY MAN
Has Muscular Strength, Mental Activity and Power.
If you are lacking in these essential elements of manhood, come to my office and consult me privately and without cost. I can and will cite you, by permission, to unnumbered cases which I have cured safely, quickly and permanently; cases which have been abandoned by family physicians and so-called experts; cases which have been aggravated and made worse by the use of Belts, Specifics, Free Samples, Electro-Medical combinations or similar devices. I will remove the evil effects of such treatment and restore to you what you have lost—your precious manhood. My cure for weak men makes the blood rich and pure, the flesh firm, the muscles solid, and the nerves strong and steady. It brightens the brain by relieving it of all despondency. It stops every drain and discharge, and gives perfect and permanent power to the organs. In a word, it builds up the physical and mental man and prepares him anew for the duties and pleasures of sturdy manhood.
I also cure to stay cured VARICOCELE, STRICTURE, SPECIFIC BLOOD POISON and all reflex complications and associate diseases and weaknesses of men. To these maladies alone I have earnestly devoted 23 of the best years of my life.
W. A. COOK, M. D.
Physicians having stubborn cases to treat are cordially invited to consult with me. I make no charge for private counsel and give to each patient a legal contract in writing backed by abundant capital, to hold for my promise. Is it not worth while to investigate a cure that has made life anew to multitudes of men?
If you cannot call at my offices, write your symptons fully. I have the most perfect system of home treatment known to medical science. Address all letters to
W. A. COOK, M. D., OR COOK MEDICAL CO., 610 Olive Street, St. Louis, Mo.

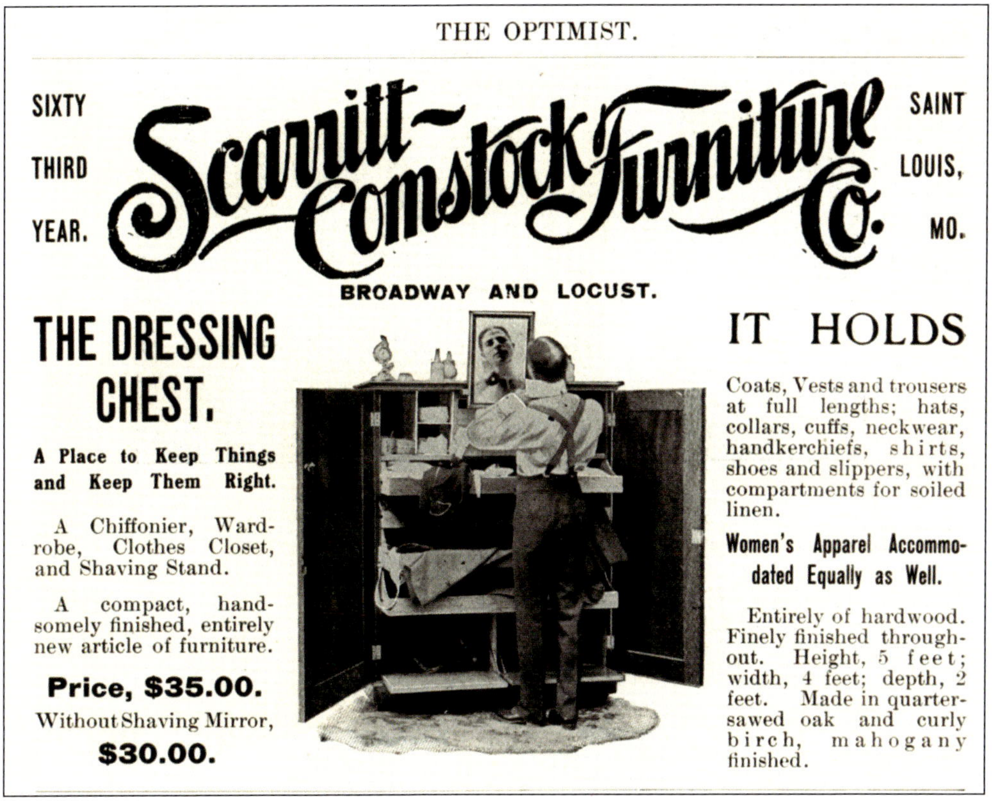
THE OPTIMIST.
SIXTY
THIRD
YEAR.
Scarritt-Comstock Furniture Co.
SAINT
LOUIS,
MO.
BROADWAY AND LOCUST.
THE DRESSING CHEST.
A Place to Keep Things and Keep Them Right.
A Chiffonier, Wardrobe, Clothes Closet, and Shaving Stand.
A compact, handsomely finished, entirely new article of furniture.
Price, $35.00.
Without Shaving Mirror,
$30.00.
IT HOLDS
Coats, Vests and trousers at full lengths; hats, collars, cuffs, neckwear, handkerchiefs, shirts, shoes and slippers, with compartments for soiled linen.
Women's Apparel Accommodated Equally as Well.
Entirely of hardwood. Finely finished throughout. Height, 5 feet; width, 4 feet; depth, 2 feet. Made in quarter-sawed oak and curly birch, mahogany finished.

Scarritt Furniture was formed in 1837 and renamed Scarritt-Comstock in 1897. The company manufactured its own wood pieces, each containing a brass nameplate with the company name emblazoned on it. The main showroom spanned three storefronts on the 800 block of Washington Avenue in downtown St. Louis. (Missouri History Museum.)

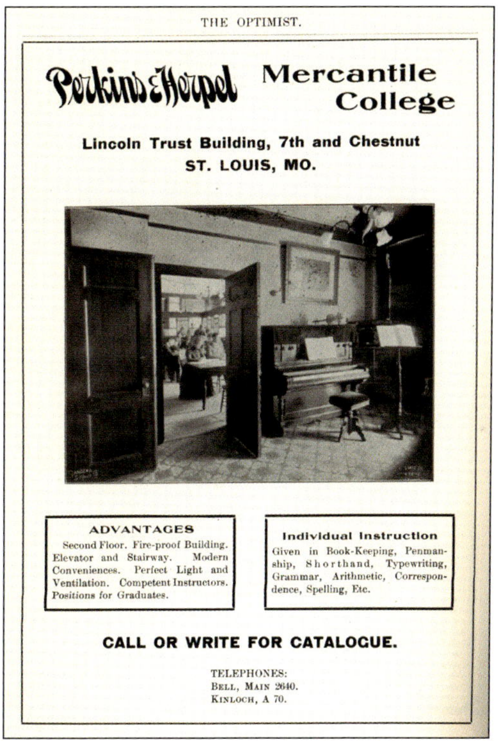
THE OPTIMIST.
Perkins & Herpel Mercantile College
Lincoln Trust Building, 7th and Chestnut
ST. LOUIS, MO.
ADVANTAGES
Second Floor. Fire-proof Building. Elevator and Stairway. Modern Conveniences. Perfect Light and Ventilation. Competent Instructors. Positions for Graduates.
Individual Instruction
Given in Book-Keeping, Penmanship, Shorthand, Typewriting, Grammar, Arithmetic, Correspondence, Spelling, Etc.
CALL OR WRITE FOR CATALOGUE.
TELEPHONES:
BELL, MAIN 2640.
KINLOCH, A 70.

Perkins and Herpel Mercantile College offered day and night classes at its downtown facility at the beginning of the 20th century. Established in 1883, the school's early advertising boasted that there were no classes; rather, each student received individualized instruction from faculty members. (Missouri History Museum.)

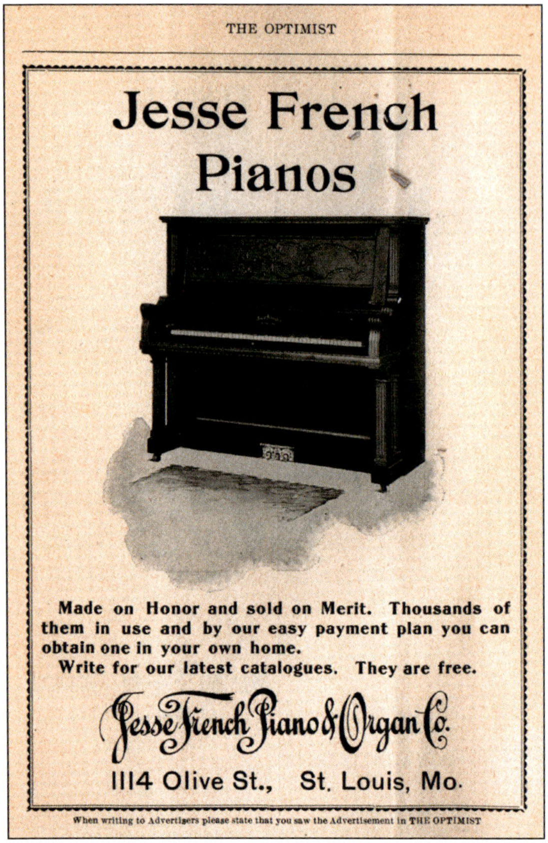
THE OPTIMIST
Jesse French Pianos
Made on Honor and sold on Merit. Thousands of them in use and by our easy payment plan you can obtain one in your own home.
Write for our latest catalogues. They are free.
Jesse French Piano & Organ Co.
1114 Olive St., St. Louis, Mo.
When writing to Advertisers please state that you saw the Advertisement in THE OPTIMIST

The Jesse French Piano and Organ Company had factories in several Midwestern cities, but Jesse French and his sons H. Edgar and Jesse Jr. were based in St. Louis. Although it originally operated as the Field-French Piano Company, the name was changed to Jesse French and Sons Piano Company in 1887. (Missouri History Museum.)

Thiebes-Stierlin Music Company began in 1894, manufacturing pianos and printing sheet music. Located on the city's music row (on Olive Street between Tenth and Twelfth Streets) with eight other music companies, Thiebes-Stierlin continued selling regular and player pianos, as well as guitars, mandolins, and strings, until the company was sold to Wurlitzer in 1919. (Missouri History Museum.)

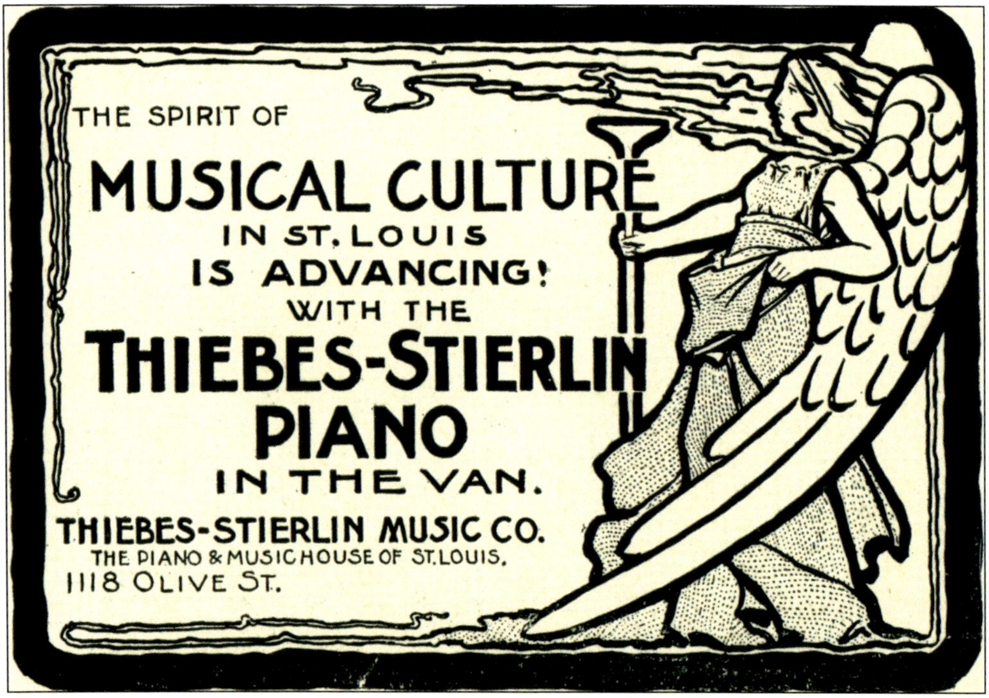
THE SPIRIT OF
MUSICAL CULTURE
IN ST. LOUIS
IS ADVANCING!
WITH THE
THIEBES-STIERLIN
PIANO
IN THE VAN.
THIEBES-STIERLIN MUSIC CO.
THE PIANO & MUSIC HOUSE OF ST. LOUIS.
1118 OLIVE ST.

Sanitol Chemical Company, a cooperative owned by dentists and druggists, moved to its distinctive building at 4264 Laclede Avenue in 1906. It made mouthwash and dental products there until 1922. Many of the company's early trade ads consisted of endorsements from dentists, but its consumer advertising in the early 20th century was filled with imaginative graphics. (St. Louis Media Archives.)

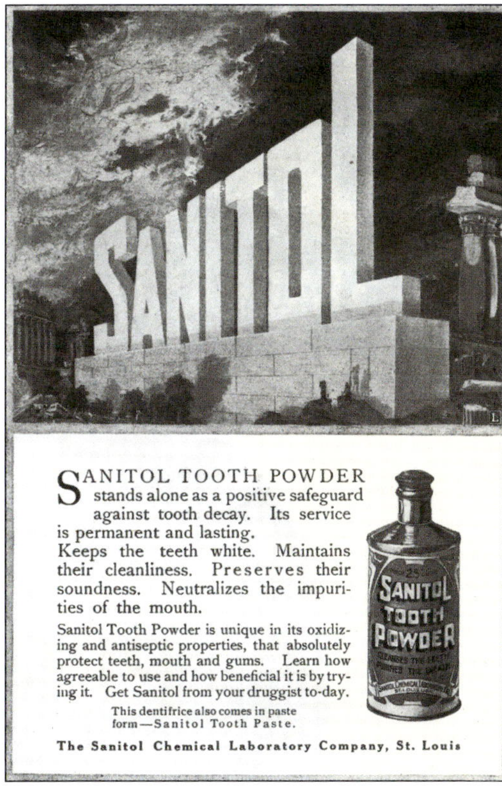
SANITOL
SANITOL TOOTH POWDER stands alone as a positive safeguard against tooth decay. Its service is permanent and lasting.
Keeps the teeth white. Maintains their cleanliness. Preserves their soundness. Neutralizes the impurities of the mouth.
Sanitol Tooth Powder is unique in its oxidizing and antiseptic properties, that absolutely protect teeth, mouth and gums. Learn how agreeable to use and how beneficial it is by trying it. Get Sanitol from your druggist to-day.
This dentifrice also comes in paste form—Sanitol Tooth Paste.
The Sanitol Chemical Laboratory Company, St. Louis
SANITOL
TOOTH
POWDER

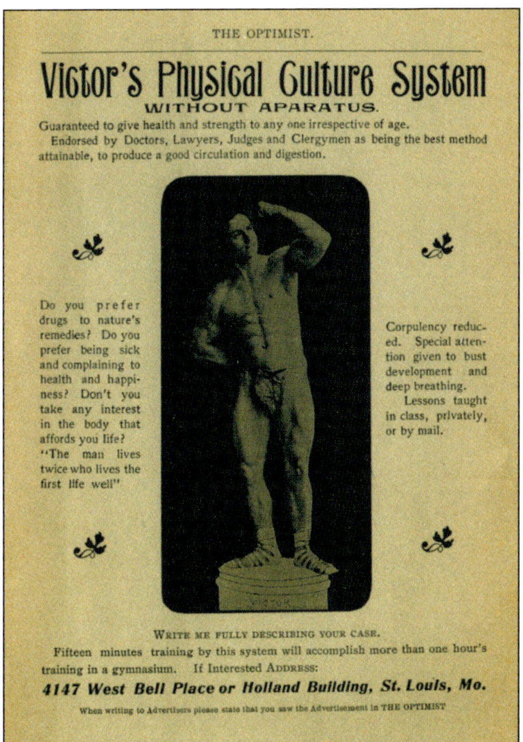
THE OPTIMIST.
Victor's Physical Culture System
WITHOUT APARATUS.
Guaranteed to give health and strength to any one irrespective of age.
Endorsed by Doctors, Lawyers, Judges and Clergymen as being the best method attainable, to produce a good circulation and digestion.
Do you prefer drugs to nature's remedies? Do you prefer being sick and complaining to health and happiness? Don't you take any interest in the body that affords you life? "The man lives twice who lives the first life well"
Corpulency reduced. Special attention given to bust development and deep breathing.
Lessons taught in class, privately, or by mail.
WRITE ME FULLY DESCRIBING YOUR CASE.
Fifteen minutes training by this system will accomplish more than one hour's training in a gymnasium. If Interested ADDRESS:
4147 West Bell Place or Holland Building, St. Louis, Mo.
When writing to Advertisers please state that you saw the Advertisement in THE OPTIMIST

In 1902, Victor's Physical Culture System promised results from individual training and a specialized series of exercises. The 24-lesson program was "guaranteed to produce increases in physical strength" and cure gout and rheumatism, as well as relieve any trouble of the stomach. The lessons could be adapted to woman and children. (Missouri History Museum.)

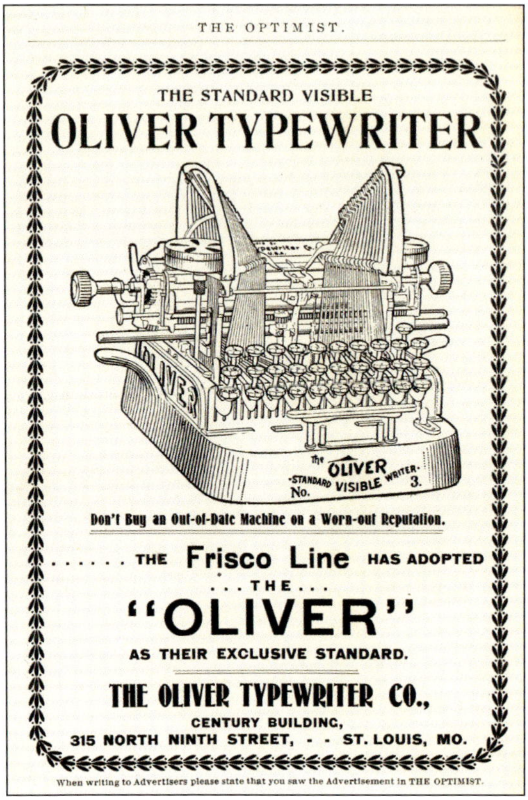
THE OPTIMIST.
THE STANDARD VISIBLE
OLIVER TYPEWRITER
OLIVER
STANDARD VISIBLE WRITER No. 3.
Don't Buy an Out-of-Date Machine on a Worn-out Reputation.
...... THE Frisco Line HAS ADOPTED
...THE...
"OLIVER"
AS THEIR EXCLUSIVE STANDARD.
THE OLIVER TYPEWRITER CO.,
CENTURY BUILDING,
315 NORTH NINTH STREET, - - ST. LOUIS, MO.
When writing to Advertisers please state that you saw the Advertisement in THE OPTIMIST.

The Oliver Typewriter Company, headquartered in Chicago, established a St. Louis office to expand the brand to different regions. The St. Louis store closed when the company changed to a mail-order firm in 1917. (Missouri History Museum.)

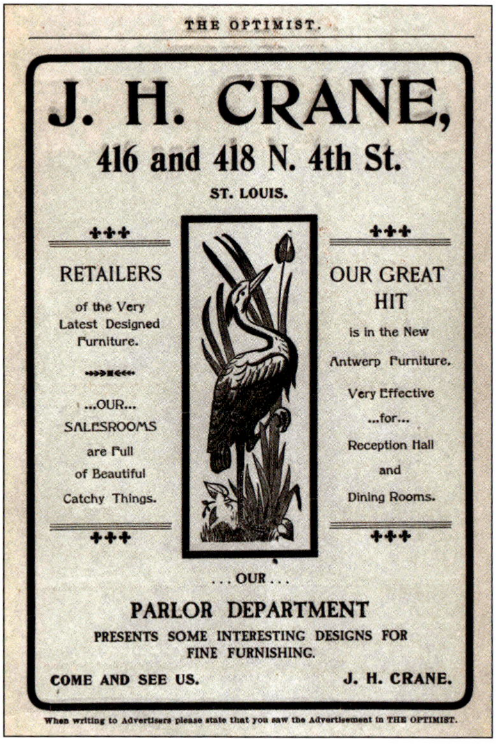
THE OPTIMIST.
J. H. CRANE,
416 and 418 N. 4th St.
ST. LOUIS.
RETAILERS
of the Very
Latest Designed
Furniture.
...OUR...
SALESROOMS
are Full
of Beautiful
Catchy Things.
OUR GREAT
HIT
is in the New
Antwerp Furniture.
Very Effective
...for...
Reception Hall
and
Dining Rooms.
...OUR...
PARLOR DEPARTMENT
PRESENTS SOME INTERESTING DESIGNS FOR
FINE FURNISHING.
COME AND SEE US.
J. H. CRANE.
When writing to Advertisers please state that you saw the Advertisement in THE OPTIMIST.

J.H. Crane Furniture, established in 1871, was incorporated in 1903. The company sold wholesale and retail furniture from the same building downtown on the 400 block of North Fourth Street. The company went bankrupt in 1907. (Missouri History Museum.)

This 1903 image ad in a women's magazine promoted the brand name found on many Ralston Purina products, as well as the checkerboard pattern that would remain the major part of the company's identity for decades. At the time, Ralston Purina's consumer product line was grain based, and this ad offered a full package of the company's cereal coffee to anyone who mailed in a dime. (St. Louis Media Archives.)

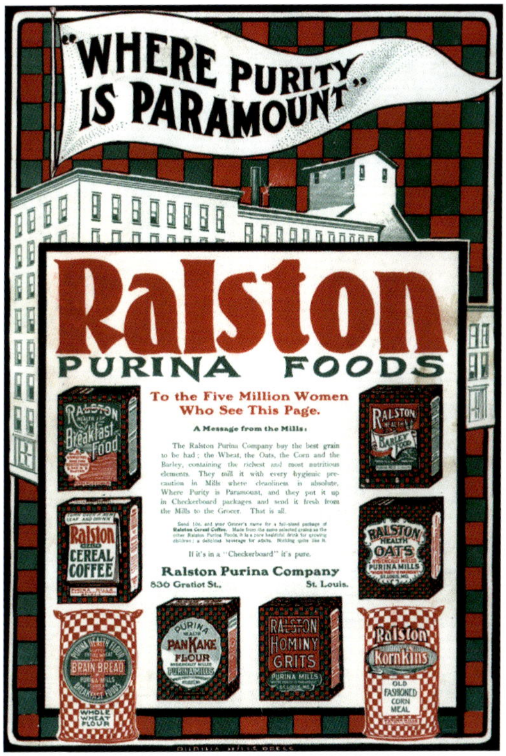

"WHERE PURITY IS PARAMOUNT"
Ralston
PURINA FOODS
To the Five Million Women Who See This Page.
A Message from the Mills:
The Ralston Purina Company buy the best grain to be had; the Wheat, the Oats, the Corn and the Barley, containing the richest and most nutritious elements. They mill it with every hygienic precaution in Mills where cleanliness is absolute, Where Purity is Paramount, and they put it up in Checkerboard packages and send it fresh from the Mills to the Grocer. That is all.
If it's in a "Checkerboard" it's pure.
Ralston Purina Company
836 Gratiot St.
St. Louis.
Ralston Breakfast Food
Ralston Cereal Coffee
Ralston Barley Food
Ralston Oats
Purina Pankake Flour
Ralston Hominy Grits
Brain Bread
Whole Wheat Flour
Ralston Kornkins
Old Fashioned Corn Meal

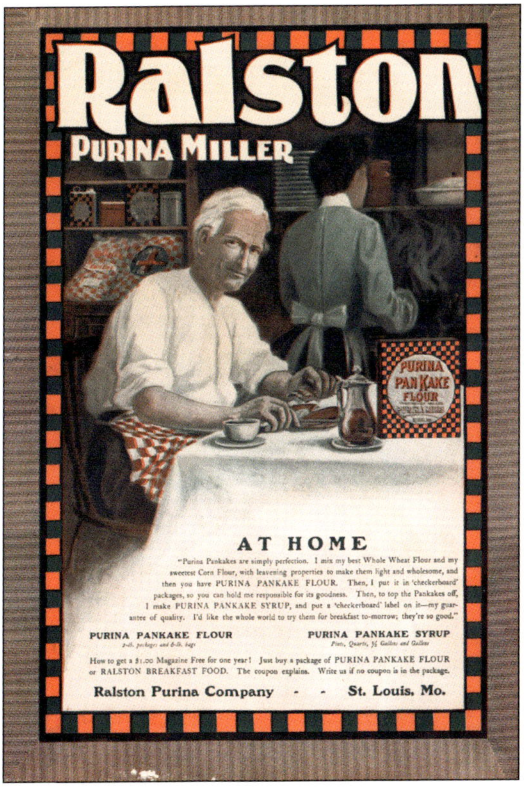

Ralston
PURINA MILLER
PURINA PANKAKE FLOUR
AT HOME
"Purina Pankakes are simply perfection. I mix my best Whole Wheat Flour and my sweetest Corn Flour, with leavening properties to make them light and wholesome, and then you have PURINA PANKAKE FLOUR. Then, I put it in 'checkerboard' packages, so you can hold me responsible for its goodness. Then, to top the Pankakes off, I make PURINA PANKAKE SYRUP, and put a 'checkerboard' label on it—my guarantee of quality. I'd like the whole world to try them for breakfast to-morrow; they're so good."
PURINA PANKAKE FLOUR
PURINA PANKAKE SYRUP
How to get a $1.00 Magazine Free for one year! Just buy a package of PURINA PANKAKE FLOUR or RALSTON BREAKFAST FOOD. The coupon explains. Write us if no coupon is in the package.
Ralston Purina Company - - St. Louis, Mo.

This Ralston Purina ad, also from 1903, focuses on fewer products, encouraging the consumer to buy Purina Pankake Flour and Syrup for the breakfast experience. The checkerboard pattern is evident, but the artwork forces a focus on the image of the man, a Ralston Purina miller, whose message is simple: because the product is so good, he is willing to put the Purina checkerboard on the label. (St. Louis Media Archives.)

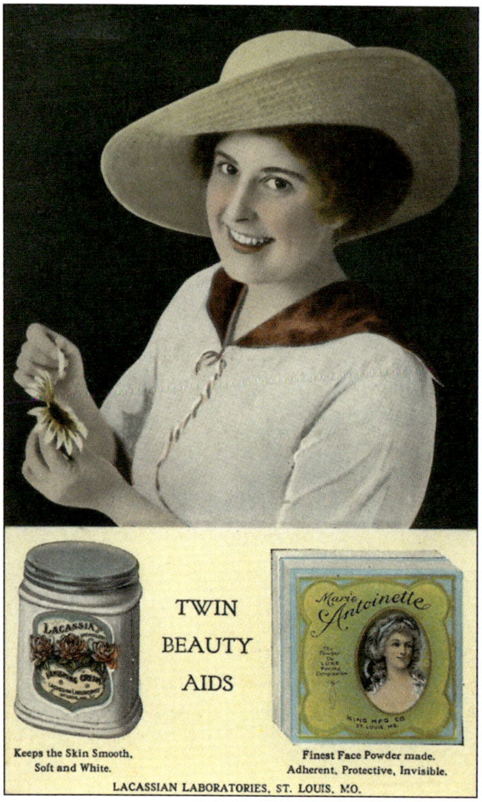

TWIN
BEAUTY
AIDS
Keeps the Skin Smooth, Soft and White.
Marie Antoinette
Finest Face Powder made. Adherent, Protective, Invisible.
LACASSIAN LABORATORIES, ST. LOUIS, MO.

Lacassian Laboratories, a maker of perfumes and women's toiletries, occupied a multistory building at 2200 Locust Street in 1916. The company ran ads in national magazines soliciting "agents" who could make up to $300 a month selling the products. High-quality art cards, like this one, could be distributed by the agents. (St. Louis Media Archives.)

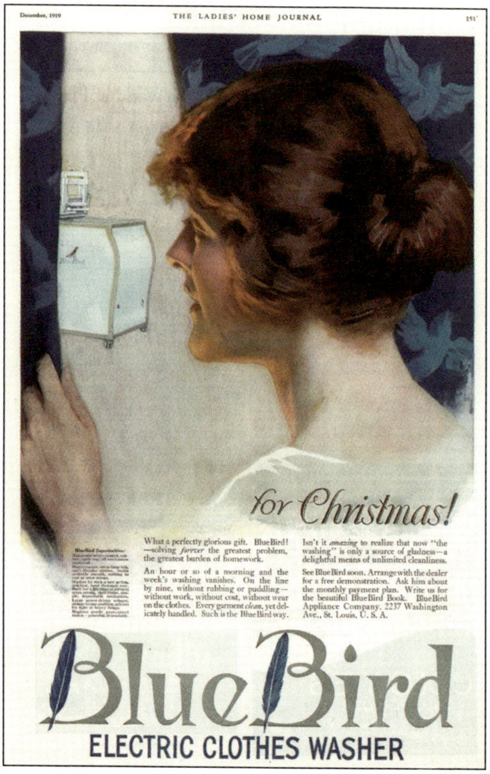

THE LADIES' HOME JOURNAL
for Christmas!
What a perfectly glorious gift. BlueBird! —solving *forever* the greatest problem, the greatest burden of homework.
An hour or so of a morning and the week's washing vanishes. On the line by nine, without rubbing or puddling—without work, without cost, without wear on the clothes. Every garment *clean*, yet delicately handled. Such is the BlueBird way.
Isn't it *amazing* to realize that now "the washing" is only a source of gladness—a delightful means of unlimited cleanliness.
See BlueBird soon. Arrange with the dealer for a free demonstration. Ask him about the monthly payment plan. Write us for the beautiful BlueBird Book. BlueBird Appliance Company, 2237 Washington Ave., St. Louis, U. S. A.
BlueBird
ELECTRIC CLOTHES WASHER

Trade ads ran in national publications three months before the first Blue Bird washer rolled off the St. Louis assembly line. By the time consumer ads like this one appeared in print, the factory had orders for 40,000 machines, and that number had doubled within 10 weeks. (St. Louis Media Archives.)

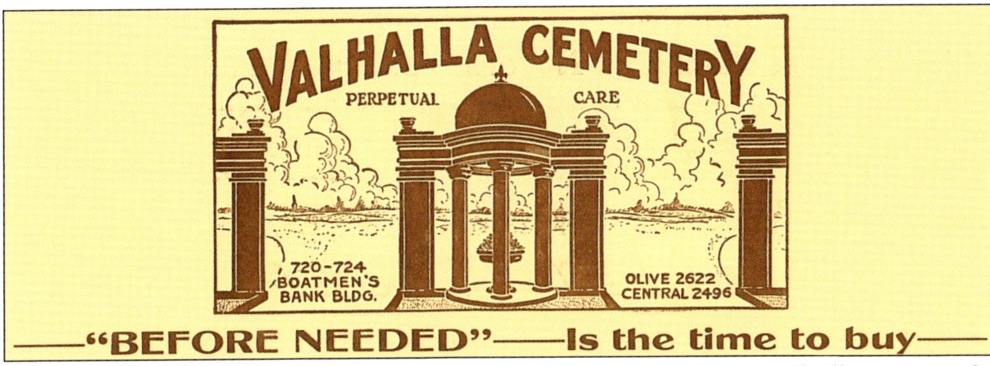
VALHALLA CEMETERY
PERPETUAL CARE
720-724
BOATMEN'S
BANK BLDG.
OLIVE 2622
CENTRAL 2496
"BEFORE NEEDED"—Is the time to buy

In this color print ad from 1920, Valhalla Cemetery is engaged in the preneed selling seen in the funeral industry today. The stark simplicity of the art and the minimal message are all that is needed to convey the image of respect and class. (St. Louis Public Library.)

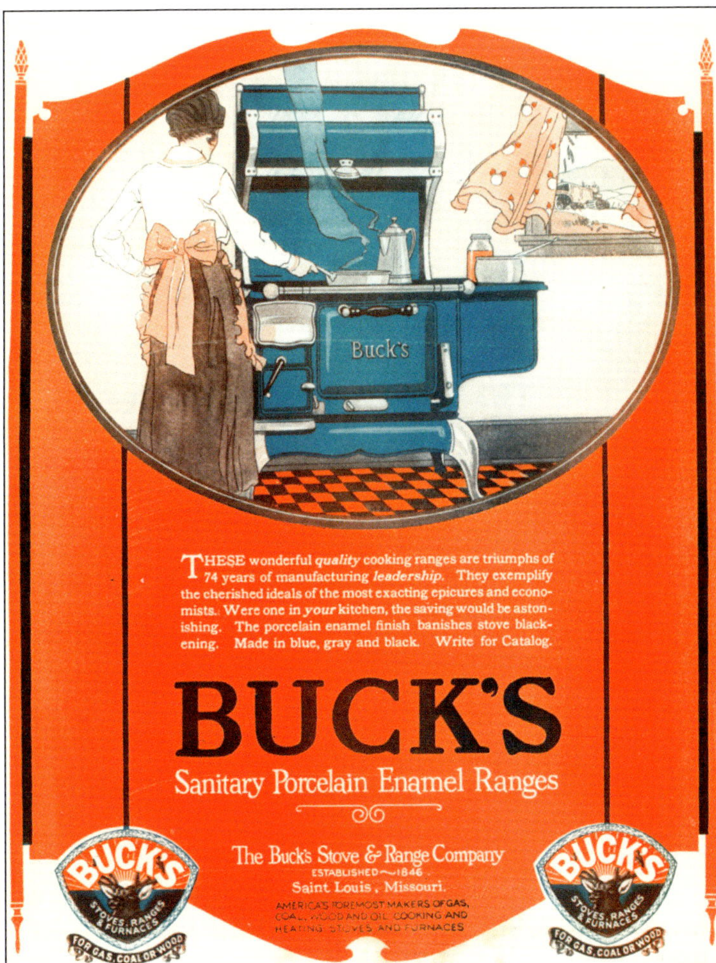
Buck's
THESE wonderful quality cooking ranges are triumphs of 74 years of manufacturing leadership. They exemplify the cherished ideals of the most exacting epicures and economists. Were one in your kitchen, the saving would be astonishing. The porcelain enamel finish banishes stove blackening. Made in blue, gray and black. Write for Catalog.
BUCK'S
Sanitary Porcelain Enamel Ranges
The Buck's Stove & Range Company
ESTABLISHED 1846
Saint Louis, Missouri.
AMERICA'S FOREMOST MAKERS OF GAS, COAL, WOOD AND OIL COOKING AND HEATING STOVES AND FURNACES
BUCK'S
STOVES, RANGES & FURNACES
FOR GAS, COAL OR WOOD

The Buck's Stove and Range Company began its manufacturing operation at 720 North First Street in 1881. Like other local competitors, Buck's advertised heavily in national publications. (St. Louis Media Archives.)

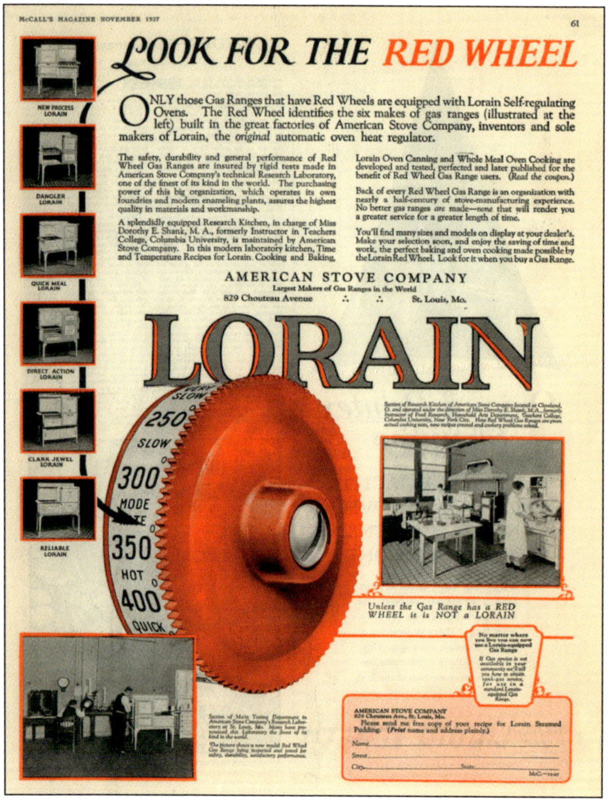

McCALL'S MAGAZINE NOVEMBER 1927
61
LOOK FOR THE RED WHEEL
ONLY those Gas Ranges that have Red Wheels are equipped with Lorain Self-regulating Ovens. The Red Wheel identifies the six makes of gas ranges (illustrated at the left) built in the great factories of American Stove Company, inventors and sole makers of Lorain, the original automatic oven heat regulator.
The safety, durability and general performance of Red Wheel Gas Ranges are insured by rigid tests made in American Stove Company's technical Research Laboratory, one of the finest of its kind in the world. The purchasing power of this big organization, which operates its own foundries and modern enameling plants, assures the highest quality in materials and workmanship.
A splendidly equipped Research Kitchen, in charge of Miss Dorothy E. Shank, M. A., formerly Instructor in Teachers College, Columbia University, is maintained by American Stove Company. In this modern laboratory kitchen, Time and Temperature Recipes for Lorain Cooking and Baking,
Lorain Oven Canning and Whole Meal Oven Cooking are developed and tested, perfected and later published for the benefit of Red Wheel Gas Range users. (Read the coupon.)
Back of every Red Wheel Gas Range is an organization with nearly a half-century of stove-manufacturing experience. No better gas ranges are made—none that will render you a greater service for a greater length of time.
You'll find many sizes and models on display at your dealer's. Make your selection soon, and enjoy the saving of time and work, the perfect baking and oven cooking made possible by the Lorain Red Wheel. Look for it when you buy a Gas Range.
AMERICAN STOVE COMPANY
Largest Makers of Gas Ranges in the World
829 Chouteau Avenue ∴ ∴ St. Louis, Mo.
NEW PROCESS LORAIN
DANGLER LORAIN
QUICK MEAL LORAIN
DIRECT ACTION LORAIN
CLARK JEWEL LORAIN
RELIABLE LORAIN
LORAIN
VERY SLOW
250
SLOW
300
MODE
350
HOT
400
QUICK
Unless the Gas Range has a RED WHEEL it is NOT a LORAIN
AMERICAN STOVE COMPANY
829 Chouteau Ave., St. Louis, Mo.
Please send me free copy of your recipe for Lorain Steamed Pudding. (Print name and address plainly.)
Name
Street
City
State

American Stove Company, which manufactured several different brands of gas stoves at plants in and around St. Louis, used ads like this one from 1920 to promote the fact that their ovens were well regulated, making baking easier. The Lorain red wheel was developed by American Stove as a signature feature of its products. (St. Louis Media Archives.)

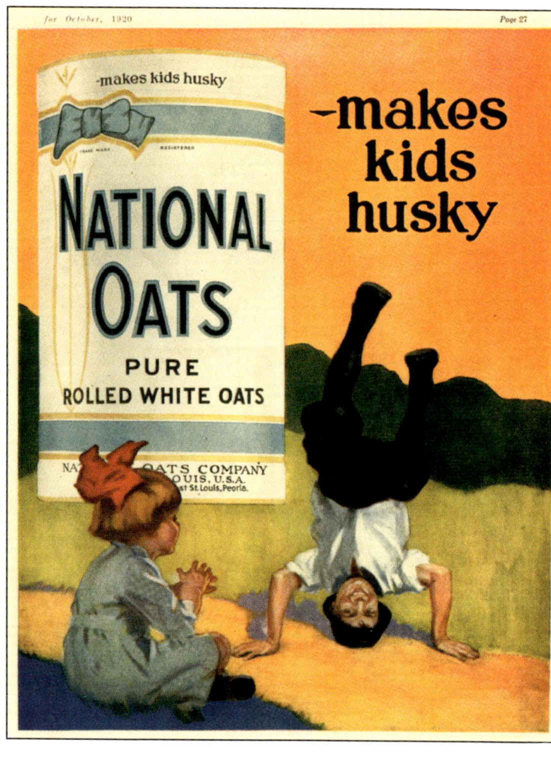

for October, 1920
Page 27
-makes kids husky
NATIONAL OATS
PURE
ROLLED WHITE OATS
-makes kids husky

National Oats approached advertising differently, to say the least. In a 1921 letter to retailers, the company stated that rolled oats were the same, no matter what the brand. Thus, they promised to meet the wholesale prices of any other company and avoid promoting their product as being different from others on the market. (St. Louis Media Archives.)

The pasta made by the Maull Brothers at their plant at 1225 St. Louis Avenue was one of many products branded as "Faust" to capitalize on the name of what was arguably St. Louis's best-known restaurant. Faust also marketed branded beer made by Anheuser-Busch and coffee, tea, chile powder, and ginger, packaged by the Blanke tea and spice company. (Duane Marburger.)

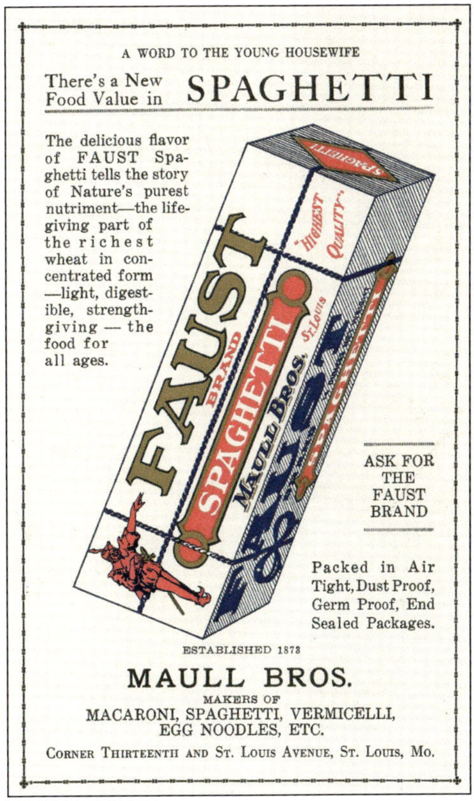

A WORD TO THE YOUNG HOUSEWIFE
There's a New Food Value in SPAGHETTI
The delicious flavor of FAUST Spaghetti tells the story of Nature's purest nutriment—the life-giving part of the richest wheat in concentrated form—light, digestible, strength-giving — the food for all ages.
FAUST BRAND SPAGHETTI
MAULL BROS. ST. LOUIS
"HIGHEST QUALITY"
ASK FOR THE FAUST BRAND
Packed in Air Tight, Dust Proof, Germ Proof, End Sealed Packages.
ESTABLISHED 1873
MAULL BROS.
MAKERS OF
MACARONI, SPAGHETTI, VERMICELLI, EGG NOODLES, ETC.
CORNER THIRTEENTH AND ST. LOUIS AVENUE, ST. LOUIS, MO.

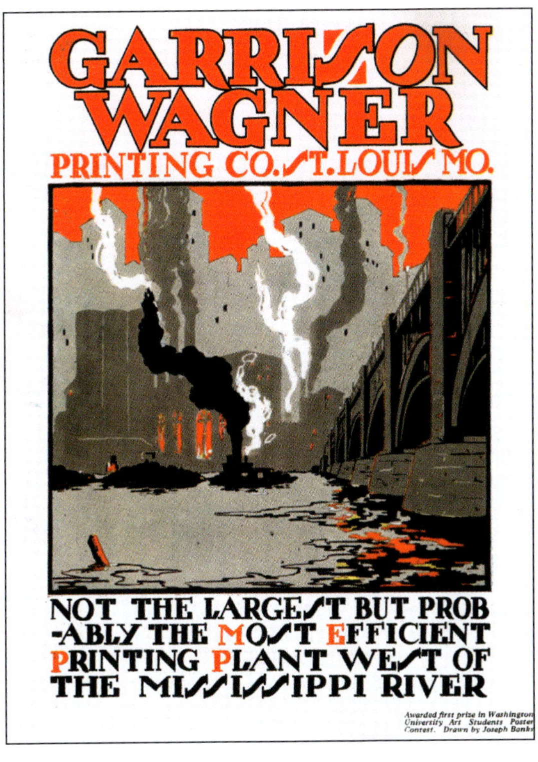

GARRISON WAGNER
PRINTING CO. ST. LOUIS MO.
NOT THE LARGEST BUT PROB-ABLY THE MOST EFFICIENT PRINTING PLANT WEST OF THE MISSISSIPPI RIVER
Awarded first prize in Washington University Art Students Poster Contest. Drawn by Joseph Banks

Garrison Wagner Printing Company used a poster that won a student art contest in this ad. Advertising professor Kristy Tucciarone is not impressed. "There is only one word to describe this ad for copy and design—nightmare. One, the city of St. Louis looks like it is on fire; two, the font is hard to read; and three, spot color is not used effectively. The 'big idea' is missing as well as the selling message. The copy attempts to play the 'underdog' card; however, the poor design overshadows this strategy." (St. Louis Media Archives.)

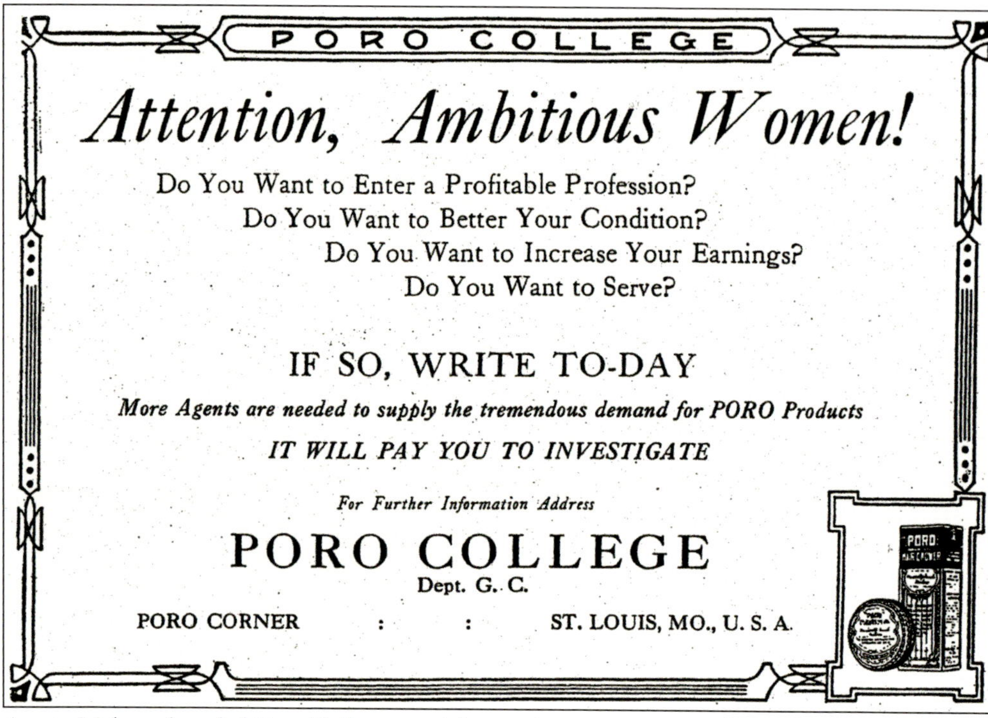
PORO COLLEGE
Attention, Ambitious Women!
Do You Want to Enter a Profitable Profession?
Do You Want to Better Your Condition?
Do You Want to Increase Your Earnings?
Do You Want to Serve?
IF SO, WRITE TO-DAY
More Agents are needed to supply the tremendous demand for PORO Products
IT WILL PAY YOU TO INVESTIGATE
For Further Information Address
PORO COLLEGE
Dept. G. C.
PORO CORNER : : ST. LOUIS, MO., U. S. A.

Annie Malone founded Poro College, an African American cosmetology school, in 1917 at St. Ferdinand and Pendleton Avenues in St. Louis. She used the school to produce her products and to train black women to sell the cosmetics door-to-door, which is how Malone had gotten her start years earlier. Ads like this were placed in African American newspapers around the country to recruit salespeople. Malone's efforts made her the first black millionaire in the nation. (Olivia Blackmore.)

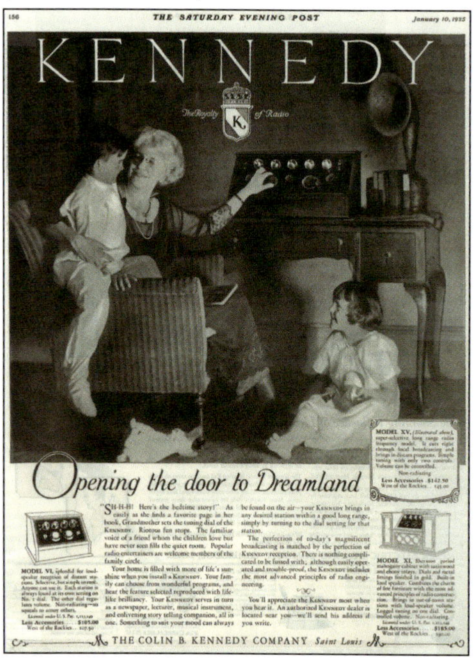
THE SATURDAY EVENING POST
KENNEDY
The Royalty of Radio
Opening the door to Dreamland
THE COLIN B. KENNEDY COMPANY Saint Louis

The California-based Colin B. Kennedy Company moved to St. Louis after it was purchased by St. Louis–based Wagner Electric. The radios it manufactured were quite sophisticated and well built for the time, but the business was not run well, and it shut down in bankruptcy in 1926. Kennedy tried to restart it by making car radios but was out of business again within five years. (St. Louis Media Archives.)

Originally incorporated in 1857 as Laclede Gas and Light Company, the utility eventually moved into in its own headquarters building at 1017 Olive Street in 1911. At the time, homes were still lit with gas fixtures, which is why "light" was included in the name. Rather than overtly encouraging people to use natural gas, many of the utility's ads promoted the purchase of appliances that used natural gas. (St. Louis Media Archives.)

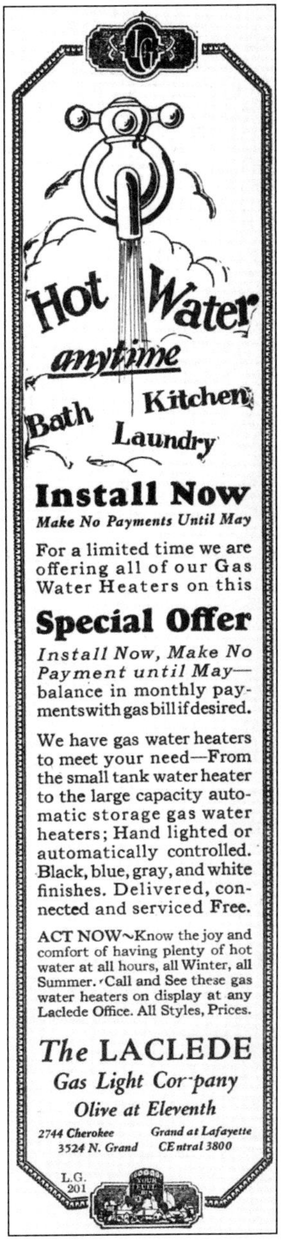

Hot Water
anytime
Bath
Kitchen
Laundry
Install Now
Make No Payments Until May
For a limited time we are offering all of our Gas Water Heaters on this
Special Offer
Install Now, Make No Payment until May—balance in monthly payments with gas bill if desired.
We have gas water heaters to meet your need—From the small tank water heater to the large capacity automatic storage gas water heaters; Hand lighted or automatically controlled. Black, blue, gray, and white finishes. Delivered, connected and serviced Free.
ACT NOW~Know the joy and comfort of having plenty of hot water at all hours, all Winter, all Summer. Call and See these gas water heaters on display at any Laclede Office. All Styles, Prices.
The LACLEDE
Gas Light Cor·pany
Olive at Eleventh
2744 Cherokee
3524 N. Grand
Grand at Lafayette
CEntral 3800
L.G.
201

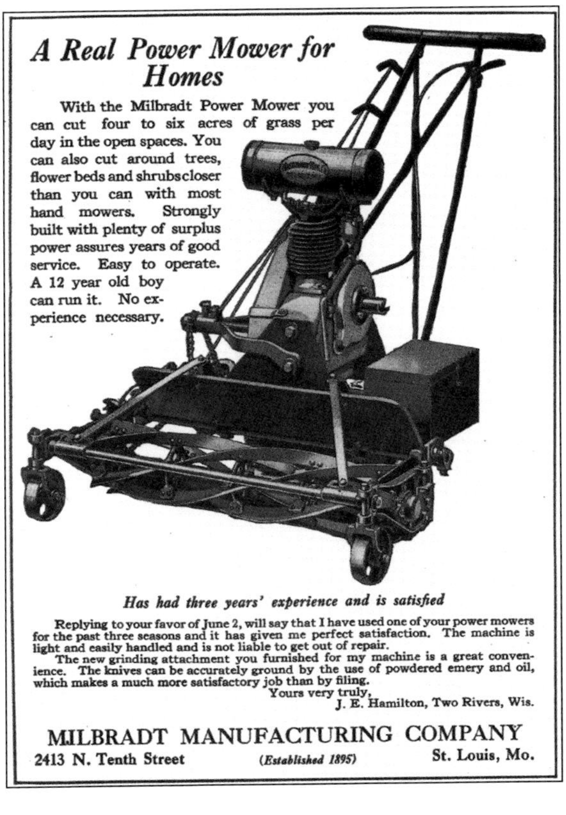

A Real Power Mower for Homes
With the Milbradt Power Mower you can cut four to six acres of grass per day in the open spaces. You can also cut around trees, flower beds and shrubs closer than you can with most hand mowers. Strongly built with plenty of surplus power assures years of good service. Easy to operate. A 12 year old boy can run it. No experience necessary.
Has had three years' experience and is satisfied
Replying to your favor of June 2, will say that I have used one of your power mowers for the past three seasons and it has given me perfect satisfaction. The machine is light and easily handled and is not liable to get out of repair.
The new grinding attachment you furnished for my machine is a great convenience. The knives can be accurately ground by the use of powdered emery and oil, which makes a much more satisfactory job than by filing.
Yours very truly,
J. E. Hamilton, Two Rivers, Wis.
MILBRADT MANUFACTURING COMPANY
2413 N. Tenth Street
(Established 1895)
St. Louis, Mo.

The Milbradt Manufacturing Company plant was at 2412 North Tenth Street in the 1920s, when this ad ran. The company manufactured power lawn equipment for consumers and corporate clients. Copy in this ad extols the ease of operation of the machine, stating, "A 12 year old boy can run it. No experience necessary." (St. Louis Media Archives.)

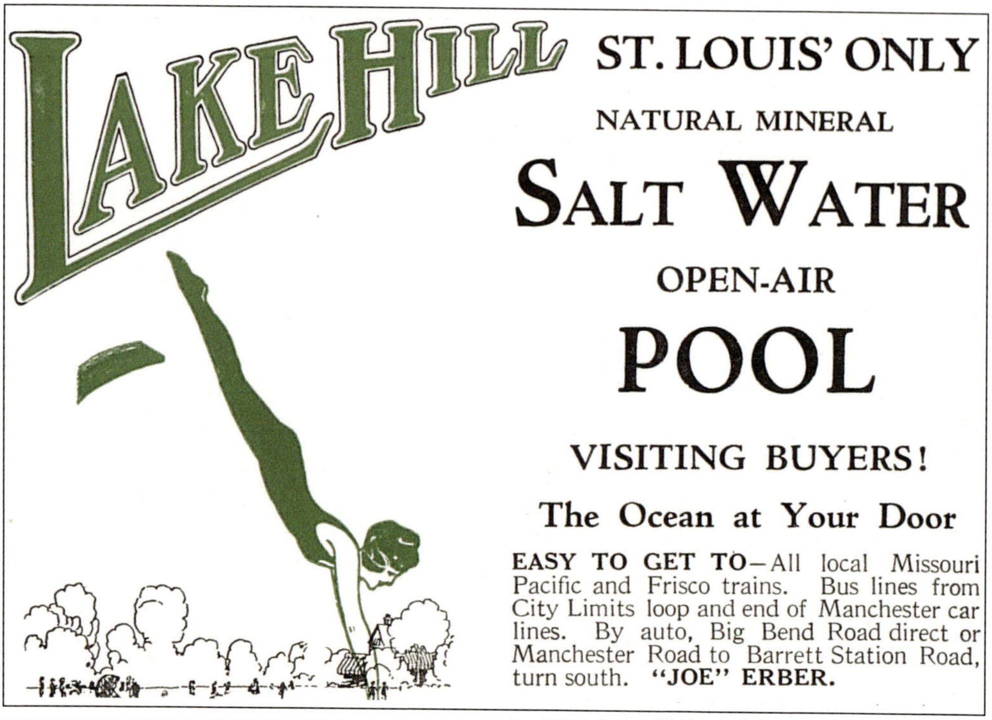
LAKE HILL
ST. LOUIS' ONLY
NATURAL MINERAL
SALT WATER
OPEN-AIR
POOL
VISITING BUYERS!
The Ocean at Your Door
EASY TO GET TO—All local Missouri Pacific and Frisco trains. Bus lines from City Limits loop and end of Manchester car lines. By auto, Big Bend Road direct or Manchester Road to Barrett Station Road, turn south. "JOE" ERBER.

In 1927, Lake Hill used spot color in this ad to lure city folks out into the country, where they could enjoy the benefits of "the ocean at your door." A saltwater pool would help them escape the ravages of Midwestern heat and leave the smoke, soot, and grime behind. (Missouri History Museum.)

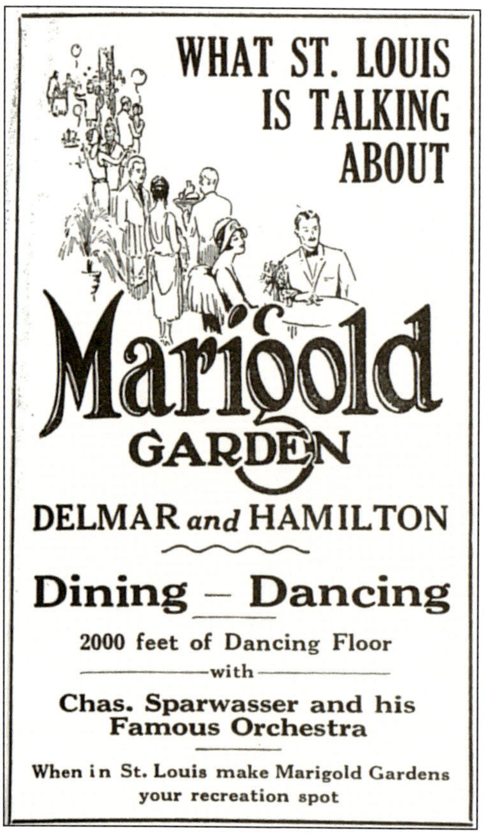
WHAT ST. LOUIS IS TALKING ABOUT
Marigold
GARDEN
DELMAR and HAMILTON
Dining – Dancing
2000 feet of Dancing Floor
with
Chas. Sparwasser and his Famous Orchestra
When in St. Louis make Marigold Gardens your recreation spot

Commercial artist R.J. Shay immediately spotted the hand-generated type on the logo of this ad for Marigold Garden. The artwork, Shay says, was done by an artist rather than an advertising agency. (St. Louis Public Library.)

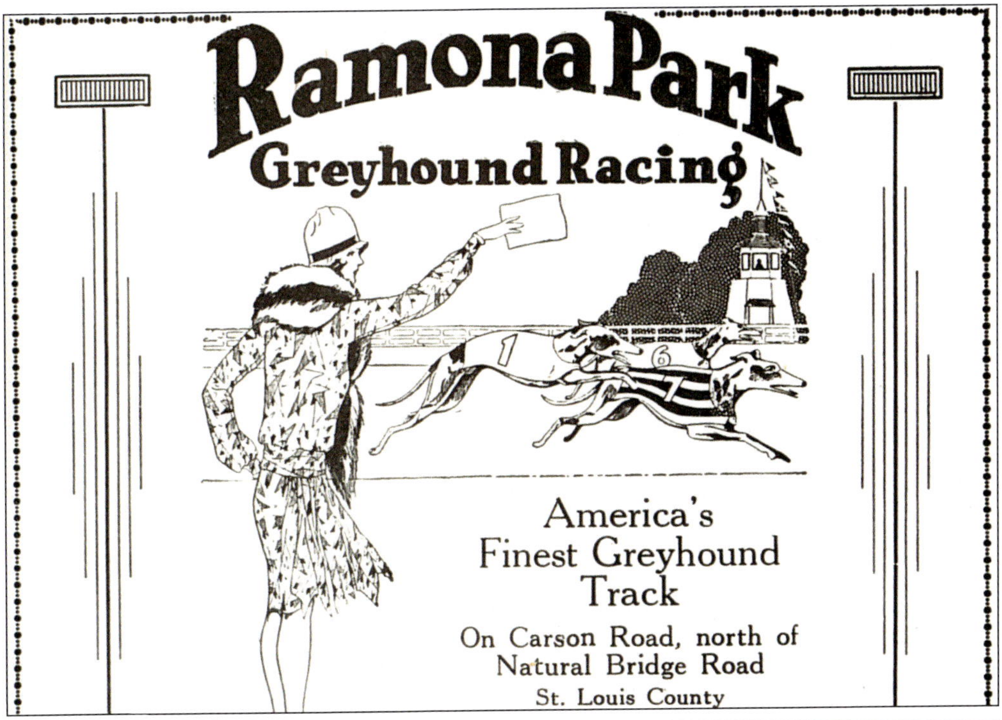
Ramona Park
Greyhound Racing
America's
Finest Greyhound
Track
On Carson Road, north of
Natural Bridge Road
St. Louis County

Ramona Park Speedway was located in Berkeley, just off Natural Bridge Road on Carson Road, in the area known as Ramona Lake Park. The oval dirt track was 5/16 of a mile long and served as a site for automobile racing for about three years, beginning in 1933. (Missouri History Museum.)

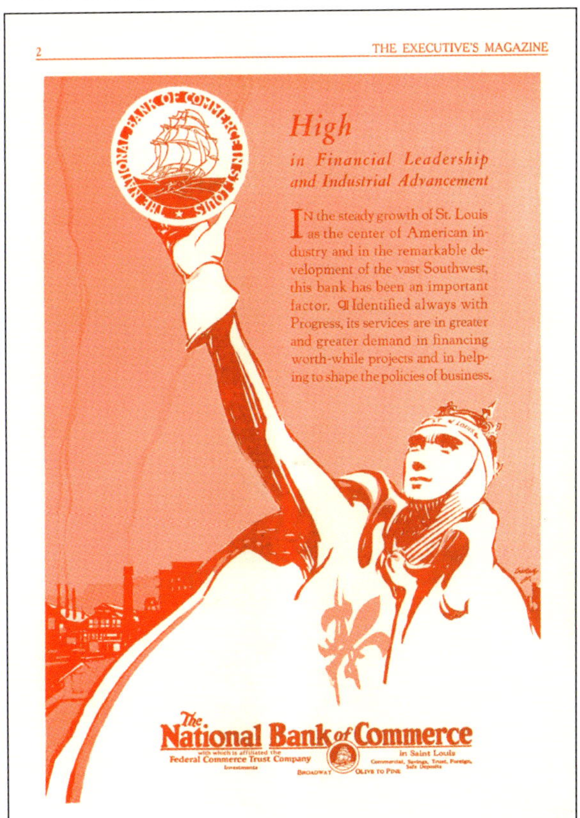
2
THE EXECUTIVE'S MAGAZINE
High
in Financial Leadership
and Industrial Advancement
IN the steady growth of St. Louis as the center of American industry and in the remarkable development of the vast Southwest, this bank has been an important factor. ¶ Identified always with Progress, its services are in greater and greater demand in financing worth-while projects and in helping to shape the policies of business.
The National Bank of Commerce
with which is affiliated the
Federal Commerce Trust Company
Investments
in Saint Louis
Commercial, Savings, Trust, Foreign, Safe Deposits
Broadway
Olive to Pine

The National Bank of Commerce was part of the St. Louis business scene in the late 1800s. As a "correspondent bank," it provided smaller banks in the area with credit and liquidity. It had a huge presence downtown, covering the entire block of Broadway between Olive and Pine Streets with a stunning, multistory edifice. (St. Louis Media Archives.)

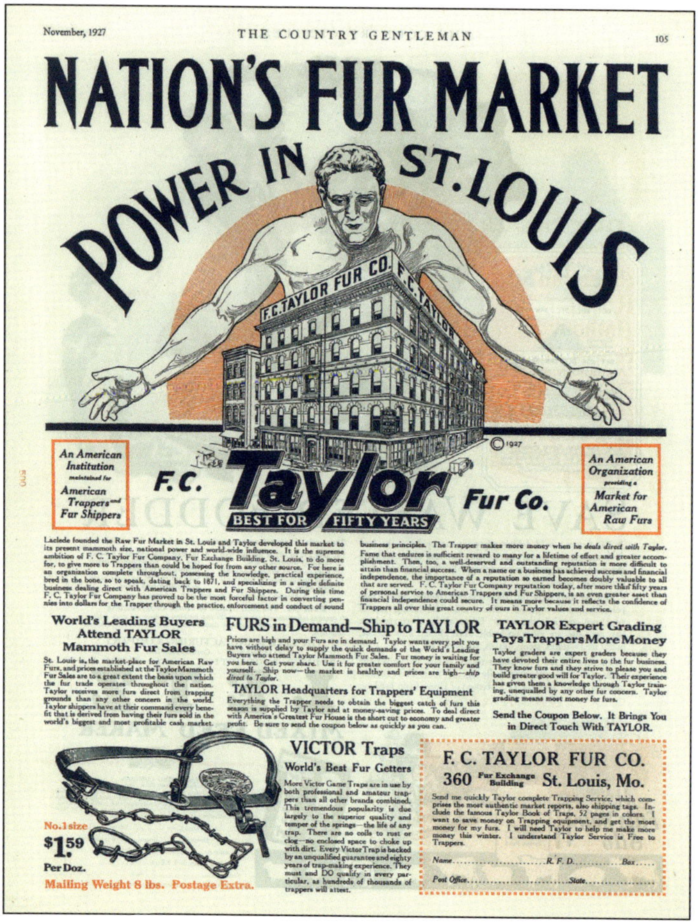
November, 1927
THE COUNTRY GENTLEMAN
105
NATION'S FUR MARKET
POWER IN ST. LOUIS
F.C. TAYLOR FUR CO.
F.C. TAYLOR FUR CO.
©1927
An American Institution maintained for American Trappers and Fur Shippers
F.C. Taylor Fur Co.
BEST FOR FIFTY YEARS
An American Organization providing a Market for American Raw Furs
Laclede founded the Raw Fur Market in St. Louis and Taylor developed this market to its present mammoth size, national power and world-wide influence. It is the supreme ambition of F. C. Taylor Fur Company, Fur Exchange Building, St. Louis, to do more for, to give more to Trappers than could be hoped for from any other source. For here is an organization complete throughout, possessing the knowledge, practical experience, bred in the bone, so to speak, dating back to 1871, and specializing in a single definite business dealing direct with American Trappers and Fur Shippers. During this time F. C. Taylor Fur Company has proved to be the most forceful factor in converting pennies into dollars for the Trapper through the practice, enforcement and conduct of sound business principles. The Trapper makes more money when he deals direct with Taylor. Fame that endures is sufficient reward to many for a lifetime of effort and greater accomplishment. Then, too, a well-deserved and outstanding reputation is more difficult to attain than financial success. When a name or a business has achieved success and financial independence, the importance of a reputation so earned becomes doubly valuable to all that are served. F. C. Taylor Fur Company reputation today, after more than fifty years of personal service to American Trappers and Fur Shippers, is an even greater asset than financial independence could secure. It means more because it reflects the confidence of Trappers all over this great country of ours in Taylor values and service.
World's Leading Buyers Attend TAYLOR Mammoth Fur Sales
St. Louis is, the market-place for American Raw Furs, and prices established at the Taylor Mammoth Fur Sales are to a great extent the basis upon which the fur trade operates throughout the nation. Taylor receives more furs direct from trapping grounds than any other concern in the world. Taylor shippers have at their command every benefit that is derived from having their furs sold in the world's biggest and most profitable cash market.
FURS in Demand—Ship to TAYLOR
Prices are high and your Furs are in demand. Taylor wants every pelt you have without delay to supply the quick demands of the World's Leading Buyers who attend Taylor Mammoth Fur Sales. Fur money is waiting for you here. Get your share. Use it for greater comfort for your family and yourself. Ship now—the market is healthy and prices are high—ship direct to Taylor.
TAYLOR Headquarters for Trappers' Equipment
Everything the Trapper needs to obtain the biggest catch of furs this season is supplied by Taylor and at money-saving prices. To deal direct with America's Greatest Fur House is the short cut to economy and greater profit. Be sure to send the coupon below as quickly as you can.
TAYLOR Expert Grading Pays Trappers More Money
Taylor graders are expert graders because they have devoted their entire lives to the fur business. They know furs and they strive to please you and build greater good will for Taylor. Their experience has given them a knowledge through Taylor training, unequalled by any other fur concern. Taylor grading means most money for furs.
Send the Coupon Below. It Brings You in Direct Touch With TAYLOR.
No. 1 size
$1.59
Per Doz.
Mailing Weight 8 lbs. Postage Extra.
VICTOR Traps
World's Best Fur Getters
More Victor Game Traps are in use by both professional and amateur trappers than all other brands combined. This tremendous popularity is due largely to the superior quality and temper of the springs—the life of any trap. There are no coils to rust or clog—no enclosed space to choke up with dirt. Every Victor Trap is backed by an unqualified guarantee and eighty years of trap-making experience. They must and DO qualify in every particular, as hundreds of thousands of trappers will attest.
F. C. TAYLOR FUR CO.
360 Fur Exchange Building St. Louis, Mo.
Send me quickly Taylor complete Trapping Service, which comprises the most authentic market reports, also shipping tags. Include the famous Taylor Book of Traps, 52 pages in colors. I want to save money on Trapping equipment, and get the most money for my furs. I will need Taylor to help me make more money this winter. I understand Taylor Service is Free to Trappers.
Name .... R. F. D. .... Box ....
Post Office .... State ....

There is a lot of copy in this 1927 ad for the F.C. Taylor Fur Company, but it is not selling furs. The target is trappers, and Taylor is trying to convince them to bring in their pelts. At the time, a lot of trapping was still done in rural areas, and a fur exchange like Taylor could provide trappers with much-needed income. (St. Louis Media Archives.)

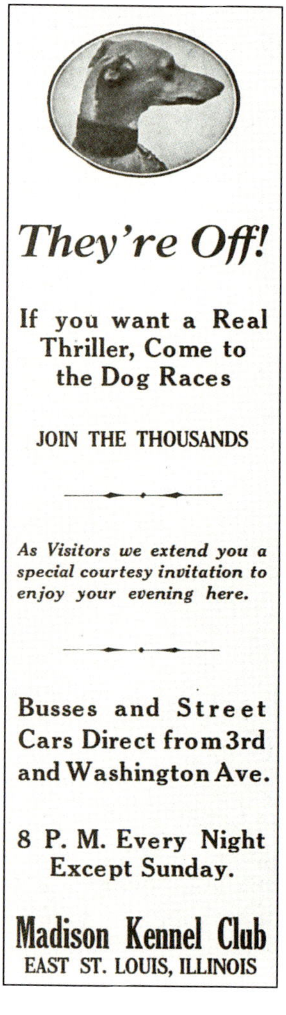
They're Off!
If you want a Real Thriller, Come to the Dog Races
JOIN THE THOUSANDS
As Visitors we extend you a special courtesy invitation to enjoy your evening here.
Busses and Street Cars Direct from 3rd and Washington Ave.
8 P. M. Every Night Except Sunday.
Madison Kennel Club
EAST ST. LOUIS, ILLINOIS

Although this venue was named Madison Kennel Club, its lure was dog racing. Madison Kennel Club used this 1927 ad to lure tourists across the river to sample the action. (St. Louis Public Library.)

This wonderful 1928 positioning ad for the *St. Louis Globe-Democrat* is copy-heavy, creating a unique selling proposition for both readers and advertisers. It also makes reference to the "49th State," which was a fictitious retail area the paper developed for use in its trade advertising. (St. Louis Media Archives.)

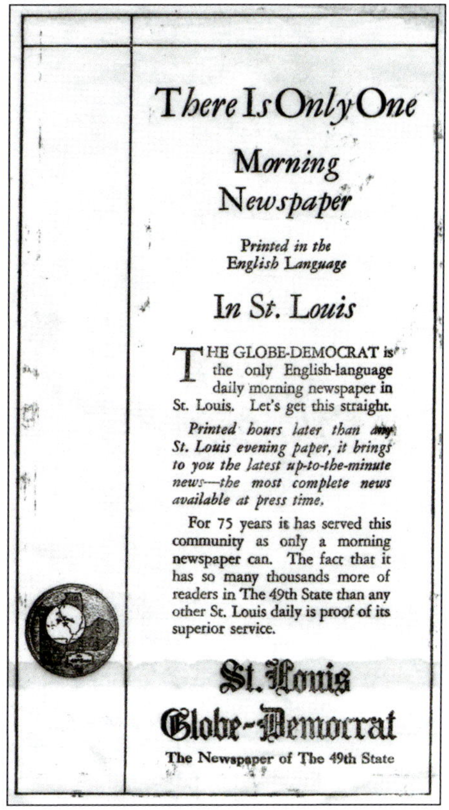

There Is Only One
Morning
Newspaper
Printed in the
English Language
In St. Louis
THE GLOBE-DEMOCRAT is the only English-language daily morning newspaper in St. Louis. Let's get this straight.
Printed hours later than any St. Louis evening paper, it brings to you the latest up-to-the-minute news—the most complete news available at press time.
For 75 years it has served this community as only a morning newspaper can. The fact that it has so many thousands more of readers in The 49th State than any other St. Louis daily is proof of its superior service.
St. Louis
Globe-Democrat
The Newspaper of The 49th State

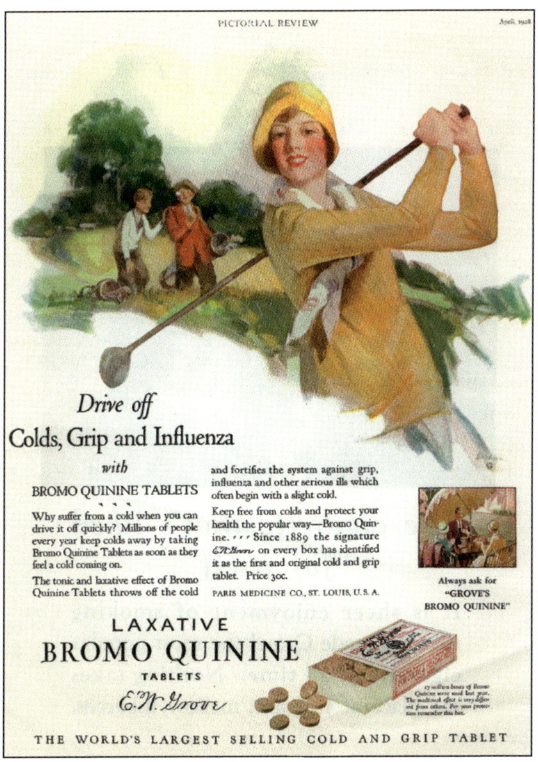

PICTORIAL REVIEW
Drive off
Colds, Grip and Influenza
with
BROMO QUININE TABLETS
Why suffer from a cold when you can drive it off quickly? Millions of people every year keep colds away by taking Bromo Quinine Tablets as soon as they feel a cold coming on.
The tonic and laxative effect of Bromo Quinine Tablets throws off the cold and fortifies the system against grip, influenza and other serious ills which often begin with a slight cold.
Keep free from colds and protect your health the popular way—Bromo Quinine. ... Since 1889 the signature E.W. Grove on every box has identified it as the first and original cold and grip tablet. Price 30c.
PARIS MEDICINE CO., ST. LOUIS, U. S. A.
Always ask for
"GROVE'S
BROMO QUININE"
LAXATIVE
BROMO QUININE
TABLETS
E.W. Grove
THE WORLD'S LARGEST SELLING COLD AND GRIP TABLET

Bromo Quinine was created and copyrighted in 1893 by St. Louis–based Grove Laboratories for its Paris Medicine Company. The tablets' laxative qualities were said to stop a cold or the flu if taken at the onset of sickness. Each box of pills contained the words: "The second or third dose will move the bowels well within 8 or 10 hours, when the cold will be relieved." Each tablet also contained ingredients intended to fight headaches. (St. Louis Media Archives.)

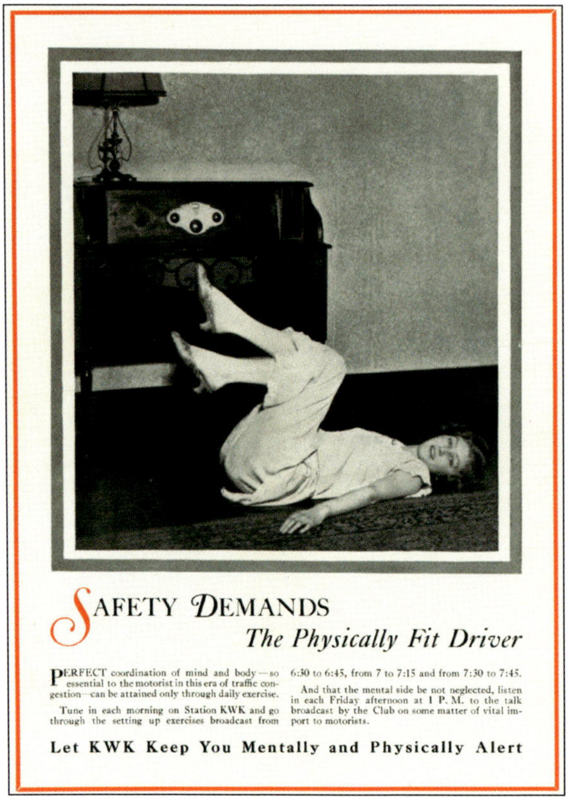
SAFETY DEMANDS
The Physically Fit Driver
PERFECT coordination of mind and body—so essential to the motorist in this era of traffic congestion—can be attained only through daily exercise.
Tune in each morning on Station KWK and go through the setting up exercises broadcast from 6:30 to 6:45, from 7 to 7:15 and from 7:30 to 7:45.
And that the mental side be not neglected, listen in each Friday afternoon at 1 P. M. to the talk broadcast by the Club on some matter of vital import to motorists.
Let KWK Keep You Mentally and Physically Alert

KWK Radio ran this ad in 1928 to capitalize on the fitness fad. The idea of exercise shows on the radio had become quite popular, although print ads being used to promote them were not common. The owner of KWK, Thomas Patrick Convey, was well known for his unconventional approach to broadcasting and marketing. (Missouri History Museum.)

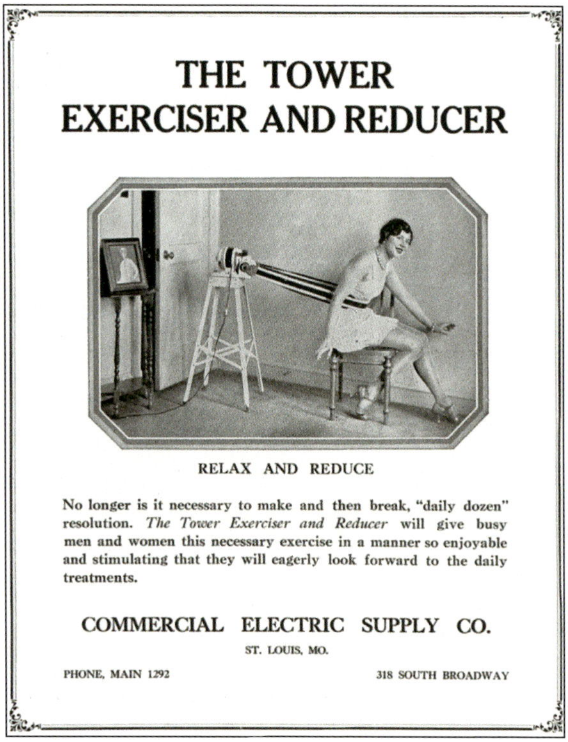
THE TOWER
EXERCISER AND REDUCER
RELAX AND REDUCE
No longer is it necessary to make and then break, "daily dozen" resolution. The Tower Exerciser and Reducer will give busy men and women this necessary exercise in a manner so enjoyable and stimulating that they will eagerly look forward to the daily treatments.
COMMERCIAL ELECTRIC SUPPLY CO.
ST. LOUIS, MO.
PHONE, MAIN 1292
318 SOUTH BROADWAY

Commercial Electric Supply Company also got involved in the fitness movement, marketing a machine that could make getting in shape a pleasant experience. At the turn of the century, the company was heavily involved in the electrical work at the 1904 World's Fair, which featured a remote switch activated by the president in Washington, DC, that turned on the lights in Forest Park. (Missouri History Museum.)

The Coronado Hotel hosted its share of celebrities during its heyday and was reportedly famous for the fact that patrons of its Coal Hole bar could get alcoholic concoctions during Prohibition. (Missouri History Museum.)

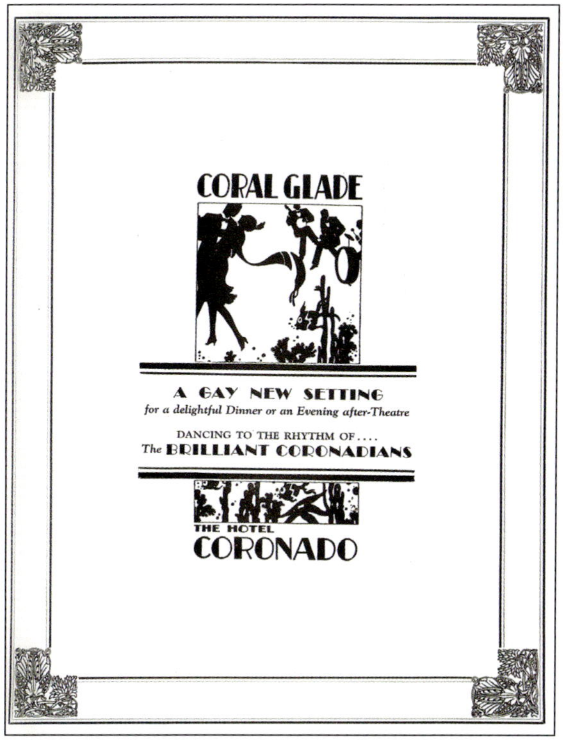

CORAL GLADE
A GAY NEW SETTING
for a delightful Dinner or an Evening after-Theatre
DANCING TO THE RHYTHM OF....
The BRILLIANT CORONADIANS
THE HOTEL
CORONADO

The Barthel-Duesenberg Piano Company did not limit its product line to pianos. By the late 1920s, it added radios to the inventory. The business had its beginnings at 1724 Olive Street before moving to a much larger space in three storefronts at 910-912-914 Pine Street. (Missouri History Museum.)

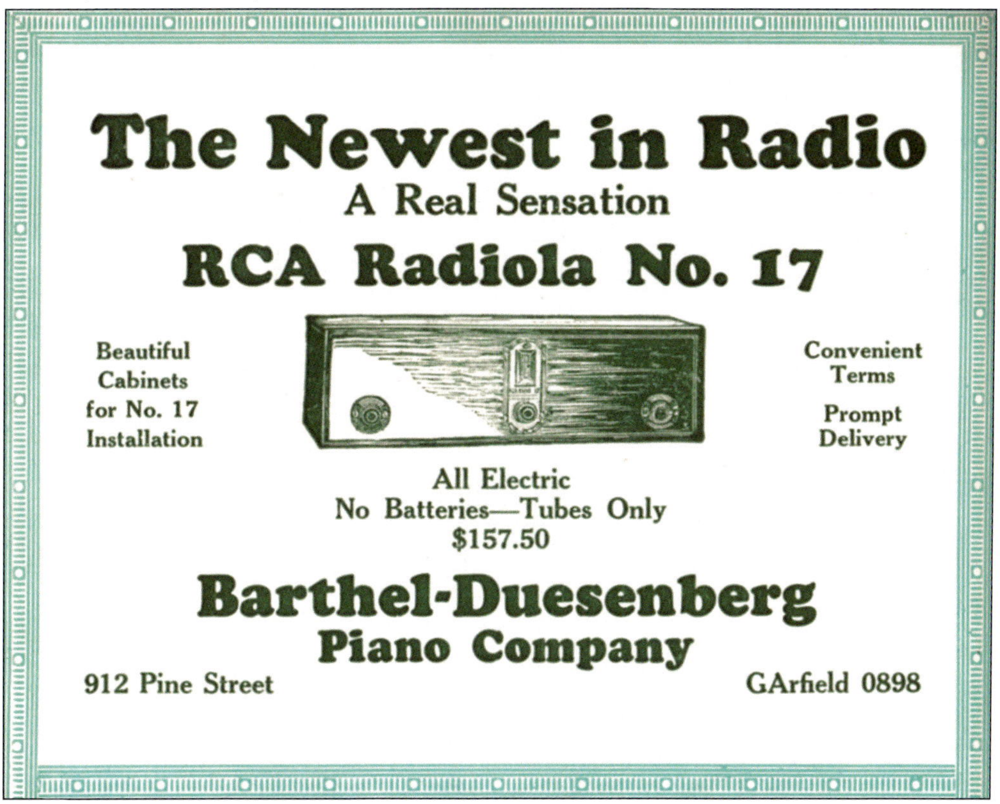

The Newest in Radio
A Real Sensation
RCA Radiola No. 17
Beautiful Cabinets for No. 17 Installation
Convenient Terms
Prompt Delivery
All Electric
No Batteries—Tubes Only
$157.50
Barthel-Duesenberg
Piano Company
912 Pine Street
GArfield 0898

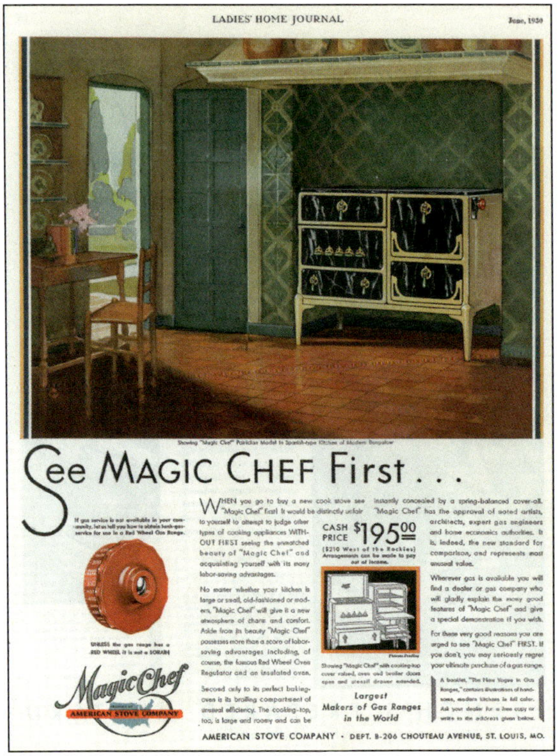
LADIES' HOME JOURNAL
June, 1930
See MAGIC CHEF First . . .
WHEN you go to buy a new cook stove see "Magic Chef" first! It would be distinctly unfair to yourself to attempt to judge other types of cooking appliances WITHOUT FIRST seeing the unmatched beauty of "Magic Chef" and acquainting yourself with its many labor-saving advantages.
No matter whether your kitchen is large or small, old-fashioned or modern, "Magic Chef" will give it a new atmosphere of charm and comfort. Aside from its beauty "Magic Chef" possesses more than a score of labor-saving advantages including, of course, the famous Red Wheel Oven Regulator and an insulated oven.
Second only to its perfect baking-oven is its broiling compartment of unusual efficiency. The cooking-top, too, is large and roomy and can be instantly concealed by a spring-balanced cover-all.
"Magic Chef" has the approval of noted artists, architects, expert gas engineers and home economics authorities. It is, indeed, the new standard for comparison, and represents most unusual value.
Wherever gas is available you will find a dealer or gas company who will gladly explain the many good features of "Magic Chef" and give a special demonstration if you wish.
For these very good reasons you are urged to see "Magic Chef" FIRST. If you don't, you may seriously regret your ultimate purchase of a gas range.
CASH PRICE $195.00
($210 West of the Rockies)
Arrangements can be made to pay out of income.
Showing "Magic Chef" with cooking-top cover raised, oven and broiler doors open and utensil drawer extended.
Largest Makers of Gas Ranges in the World
A booklet, "The New Vogue in Gas Ranges," contains illustrations of handsome, modern kitchens in full color. Ask your dealer for a free copy or write to the address given below.
If gas service is not available in your community, let us tell you how to obtain tank-gas service for use in a Red Wheel Gas Range.
UNLESS the gas range has a RED WHEEL it is not a LORAIN
Magic Chef
AMERICAN STOVE COMPANY
AMERICAN STOVE COMPANY · DEPT. B-206 CHOUTEAU AVENUE, ST. LOUIS, MO.

The American Stove Company, founded by Charles Stockstrom, began making the Magic Chef gas stove in 1929. This product was so successful that the parent company changed its name to Magic Chef. (Shelly Donaho.)

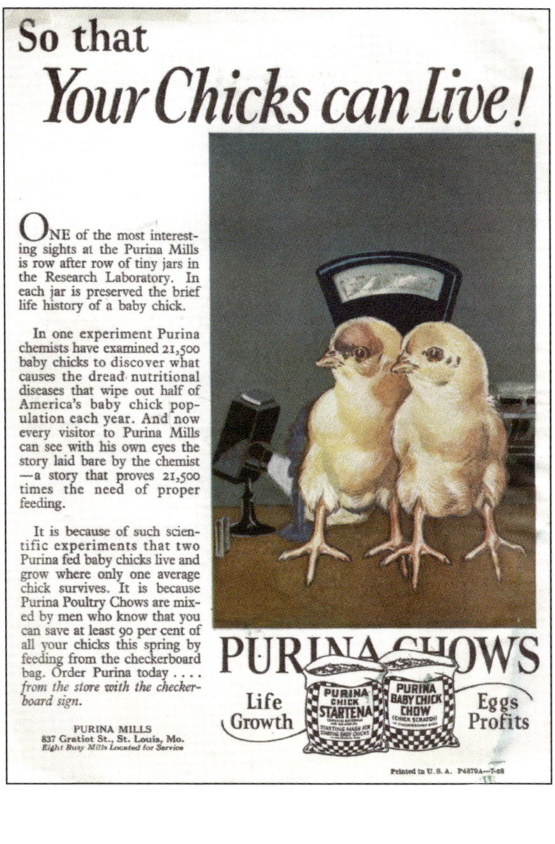
So that
Your Chicks can Live!
ONE of the most interesting sights at the Purina Mills is row after row of tiny jars in the Research Laboratory. In each jar is preserved the brief life history of a baby chick.
In one experiment Purina chemists have examined 21,500 baby chicks to discover what causes the dread nutritional diseases that wipe out half of America's baby chick population each year. And now every visitor to Purina Mills can see with his own eyes the story laid bare by the chemist —a story that proves 21,500 times the need of proper feeding.
It is because of such scientific experiments that two Purina fed baby chicks live and grow where only one average chick survives. It is because Purina Poultry Chows are mixed by men who know that you can save at least 90 per cent of all your chicks this spring by feeding from the checkerboard bag. Order Purina today . . . . from the store with the checkerboard sign.
PURINA MILLS
837 Gratiot St., St. Louis, Mo.
Eight Busy Mills Located for Service
PURINA CHOWS
Life Growth
Eggs Profits
PURINA CHICK STARTENA
PURINA BABY CHICK CHOW
Printed in U. S. A. P4879A—7-28

The manufacture of Purina animal feed in St. Louis dates back to the company's founding in 1894 under the name Robinson-Danforth Commission Company. When the company's product line expanded to include breakfast cereal, the corporation changed its name to the Ralston Purina Company. (Duane Marburger.)

Retired ad man Gerry Mandel says, "I love this ad! Margaret may not be a beauty, but I bet she had a marvelous voice and an effective teaching technique. A quote by Tennyson: 'nice, classy touch.' Way to go, Margaret. Hope you got a lot of students with this." (St. Louis Media Archives.)

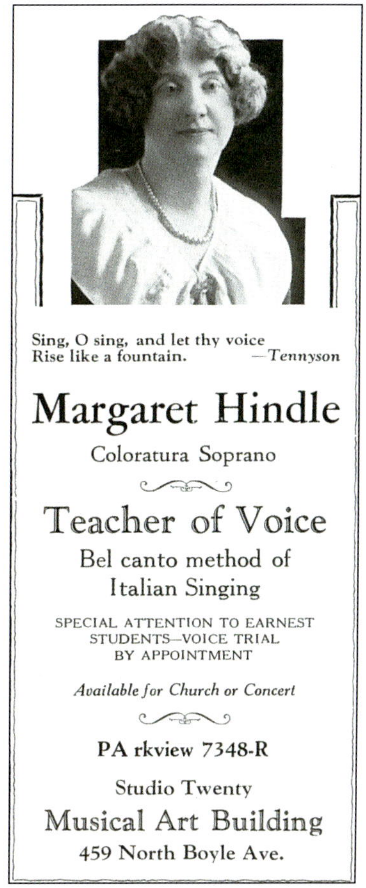

Sing, O sing, and let thy voice
Rise like a fountain. —Tennyson
Margaret Hindle
Coloratura Soprano
Teacher of Voice
Bel canto method of
Italian Singing
SPECIAL ATTENTION TO EARNEST STUDENTS—VOICE TRIAL BY APPOINTMENT
Available for Church or Concert
PA rkview 7348-R
Studio Twenty
Musical Art Building
459 North Boyle Ave.

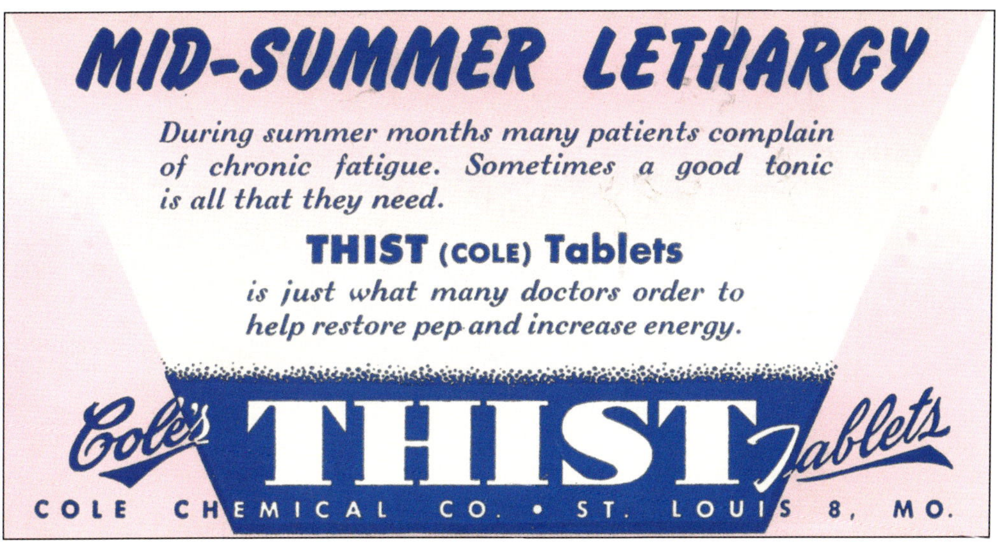

MID-SUMMER LETHARGY
During summer months many patients complain of chronic fatigue. Sometimes a good tonic is all that they need.
THIST (COLE) Tablets
is just what many doctors order to help restore pep and increase energy.
Cole's THIST Tablets
COLE CHEMICAL CO. • ST. LOUIS 8, MO.

Cole Chemical Company was located at 3721 Laclede Avenue, near the city's pharmaceutical manufacturing district, and was incorporated in 1920. Along with medicines like Thist, Cole made disinfectants and antiseptics in its laboratories. Thist tablets, which promised to restore pep, contained a small dose of strychnine. (St. Louis Media Archives.)

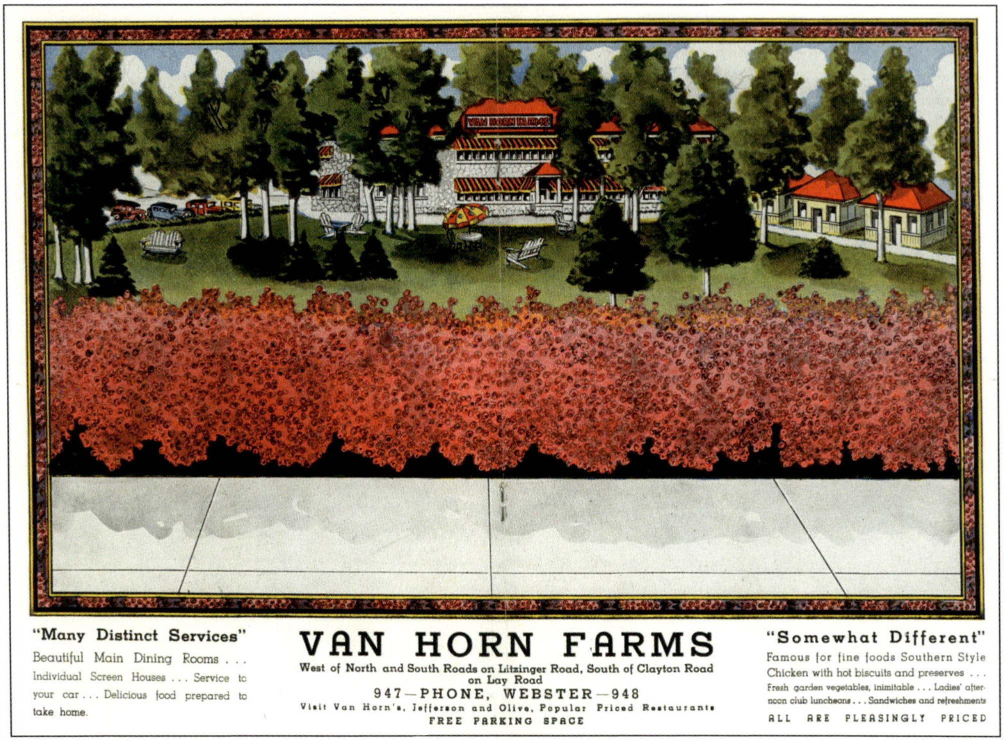
"Many Distinct Services"
Beautiful Main Dining Rooms . . . Individual Screen Houses . . . Service to your car . . . Delicious food prepared to take home.
VAN HORN FARMS
West of North and South Roads on Litzinger Road, South of Clayton Road on Lay Road
947—PHONE, WEBSTER—948
Visit Van Horn's, Jefferson and Olive, Popular Priced Restaurants
FREE PARKING SPACE
"Somewhat Different"
Famous for fine foods Southern Style Chicken with hot biscuits and preserves . . . Fresh garden vegetables, inimitable . . . Ladies' afternoon club luncheons . . . Sandwiches and refreshments
ALL ARE PLEASINGLY PRICED

This colorful ad, run as a double-page spread in the 1933 Municipal Opera program, was an attention-getter. Van Horn Farms was then in an environment that was semi-rural, making it a great weekend destination. (St. Louis Media Archives.)

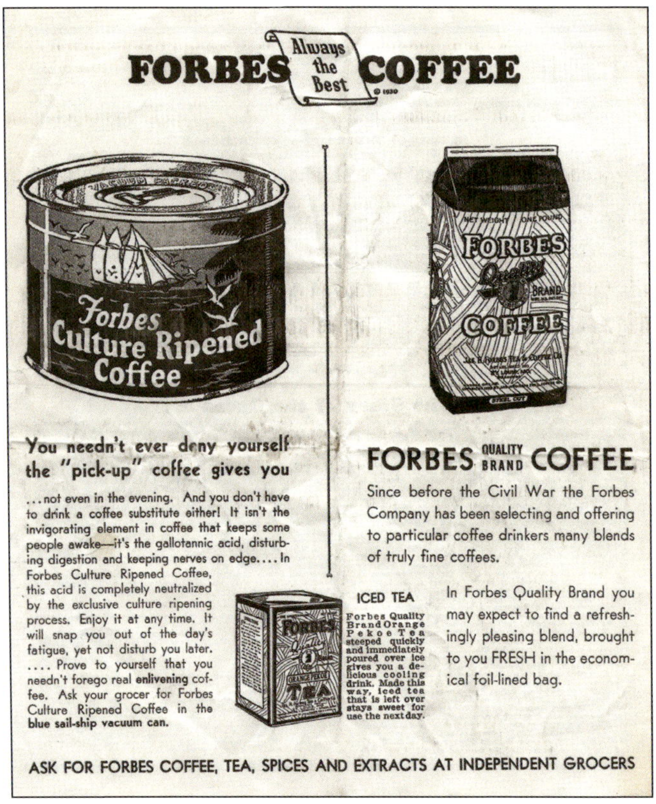
FORBES Always the Best COFFEE
Forbes Culture Ripened Coffee
FORBES Quality Brand COFFEE
You needn't ever deny yourself the "pick-up" coffee gives you
. . . not even in the evening. And you don't have to drink a coffee substitute either! It isn't the invigorating element in coffee that keeps some people awake—it's the gallotannic acid, disturbing digestion and keeping nerves on edge. . . . In Forbes Culture Ripened Coffee, this acid is completely neutralized by the exclusive culture ripening process. Enjoy it at any time. It will snap you out of the day's fatigue, yet not disturb you later. . . . Prove to yourself that you needn't forego real enlivening coffee. Ask your grocer for Forbes Culture Ripened Coffee in the blue sail-ship vacuum can.
FORBES QUALITY BRAND COFFEE
Since before the Civil War the Forbes Company has been selecting and offering to particular coffee drinkers many blends of truly fine coffees.
ICED TEA
Forbes Quality Brand Orange Pekoe Tea steeped quickly and immediately poured over ice gives you a delicious cooling drink. Made this way, iced tea that is left over stays sweet for use the next day.
In Forbes Quality Brand you may expect to find a refreshingly pleasing blend, brought to you FRESH in the economical foil-lined bag.
ASK FOR FORBES COFFEE, TEA, SPICES AND EXTRACTS AT INDEPENDENT GROCERS

Founded in 1853, the James H. Forbes Tea and Coffee Company's first headquarters was near Fourth Street a few doors west of Broadway. Expansion of the business necessitated several subsequent moves. In 1898, it added spices to the inventory. The company even sold its roasted peanuts at Sportsman's Park. In 1963, more than 110 years after Forbes was founded, a buyer moved the company to Ohio. (St. Louis Media Archives.)

Retired ad man Charlie Claggett Jr. says, "I think my father probably wrote this ad. It's hard to believe today that anyone would ever take the time to read so much about cereal! But wait! It's not just about cereal, it's about doing something good for your child: making 'Young America huskier, hardier, happier,' and building strong bodies, eager appetites, rosy cheeks; providing energy; even building resistance to colds and disease. Talk about benefits! And not only does Ralston have the endorsement of America's cowboy hero, Tom Mix, but also 'thousands of mothers' who wrote in to tell Tom how much their children love the taste. One mother even claimed that Ralston has 'improved her child's disposition so much, even his teacher noticed!' And let's be sure to also note that 84 out of 100 doctors—dietitians and teachers, too)—prefer it. Oh, and don't forget to tune in to the *Tom Mix Radio Program* three days a week and watch for Tom's adventures in the Sunday comics. This is one hardworking, persuasive ad." (St. Louis Media Archives.)

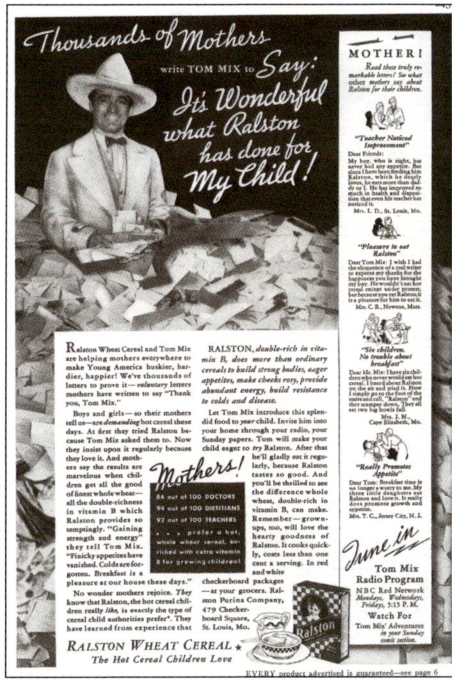
Thousands of Mothers
write TOM MIX to Say:
It's Wonderful what Ralston has done for My Child!
Ralston Wheat Cereal and Tom Mix are helping mothers everywhere to make Young America huskier, hardier, happier! We've thousands of letters to prove it—voluntary letters mothers have written to say "Thank you, Tom Mix."
Boys and girls—so their mothers tell us—are demanding hot cereal these days. At first they tried Ralston because Tom Mix asked them to. Now they insist upon it regularly because they love it. And mothers say the results are marvelous when children get all the good of finest whole wheat—all the double-richness in vitamin B which Ralston provides so temptingly. "Gaining strength and energy" they tell Tom Mix. "Finicky appetites have vanished. Colds are forgotten. Breakfast is a pleasure at our house these days."
No wonder mothers rejoice. They know that Ralston, the hot cereal children really like, is exactly the type of cereal child authorities prefer*. They have learned from experience that
RALSTON, double-rich in vitamin B, does more than ordinary cereals to build strong bodies, eager appetites, make cheeks rosy, provide abundant energy, build resistance to colds and disease.
Let Tom Mix introduce this splendid food to your child. Invite him into your home through your radio, your Sunday papers. Tom will make your child eager to try Ralston. After that he'll gladly eat it regularly, because Ralston tastes so good. And you'll be thrilled to see the difference whole wheat, double-rich in vitamin B, can make. Remember—grown-ups, too, will love the hearty goodness of Ralston. It cooks quickly, costs less than one cent a serving. In red and white checkerboard packages—at your grocers. Ralston Purina Company, 479 Checkerboard Square, St. Louis, Mo.
Mothers!
84 out of 100 DOCTORS
94 out of 100 DIETITIANS
92 out of 100 TEACHERS
. . . prefer a hot, whole wheat cereal, enriched with extra vitamin B for growing children!
RALSTON WHEAT CEREAL ★
The Hot Cereal Children Love
MOTHER!
Read these truly remarkable letters! See what other mothers say about Ralston for their children.
"Teacher Noticed Improvement"
Dear Friends:
My boy, who is eight, has never had any appetite. But since I have been feeding him Ralston, which he dearly loves, he eats more than daddy or I. He has improved so much in health and disposition that even his teacher has noticed it.
Mrs. I. D., St. Louis, Mo.
"Pleasure to eat Ralston"
Dear Tom Mix: I wish I had the eloquence of a real writer to express my thanks for the happiness you have brought my boy. He wouldn't eat hot cereal except under protest, but because you eat Ralston it is a pleasure for him to eat it.
Mrs. C. B., Newton, Mass.
"Six children. No trouble about breakfast"
Dear Mr. Mix: I have six children who never would eat hot cereal. I heard about Ralston on the air and tried it. Now I simply go to the foot of the stairs and call, "Ralston" and they scamper down. They all eat two big bowls full.
Mrs. J. M., Cape Elizabeth, Mo.
"Really Promotes Appetite"
Dear Tom: Breakfast time is no longer a worry to me. My three little daughters eat Ralston and love it. It really does promote growth and appetite.
Mrs. T. C., Jersey City, N. J.
Tune in
Tom Mix Radio Program
NBC Red Network
Mondays, Wednesdays, Fridays, 5:15 P. M.
Watch For
Tom Mix' Adventures in your Sunday comic section.
EVERY product advertised is guaranteed—see page 6

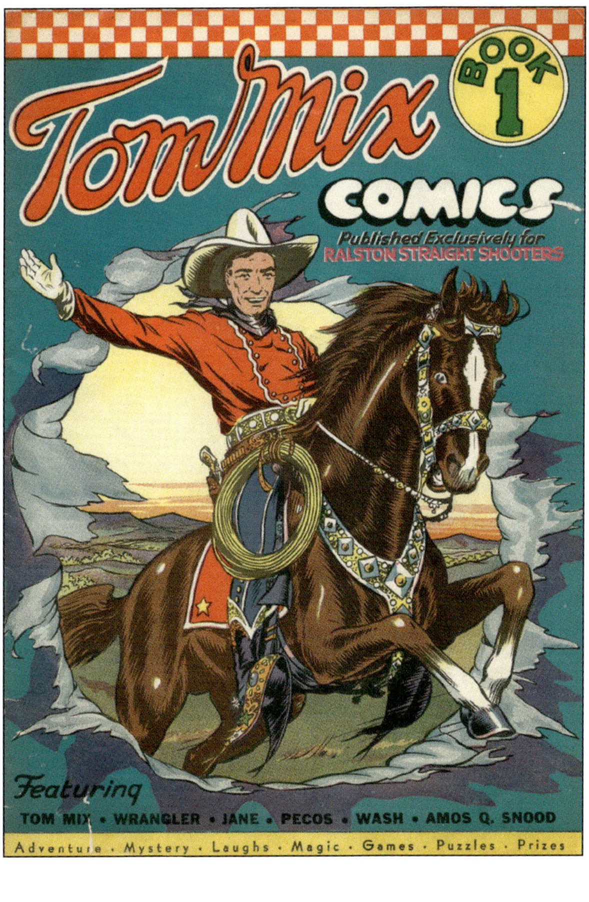
Tom Mix
BOOK 1
COMICS
Published Exclusively for
RALSTON STRAIGHT SHOOTERS
Featuring
TOM MIX • WRANGLER • JANE • PECOS • WASH • AMOS Q. SNOOD
Adventure • Mystery • Laughs • Magic • Games • Puzzles • Prizes

This *Tom Mix* comic—volume 1, no. 1—is another example of just how well the makers of Hot Ralston developed their market. Charles Claggett's radio creation expanded to include comics and premiums, both of which were in high demand among youngsters. The Tom Mix trinkets, advertised on the radio show, could be had by sending a box top from the product to "Checkerboard Square" in St. Louis. (St. Louis Media Archives.)

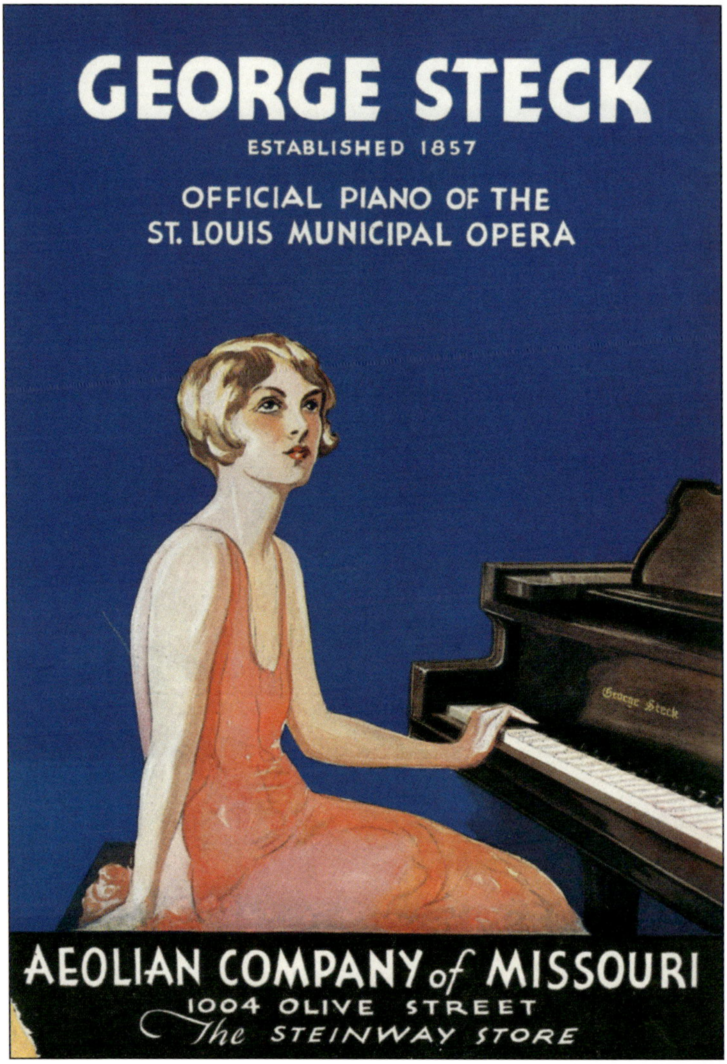

The Balmer and Weber Music Company building was originally located in the area known as St. Louis's music district. The company was bought out by Aeolian Company of Missouri in 1907, and the building was renamed Aeolian Hall; it was then renamed Ludwig-Aeolian in 1970. Professor Kristy Tucciarone says, "George Steck uses an advertising technique still popular today: expert testimony. The ad states, 'The Official Piano of the St. Louis Municipal Opera.' The opera can be classified as an 'expert' on vocals and music. The ad is effective because the use of expert testimony offers ethos." (St. Louis Media Archives.)

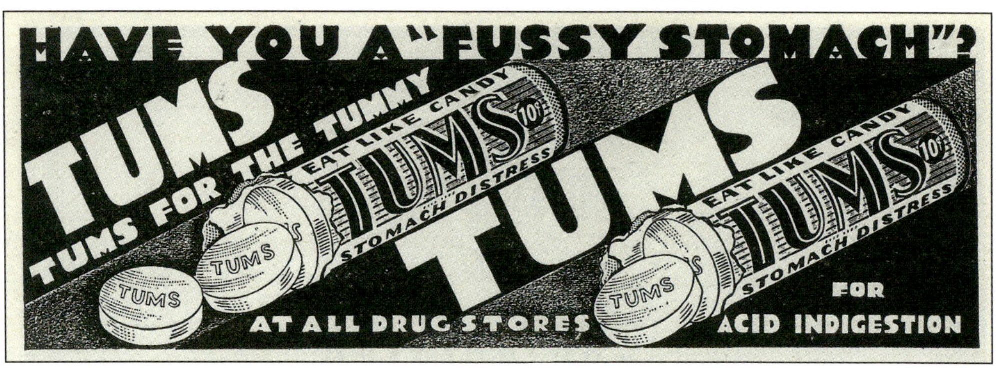

The St. Louis Tums factory, located at 320 South Broadway, produces nearly all of the Tums product consumed around the world, as it has since the formula for the pills was developed in St. Louis in 1928. Simple ads, like this one from 1935, conveyed the basic message that made the product the best-selling antacid in the nation. (St. Louis Media Archives.)

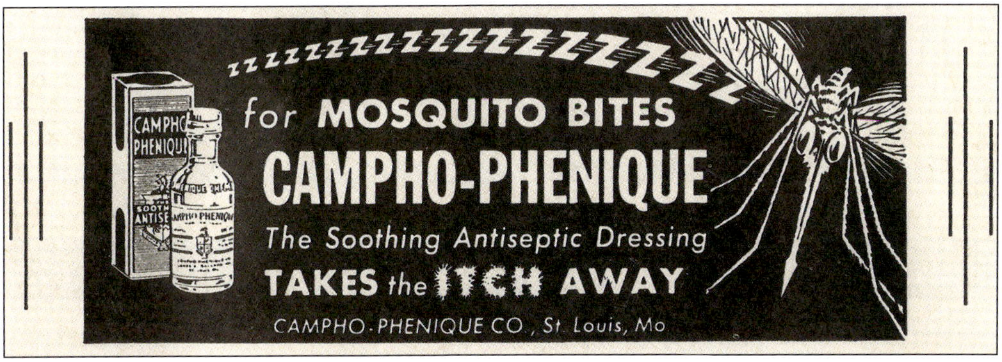
zzzzzzzzzzzzzzzZZZZZZ
for MOSQUITO BITES
CAMPHO-PHENIQUE
The Soothing Antiseptic Dressing
TAKES the ITCH AWAY
CAMPHO-PHENIQUE CO., St. Louis, Mo

Manufactured by the James F. Ballard Company in its plant at 500-502 North Second Street, the proprietary remedy Campho-Phenique became a national product used for everything from chapped lips to mosquito bites and relief from itchy rashes. It made a fortune for Ballard. (St. Louis Public Library.)

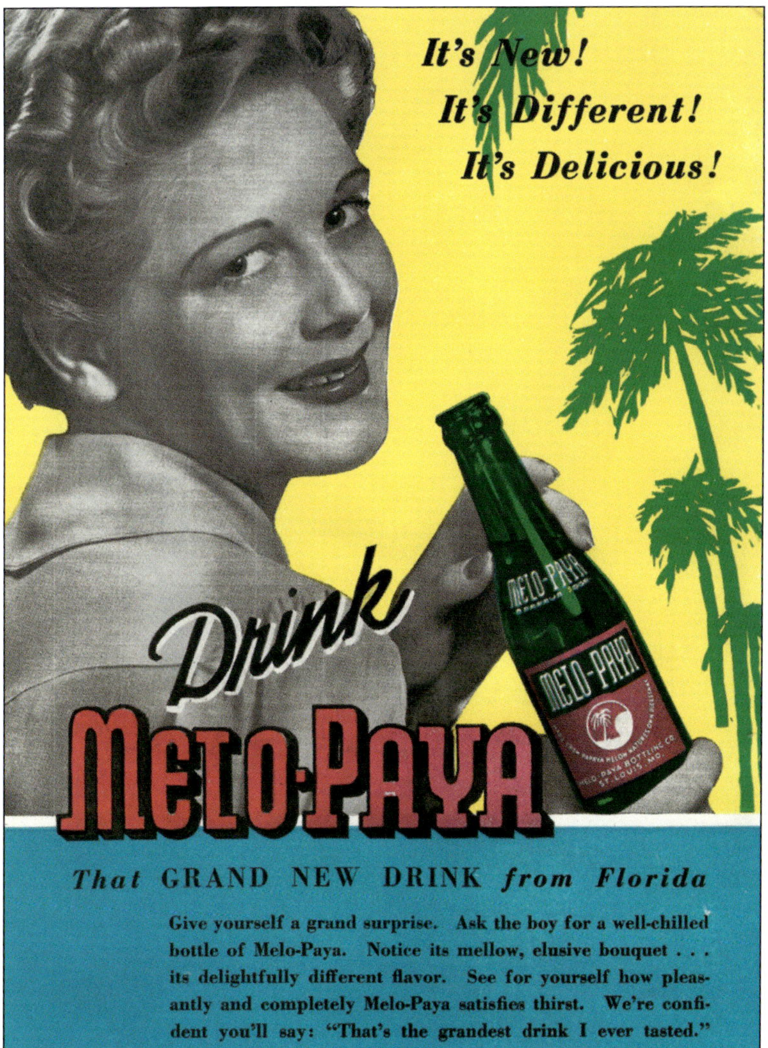
It's New!
It's Different!
It's Delicious!
Drink
MELO-PAYA
That GRAND NEW DRINK from Florida
Give yourself a grand surprise. Ask the boy for a well-chilled bottle of Melo-Paya. Notice its mellow, elusive bouquet . . . its delightfully different flavor. See for yourself how pleasantly and completely Melo-Paya satisfies thirst. We're confident you'll say: "That's the grandest drink I ever tasted."

Melo-Paya was the "different" tropical drink. It was made with papaya melon, nature's own digestive. This soft drink was bottled in franchises around the country, including St. Louis, in the late 1930s. (St. Louis Public Library.)

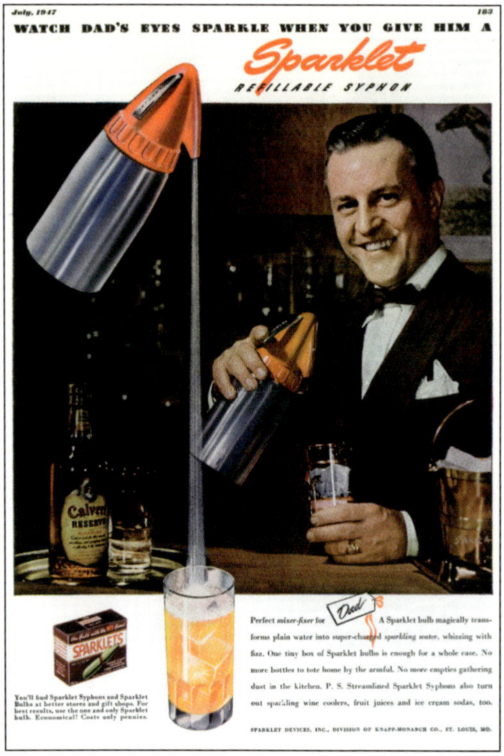
July, 1947
183
WATCH DAD'S EYES SPARKLE WHEN YOU GIVE HIM A
Sparklet
REFILLABLE SYPHON
Perfect mixer-fixer for Dad! A Sparklet bulb magically transforms plain water into super-charged sparkling water, whizzing with fizz. One tiny box of Sparklet bulbs is enough for a whole case. No more bottles to tote home by the armful. No more empties gathering dust in the kitchen. P. S. Streamlined Sparklet Syphons also turn out sparkling wine coolers, fruit juices and ice cream sodas, too.
SPARKLETS
You'll find Sparklet Syphons and Sparklet Bulbs at better stores and gift shops. For best results, use the one and only Sparklet bulb. Economical! Costs only pennies.
SPARKLET DEVICES, INC., DIVISION OF KNAPP-MONARCH CO., ST. LOUIS, MO.

This Sparklet ad from 1947 promotes a concept that had not yet found a niche. Over 60 years later, different companies are still trying to persuade consumers to buy devices that add carbonation to drinks at home. (St. Louis Media Archives.)

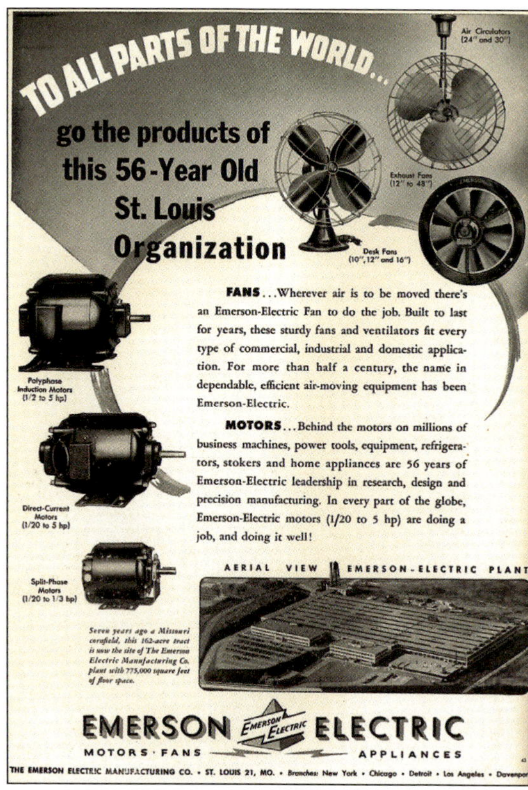
TO ALL PARTS OF THE WORLD...
go the products of this 56-Year Old St. Louis Organization
Air Circulators (24" and 30")
Exhaust Fans (12" to 48")
Desk Fans (10", 12" and 16")
FANS...Wherever air is to be moved there's an Emerson-Electric Fan to do the job. Built to last for years, these sturdy fans and ventilators fit every type of commercial, industrial and domestic application. For more than half a century, the name in dependable, efficient air-moving equipment has been Emerson-Electric.
MOTORS...Behind the motors on millions of business machines, power tools, equipment, refrigerators, stokers and home appliances are 56 years of Emerson-Electric leadership in research, design and precision manufacturing. In every part of the globe, Emerson-Electric motors (1/20 to 5 hp) are doing a job, and doing it well!
Polyphase Induction Motors (1/2 to 5 hp)
Direct-Current Motors (1/20 to 5 hp)
Split-Phase Motors (1/20 to 1/3 hp)
AERIAL VIEW EMERSON-ELECTRIC PLANT
Seven years ago a Missouri cornfield, this 162-acre tract is now the site of The Emerson Electric Manufacturing Co. plant with 775,000 square feet of floor space.
EMERSON ELECTRIC
MOTORS · FANS
APPLIANCES
THE EMERSON ELECTRIC MANUFACTURING CO. • ST. LOUIS 21, MO. • Branches: New York • Chicago • Detroit • Los Angeles • Davenport

Emerson Electric Manufacturing Company was founded in 1890 and made electric motors and fans. Through decades of growth, the company became a major multinational corporation employing thousands of people around the world. (St. Louis Media Archives.)

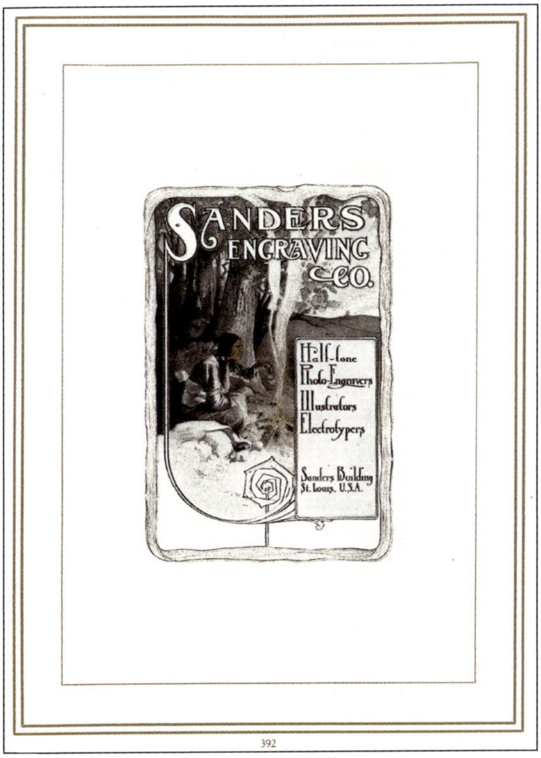

Sanders Engraving Company, a long-standing high-end engraving business, ran ads like this to demonstrate the quality of its work. The company was organized in 1887 and, at one point, also had plants in Memphis and Chattanooga. The company's operation in St. Louis was at 400 North Third Street and later listed at 221 Olive Street. Work by Sanders Engraving was seen in some of St. Louis's most prestigious publications. (St. Louis Media Archives.)

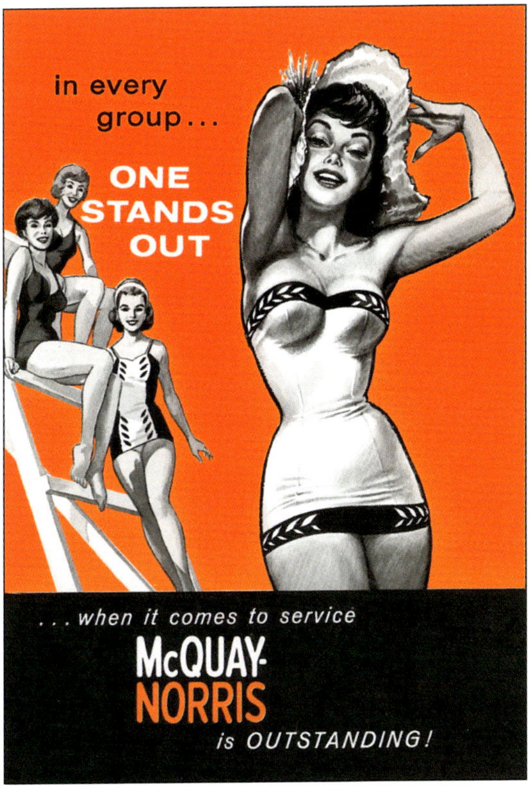

Dr, Kristy Tucciarone has strong opinions about this ad. "Ah, a trap! Show an ad with voluptuous women, and people will notice. The fact is sex does not sell all products. Does the brand have enough pull power to illustrate a 'big idea' that does not feature the business of the brand? Is the ad selling swimsuits? The fact is McQuay-Norris was a maker of automobile engine parts such as piston rings and chassis parts like steering wheel knuckle bolts. It also produced and distributed electrical controls for gas appliances." (St. Louis Media Archives.)

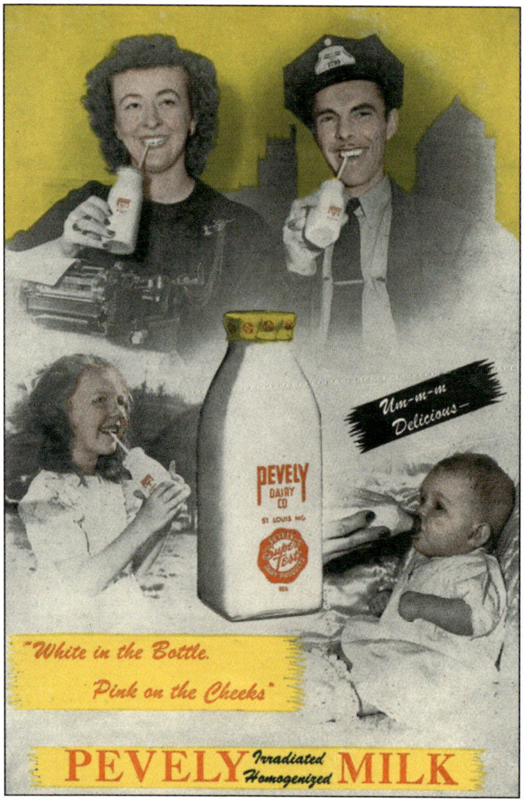

Pevely Dairy Company began as a dairy farm near the village of Pevely, Missouri, around 1882. Owner Martin Kerckhoff started delivering dairy products to the St. Louis area, and his customers called them Pevely Dairy products. Pevely's popularity grew when the family got the dairy concession at the 1904 World's Fair in Forest Park. After establishing its business in a building on South Seventh Street, Pevely Dairy ended up at the corner of Grand Boulevard and Chouteau Avenue. The huge Prairie Farms Dairy co-op purchased Pevely in 1989. (St. Louis Public Library.)

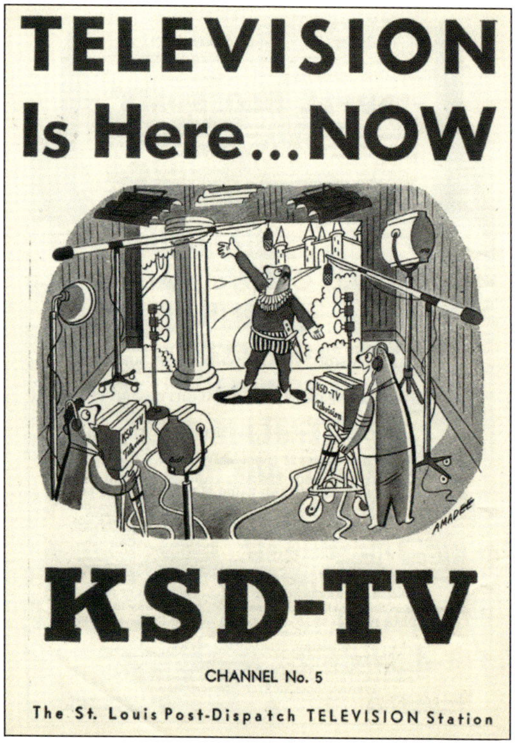

KSD-TV was the first television station in the St. Louis market, signing on February 8, 1947, when the number of local television receivers could be counted on two hands. Essentially, this ad, illustrated by Amadee Wohlschlaeger of the co-owned *St. Louis Post-Dispatch*, was meant to sell television sets to ensure that there would be viewers to watch the station. (St. Louis Media Archives.)

KSD-TV -4-

Rutledge & Lilienfeld, Inc.

ADVERTISING·MERCHANDISING

7 NORTH ELEVENTH STREET • ST. LOUIS 1 • TELEPHONE MAIN 1-3252

T. V. COPY FOR MY LITTLE MARGIE DATE

CLIENT PEVELY DAIRY CO. - COTTAGE CHEESE #3 STATION

Source	VIDEO	Source	AUDIO
STU	DIS TO ECU PYRAMID OF EASTER BASKET CARTONS OF PEVELY COTTAGE CHEESE	STU	Here's something that's just right for the Lenten season and those hard-to-plan meals.... delicious Pevely New Fashioned Cottage Cheese!!
	HAND REACHES IN FRAME, PICKS UP CARTON, DISPLAYS IT TO CAMERA		And look how it's packaged -- in gay, colorful Easter basket cartons!
	PAN TO EASTER BASKET CARTON WITH PIPE CLEANER FOR HANDLE, FILLED WITH EASTER CANDY		And this is how the Pevely Easter Basket Carton looks when you add a handle....
	HAND INDICATES HANDLE		(this one is a pipe cleaner).....
	HAND TIPS BASKET TOWARDS CAMERA TO SHOW CANDY		and fill it with Easter candy! Children just love the Pevely Easter Basket Carton....your child will want to collect a whole set for they come in so many bright colors!!!
	PAN TO OPEN CARTON PEVELY COTTAGE CHEESE. HAND ENTERS FRAME, PICKS UP CARTON, SPOONS IT TO SHOW TEXTURE OF COTTAGE CHEESE		And you'll love Pevely New Fashioned Cottage Cheese for it's such a help in planning Lenten meals. See how creamy it is.... look at those big, tender king-size curds... yes, you'll delight the whole family when you

This is a page from the script for a 1956 commercial for Pevely Dairy Company. The writing in the left column is the video instruction, while the words on the right are the audio script. This commercial was probably performed live when it was seen on the *My Little Margie* program on KSD-TV. (St. Louis Media Archives.)

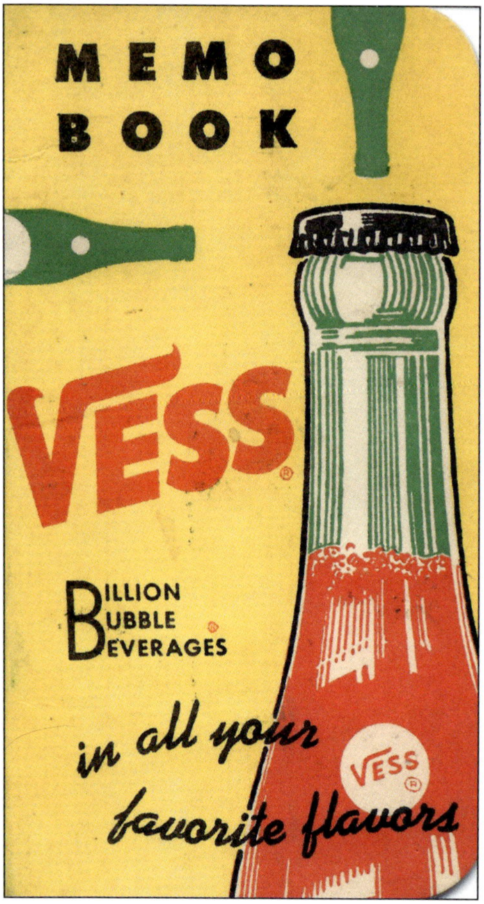

Vess was founded as the Orange Whistle Company in 1916 by a man named Vess Jones. When the stock market crashed in 1929, the company, then known as Vess, was purchased by the Schneeberger family. (St. Louis Media Archives.)

KMOX, the area's most successful radio station in the 1970s and 1980s, broke one of the cardinal rules of advertising in most of its ads during that period by neglecting to provide all pertinent information (such as the station's spot on the radio dial), but it did not matter. The station was so pervasive in the market at the time that advertisements did not even have to tell people the station's dial location (1120 AM) because everyone knew it. (St. Louis Media Archives.)

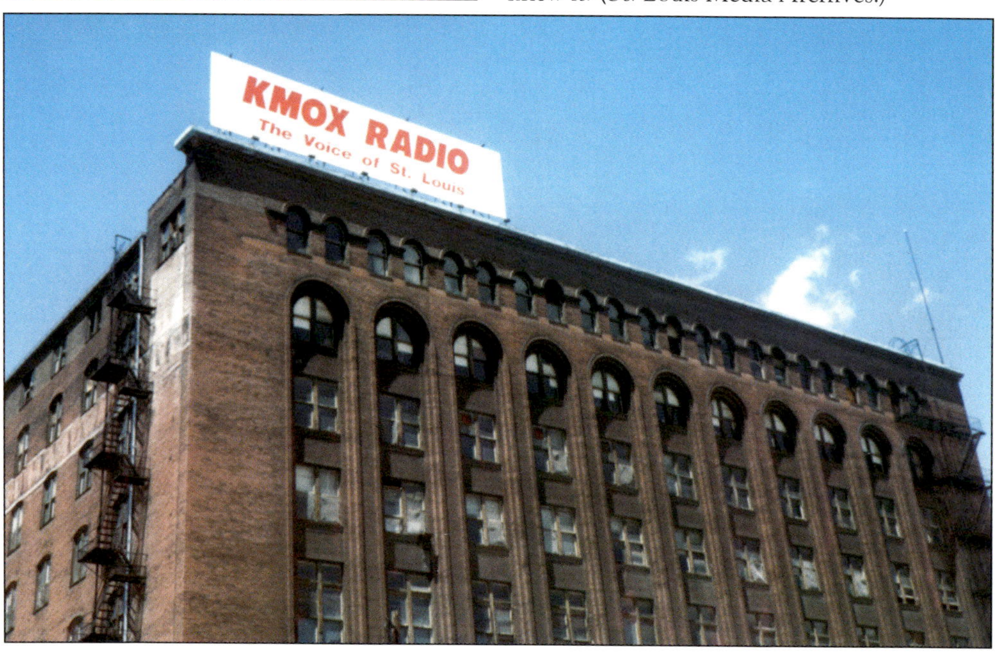

New Deal advertising in St. Louis reached an iconic level on radio and television. Steve Mizerany broke every rule in the book but achieved important name recognition that differentiated his business from other appliance sellers. This print ad from 1977 is much too cluttered, but it furthered the names of Mizerany, Joe Farhatt, and the "First String Boys." (Missouri History Museum.)

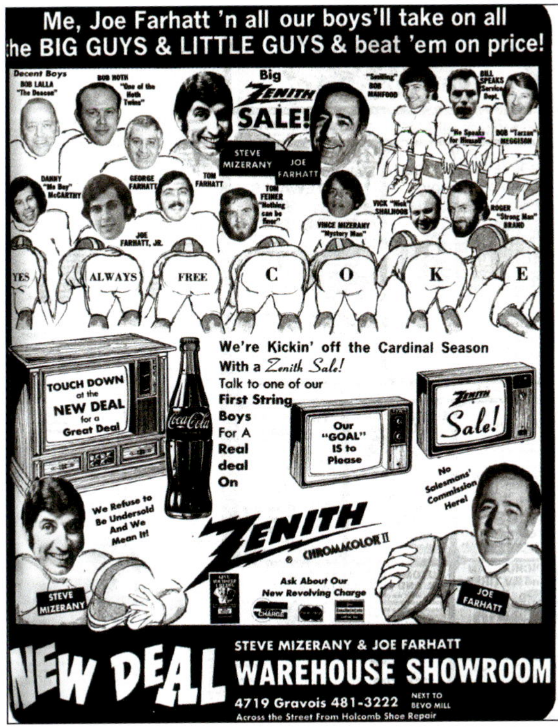

Me, Joe Farhatt 'n all our boys'll take on all the BIG GUYS & LITTLE GUYS & beat 'em on price!
Decent Boys
BOB LALLA "The Deacon"
Big ZENITH SALE!
STEVE MIZERANY
JOE FARHATT
DANNY
GEORGE FARHATT
TOM FARHATT
JOE FARHATT, JR.
VINCE MIZERANY "Mystery Man"
ROGER "Strong Man" BRAND
YES ALWAYS FREE C O K E
We're Kickin' off the Cardinal Season
With a Zenith Sale!
Talk to one of our
First String
Boys
For A
Real
deal
On
TOUCH DOWN at the NEW DEAL for a Great Deal
Coca-Cola
Our "GOAL" IS to Please
ZENITH Sale!
No Salesmans' Commission Here!
We Refuse to Be Undersold And We Mean It!
ZENITH CHROMACOLOR II
Ask About Our New Revolving Charge
STEVE MIZERANY
JOE FARHATT
NEW DEAL
STEVE MIZERANY & JOE FARHATT
WAREHOUSE SHOWROOM
4719 Gravois 481-3222
NEXT TO BEVO MILL
Across the Street From Holcomb Shoe Repair

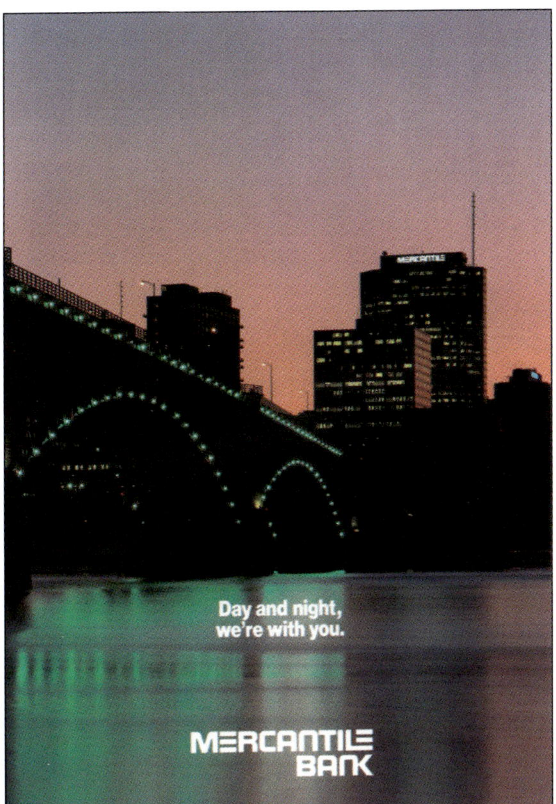

Day and night,
we're with you.
MERCANTILE
BANK

In the opinion of Dr. Kristy Tucciarone, "This ad attempts to capture the spirit of downtown while communicating to consumers the bank can take care of their needs 24 hours a day. I appreciate the use of 'you' language, as it puts me, the consumer, as the top priority." (St. Louis Media Archives.)

IMAGES
of Modern America

St. Louis Advertising

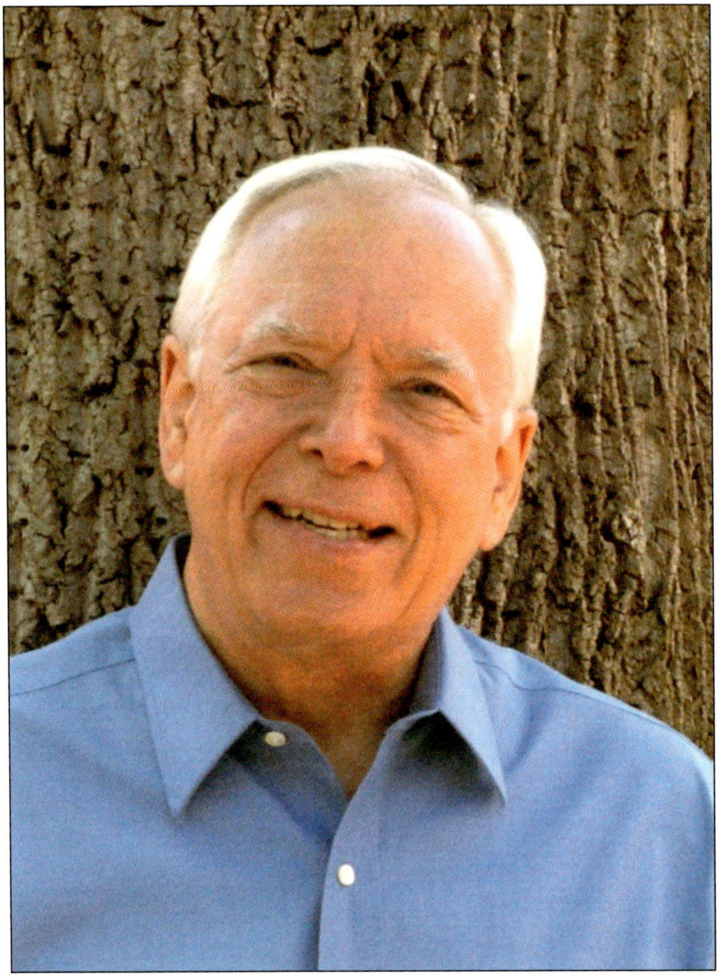

The St. Louis Media History Foundation (stlmediahistory.com) was formed by author Frank Absher (pictured) to accumulate and preserve media history and artifacts. Working in conjunction with area institutions such as the St. Louis Public Library, the foundation continues to promote the storied past of media in the St. Louis area. (Robert Byrne.)

ON THE FRONT COVER: (clockwise from top left) InSinkErator, owned by Emerson, used hometown comedienne Phyllis Diller in this classic ad (St. Louis Media Archives); the Vess Lemon Lime Soda bottle has been coined a "roadside wonder" that contained 600 feet of neon tubes and revolved on its pole (Wm. Stage); the Budweiser Clydesdales provide Anheuser-Busch with an iconic, unique advertising vehicle (Copyright © Anheuser-Busch, LLC. Used with permission of Anheuser-Busch, LLC. All rights reserved.); The big Schnuck's clock, which once could be seen atop a building just north of the Milles fountain at Union Station, was removed by the building's owner in 1992 (Schnuck's Markets); local baseball hero Stan Musial was one of many pro athletes used to promote Rawlings sporting goods (St. Louis Media Archives).

ON THE BACK COVER: (clockwise from top left) In the early 1900s, Dad's Cookie Company was a California-based franchise, but Henry Renz's bakery—at the corner of Keokuk Street and Louisiana Avenue—is still the St. Louis home of Dad's Cookies (Lonnie Tettaton); this Switzer's Licorice advertisement is from 1958 (Switzer Candy Company Archives); this is a Downtown St. Louis, Inc., window sticker for display at the businesses of members (Duane Marburger).